2007 752 10-17-1

Reference Books in International Education
(Vol. 37)
Garland Reference Library of Social Science
(Vol. 1130)

Social Justice and Third World Education

edited by
Timothy J. Scrase

GARLAND PUBLISHING, INC.
New York & London
1997

Library of Congress Cataloging-in-Publication Data

Social justice and Third World education / edited by Timothy J. Scrase.
      p.   cm. — (Reference books in international education ; vol.
37. Garland reference library of social science ; vol. 1130)
    Includes bibliographical references and index.
    ISBN 0-8153-1168-0 (alk. paper)
    1. Education—Social aspects—Developing countries.   2. Social
justice.   3. Educational equalization—Developing countries.   4. Politics and education—Developing countries.   I. Scrase, Timothy J.
II. Series: Garland reference library of social science ; v. 1130.
III. Series: Garland reference library of social science.   Reference books
in international education ; vol. 37.
LC191.8.D44S63   1997
370.11'5'091724—dc20   96–20094
                                       CIP

Printed on acid-free, 250-year-life paper
Manufactured in the United States of America

Contents

Series Editor's Preface

This series of scholarly works in comparative and international education has grown well beyond the initial conception of a collection of reference books. Although retaining its original purpose of providing a resource to scholars, students, and a variety of other professionals who need to understand the role played by education in various societies or world regions, it also strives to provide accurate, relevant, and up-to-date information on a wide variety of selected educational issues, problems, and experiments within an international context.

Contributors to this series are well-known scholars who have devoted their professional lives to the study of their specializations. Without exception these men and women possess an intimate understanding of the subject of their research and writing. Without exception they have studied their subject not only in dusty archives, but have lived and traveled widely in their quest for knowledge. In short, they are "experts" in the best sense of that often overused word.

In our increasingly interdependent world, it is now widely understood that it is a matter of military, economic, and environmental survival that we not only understand better what makes other societies tick, but that we make a serious effort to understand how others, be they Japanese, Hungarian, South African, or Chilean, attempt to solve the same kinds of educational problems that we face in North America. As the late George Z.F. Bereday wrote more than three decades ago: "[E]ducation is a mirror held against the face of a people. Nations may put on blustering shows of strength to conceal public weakness, erect grand façades to conceal shabby backyards, and profess peace while secretly arming for conquest, but how they take care of their children tells unerringly who they are" (*Comparative Methods in Education*, New York: Holt, Rinehart and Winston, 1964, p. 5).

Perhaps equally important, however, is the valuable perspective that studying another education system (or its problems) provides us in understanding our own system (or its problems). When we step beyond our own limited experience and our commonly held assumptions about schools and learning in order to look back at our system in contrast to another, we see it in a very different light. To learn, for example, how China or Belgium handles the education of a multilingual society; how the French provide for the funding of public education; or how the Japanese control access to their universities enables us to better understand that there are reasonable alternatives to our own familiar way of doing things. Not that we can *borrow* directly from other societies. Indeed, educational arrangements are inevitably a reflection of deeply embedded political, economic, and cultural factors that are unique to a particular society. But a conscious recognition that there are other ways of doing things can serve to open our minds and provoke our imaginations in ways that can result in new experiments or approaches that we may not have otherwise considered.

Since this series is intended to be a useful research tool, the editor and contributors welcome suggestions for future volumes, as well as ways in which this series can be improved.

Edward R. Beauchamp
University of Hawaii

Acknowledgments

This book has been a long time in the making. As such, I would first wish to acknowledge the patience of the contributors, editors, and those at Garland for their faith in seeing the project completed. I am grateful to the School of Social Sciences and Liberal Studies at Charles Sturt University–Mitchell, my former employer, for financial assistance to cover overseas research and consultations with some of the contributors. Their funds also enabled the translation of Carlos Marin's chapter. For his translation, I would like to thank Andrew Batchelor of Bathurst, New South Wales. Colleagues at my present employer, the Sociology Department, University of Tasmania in Hobart, have been a constant source of support and encouragement. Ruchira has given unswerving support and provided me with the confidence to complete this project, even when I had my doubts. To all, thank you.

Introduction: Social Justice, Education and the Third World[1]

Timothy J. Scrase

> *A goal of social justice, I will assume, is social equality. Equality refers not primarily to the distribution of social goods, though distributions are certainly entailed by social equality. It refers primarily to the full participation and inclusion of everyone in a society's major institutions, and the socially supported substantive opportunity for all to develop and exercise their capacities and realize their choices.*
>
> *Iris Marion Young,* Justice and the Politics of Difference

> *The issue of social justice is not an add-on. It is fundamental to what good education is about.*
>
> *R. W. Connell,* Schools and Social Justice

In much of the comparative education literature, questions of educational inequality and lack of educational opportunity in the developing world stand as perplexing, complex, and difficult problems. Yet, while inequality in education remains one of the most researched and written about topics in the discipline, the question of social justice and its relationship to education remains implicit. This volume aims to reverse this trend—to make the issue of social justice, both in theory and practice, central and explicit. It seeks to unravel the claims of Young (1990, p. 193), above, that social justice in education is not simply met by providing a large number of schools, institutions, and training programs. Rather, and in addition, educational justice has to be linked to broader social justice imperatives like the full and unhindered opportunity to participate in society's major institutions regardless of class, color, or gender. From this perspective, education is not a separate social institution, but one that is intrinsically linked to politics, welfare, employment, and morality. This perspective stands as a challenge to policy makers. Education is continually being called upon to meet the demands of politicians and, increasingly, economists and economic rationalists, both in the First World and the Third World, to produce an ever more talented, literate, and independent graduate ready for the world of business and enterprise. Across the globe, educational success now has come to mean employment success. Education has come to mean jobs and careers. But, is this *education?* It would seem that we are short-changing our children and youth, playing a kind of charade in which we are telling them and compelling them to "get an education" when what we are in fact doing is, fundamentally, schooling and training them.

This raises a further interesting question as to the uneasy relationship between social justice and schooling. Connell (1993, pp. 15–19), on this question, explains that governments have long been operating from a perspective of distributive justice.[2] That is, as long as enough schools are provided, or universal literacy programs put in place, or compensatory and affirmative action programs established, governments are satisfied that they have met their social justice requirements. However,

The underlying weakness of this approach to educational justice is its indifference to the nature of education itself. For education is a social process in which the "how much" cannot be separated from the "what." There is an inescapable link between distribution and content. (Connell, 1993, p. 18)

What Connell is pointing out is that an education system, and hence government and state, that merely trains children and youth irrespective of, or with little consideration to, issues of what actually happens *in schools* in terms of the curriculum content, pedagogy, or the relationships between pupils and teachers, has an inherently flawed view of what social justice in education implies. The very essence of social justice in education is one that is not just concerned with outcomes, but encompasses inclusiveness, difference, and democratic participation and decision making at all levels. As Connell (1993, p. 19) remarks:

Justice cannot be achieved by distributing the same amount of a standard good to children of all social classes and colour. Education is a process operating through relationships, which cannot be neutralized or obliterated to allow equal distribution of the social good at the core (original emphasis).

The relationship of social justice to education, then, is one that is concerned with fairness, rights, and the [equal] opportunity to participate in one of society's most fundamental institutions. For researchers, it is about uncovering and reflecting upon the seemingly perpetuating problems of poverty, of inequality, and of an undemocratic and often alienating system of learning. And for policy makers, there is the unenviable, and so far unsuccessful, task of providing resources and facilities and appropriate policies to effectively meet not only the distributive aspects of educational justice, but also content, or curriculum justice. Fundamentally, the view advocated throughout the various chapters of this book is that social justice is not merely about individual justice. Rather, justice should be understood in terms of the needs of marginalized classes and groups. In other words, this view of social justice is rather more *collectivist* in nature.[3] This view " . . . gives prominence to the justice needs of social groups, alongside, and sometimes ahead of, the needs of individuals" (Corson, 1992, p. 181).

Rationale for this Volume

Across the Third World, from sub-Saharan Africa to Cost Rica, the costs of providing a basic education are rising. Education is no longer a taken-for-granted right for the simple fact that it has become expensive. It is expensive for governments as well as for parents and family members. Additionally, classes are overcrowded, graduates do not want to teach, especially in rural areas, and increasing family debt is forcing children, particularly girls, to leave school prematurely. The decade for "development" is well and truly over. The following scene in Kenya exemplifies the plight of families throughout the underdeveloped world in trying to keep their children educated:

In Kenya's capital, Nairobi, 14-year-old Mwangi and his younger sister

*Wangoi confide their prayer-like hope that their mother will earn enough
selling peanuts in Uhuru Park to return them to their village home and
to primary school. And Serah Wanjira, labouring through the city's wealthy
Westlands suburb to sell her burden of vegetables, speaks angrily of the
rising costs which are taking secondary education out of her children's
reach. (Sayer, 1993, p. 15)*

For these Kenyans, a large part of the reason for their increasing
pauperization can be explained by globalization, a process of increasing economic, cultural, and social interconnectedness across the globe
(see, for instance, Sklair, 1991; Tomlinson, 1991; McGrew, 1992)
Globalizing forces are having far reaching effects in the periphery,
not the least being rising national and individual debt, increased
daily costs of living and increasing competition for scarce resources
(such as a good education). This has been aptly described as
maldevelopment (Amin, 1990).

Succumbing to the pressures of global economic competition,
Third World governments have resorted to liberalizing their economies and opening them up to the vagaries of the capitalist world
economy. In India, for instance, I have argued elsewhere that the
middle classes view education as *their* privilege and right, as *their*
avenue to the better paying and higher status positions in the rapidly globalized and liberalized Indian market. Thus, in this context,
globalization has engendered localized forms of cultural politics in
that education becomes increasingly monopolized and protected by
a privileged elite at the expense of the disempowered and the poor
(Scrase, 1995). Consequently, the notion of a social justice imperative in education, even in terms of distributive justice, is overridden
by concerns of national debt repayment, loan servicing, and economic and development programs that privilege industry and profit
above basic needs.

It is within this context that the present volume was assembled.
A number of fundamental questions are addressed in terms of the
way social justice intersects with education in the Third World in
the 1990s. Will education remain at the forefront of social growth
and development in Third World countries during this decade? How
will the processes of globalization and the rise of the new world
order affect the structure of Third World education? Have Third

World governments already relegated their mass education programs to a secondary status in order to invest their limited revenue in perceived high-growth, income generating industries like computers and tourism? Have the Third World elite maintained their control over education? How have they maintained this control? And will they continue to do so? And, significantly, how have, or can, the marginalized and impoverished Third World masses have their interests, needs, and inequalities redressed in education and schooling in the 1990s?

The Individual Contributions

This book is organized into two sections. In Part I, four chapters are devoted to explorations of problems and issues, exploring in depth theoretical positions, problems of policy, and its implementation. Bacchus begins his essay by exploring the complexities of development and the inherent inequalities among nations. At the global level, as he points out, various programs and policies have been put in place in an attempt to resolve the growing disparities between rich and poor nations, but these have largely failed. He then asks the important question: "what role can education play in reducing global inequality?" He again reviews a number of approaches such as mutual self-interest, those proffered in the Brandt report, the role of the elite, and possibilities for reversing inequalities in less developed countries given historical forces, and global economic and geopolitical realities. He offers an argument in support of education for development and social justice in which effective education is that which is relevant to the needs and interests of the population and where there are useful knowledge and skills imparted. Finally, he presents some thoughts on the usefulness and importance of critical emancipatory knowledge that can better prepare students to transform their reality. For Bacchus, educational justice is exclusively connected to issues of political justice, fundamental human rights, and democratic participation in development.

Martino explores the problems of social justice and education in the Third World from a somewhat different angle. In reviewing the current global trend for structural adjustment and capitalist liberalization of their economies, he argues that the majority of Third World nations have all but abandoned their commitment to maintaining educational justice. Fundamentally, the pressures of debt servicing, coupled with the collapse of the Soviet socialist empire, have led to a virtual back draft in which Third World governments have had to drastically cut and redirect funds away from an array of social programs, including those concerning education. This shift in policy has fundamentally benefited the children of the new entrepreneurs, the middle classes, and the elite at the expense of the marginalized and the poor. Martino focuses on two key elements to this shift—the implementation of Fordist regimes of accumulation and the role played by the World Bank and the IMF. Ultimately, Martino argues that social justice through education, at least at the national level, is a lost cause and, perhaps, the reflections of Bacchus on the role and place of critical pedagogy, or nonformal forms of education, can provide a solution to this complex problem.

Metaphors of development pervade the discourse of educational planners at the national and supranational level. To be developed, a nation has to be industrialized, urban, technically advanced, nontraditional, rational, and modern. In her chapter, Fox investigates the linkages and intersections between these metaphors of development and those of social justice. The language of development has been all pervasive from colonial times and thus renders ineffective cross-national, intercultural discourse on justice and development. Fox argues that, by opening up genuine dialogue among education planners, development experts, and government officials, development assistance will then be able to positively contribute to social justice in the Third World. If educational planning in the Third World is to succeed, Fox argues that the consultants and planners must begin to move toward *authentic* intercultural communication in which there is an acceptance of equal validity claims from all the participants in the planning and developmental process.

In one sense, Fox is addressing the point that the marginalized and excluded attain recognition as equal participants in the educational process. This view is also forwarded by Alladin where he argues that only through the sociocultural integration of ethnic minorities can Third World states truly claim to have democratic participation and resolve their lingering problems of underdevelopment. The problem, as he points out, is that for many Third World countries this issue has not been resolved. Ethnic minorities expediently become "the problem" in times of economic crisis or political instability. In the first part of his paper, Alladin reviews the two dominant perspectives of ethnicity and ethnic difference—assimilationist and cultural pluralist. He then explores ethnic difference in terms of the politics of postcolonial development and the role of education in fostering "national unity," using Malaysia as a case study. While schools remained important for the fostering of government integration policies, they ultimately polarized the community in terms of Malay and non-Malays. The solution, he suggests, is through developing effective policies of redistribution to enhance successful economic and social development of the society as a whole. Drawing on the work of Freire, Alladin concludes that education can play a significant role in the transformation of underdeveloped societies, and their marginalized populations, toward one where their is more equality and social justice, and this will reduce the lingering ethnic tensions within the nation more generally.

The case studies presented in Part II focus specifically on a range of issues and problems in education that impinge on the policies, practices, and theories of social justice articulated in Part I. Drawing upon her experiences in Africa, Davies explores the ways practitioners of education, particularly teachers, can come to terms with implementing social justice in their educational practice, especially within the context of gender relations and gender inequality. She views equality as being fundamental to justice but, like Connell, argues that it is essential to know how practitioners define it, interpret it, and what they are doing about it. "Doing justice," as the title of her chapter suggests, thereby reflects her concern that we all need to take responsibility for changing gender relations, and that the individual accounts outlined in her chapter are as important, if not more so, than grand policy statements and initiatives. How, then, can gender justice be met in the context of African women's education? According to Davies, it is through a personal agency perspective in which account is made, and, moreover, action taken, on the views of both women and men that gender justice can be met. In this way, education can be a transformative and liberating experience.

The ethnographic method, together with a consideration of agency, is also taken up by Ganguly-Scrase, this time in the context of schooling among a group of marginalized, low-caste Indian leather workers. In particular, Ganguly-Scrase privileges the children's accounts of their school, neighborhood, and community, showing how they are able to interpret their lived conditions, often in contradiction to views demanded of them from their school teachers, the local elite, and the education system more generally. In a sense, she presents a "bottom-up" account of educational justice, eliciting the views of the marginalized and impoverished to show how they, at least symbolically, challenge both the hegemonic domination of the state and the ideals of the social reformers so concerned with their social upliftment. As such, Ganguly-Scrase highlights the inherent problems of meeting social justice through education in India when schooling is fundamentally a top-down, elite-driven, and alienating experience for most socially marginal children.

The next three essays investigate the politics of education in the context of government agendas to meet social justice imperatives. Hickling-Hudson addresses the way in which postrevolutionary Grenada devised and implemented a range of social justice initiates in their educational policies. Of importance to the Grenadan government was the key role of education in uplifting the masses, reducing long-established and persistent social inequalities, and fostering a range of government development policies. For revolutionary governments, expeditiously undoing the wrongs of the past is imperative. For Grenada, and for its education system, this involved tackling the immense problems of lack of adequate resources and facilities, lack of suitably trained teachers, no clearly articulated policy of universal education, and so forth. In short, Grenada was a country racked by educational underdevelopment. Hickling-Hudson sets about describing and analyzing the New Jewel Movement's agenda for radical educational change with an explicit social justice imperative, highlighting the innovations, difficulties, and achievements in its tragic five years in power. Education in Grenada was essentially political, political in that for the first time the large majority of its citizens gained access to the world of literacy, knowledge, and personal and social empowerment.

The analysis of social justice and education in socialist states is also presented by Price in his essay on teaching and learning in postrevolutionary China. Importantly, he argues that the discourse of social justice emanating from Europe has been largely ignored in China. Instead, justice is implied in the various statements on rights and duties of citizens outlined in an array of pamphlets, policies, and political documents. Inequality is inherent in Chinese society—in terms of gender, urban and rural differences, the educated and the illiterate, and between different types of workers. Yet, while there is no clear policy on social justice, it is alluded to in various educational forms, especially textbooks, which prescribe the moral obligations of Chinese citizens for duty to the state, the Party, and to each other. In the last section of his paper, Price analyzes the pro-democracy movement in light of justice and human rights, and questions whether this movement represents the interests of all Chinese or simply those of a vocal and educated minority.

In the Middle East social justice has never been an explicit educational outcome. Safwat, in her discussion of the limitations for women to gain equal justice in Arab states, highlights the complexities of Arab politics and the desire for increasing women's participation in the workforce and in political life more generally. Importantly, she stresses that we need to deconstruct the notion of an "Arab world," arguing instead that each country must be examined separately in light of historical forces, contemporary geopolitics, and various interpretations of Islam. Arab women's gains through education must therefore be analyzed within this context of shifting alliances and external pressures—political, cultural, and economic. While an education is fundamental to women gaining status and employment in Arab states, their social mobility is strongly determined by the current economic climate. Educated women are seen to be competing with men, especially in the higher-paid positions, whereas illiterate women are marginalized into the skilled and nonunionized jobs, in many cases competing with male expatriate labor. She argues, therefore, that education for women does not necessarily correlate positively with social justice for women, especially as many of the political struggles in the Arab states are expressed as gender struggles, with women coming off second best.

The final chapter reflects the views of an activist involved in the education and social upliftment of South America's poor. Marin describes the rationale and guiding principles for action through which he, and those in his organization, operate. In this perspective, social justice, education, and national development are interlinked. While formal education has its role, education must be all-encompassing and lifelong. It must also generate, as he says, a culture of human life, a culture of human rights and duties, and of fundamental liberties. Marin proposes a proactive education—one that empowers and liberates; one whereby content must be enriched and the educational process must become clear.

Although the problems, issues, and case studies raised in this book are not exhaustive, they do provide a range of diverse ways comparative educationists, from a range of disciplines, address the issue of social justice and Third World education. Despite the different approaches, however, there is a common thread running through these essays. That is, there is an overwhelming commitment by the authors to the view that social justice must be included as part of any educational program for effective education, in the full sense of the term, to take place. Moreover, this view of social justice must not only be concerned with distributive mechanisms to achieve equality of educational outcomes, but rather the practice of justice in education must be inclusive, taking in the views and needs of the full range of educational actors—the children and students, the ethnic minorities, the marginalized, and the impoverished.

Notes

1. While the term the "Third World" is used both in the title and extensively throughout this book, I do acknowledge the remarks of Zachariah (1992) on the current inappropriateness of this term in that, as he pointed out, the term has come to mean "third rate" and "third class." Also, geopolitical changes have led to the redundancy of the term. Of course, many terms are loaded: "developing nations" implies "catching-up nations"; "the South" stereotypes most southern hemisphere nations (e.g,. Brazil compared to Sudan); and so forth. While I fundamentally agree with his point, however, in that we need to find a new, all-encompassing term to replace "Third World," I do not think the title of the book, following his suggestions (1993, p. 553) would be appropriate: *Social Justice and Education in Most Countries in the Southern Hemisphere*!
2. That is, the approach outlined by Rawls (1972).
3. For an excellent discussion of the inherent problems of individualist accounts of justice and the way collectivist accounts can be a more useful framework for understanding the rights of the marginalized see Corson (1992).

References

Amin, Samir (1990). *Maldevelopment: Anatomy of a Global Failure*. London: Zed.
Connell, R.W. (1993). *Schools and Social Justice*. Leichardt, New South Wales: Pluto Press.
Corson, David J. (1992). "Social Justice and Minority Language Policy." *Educational*

Theory, vol. 42, no. 2.

McGrew, Anthony (1992). "A Global Society?" In S. Hall, D. Held, and A. McGrew (eds.), *Modernity and Its Futures.* Cambridge, U.K.: Polity.

Rawls, John (1972). *A Theory of Justice.* Oxford: Oxford University Press.

Sayer, Geoff (1993). "Peanuts and Prayers." In *New Internationalist,* October.

Scrase, Timothy J. (1995). "Globalization, India and the Struggle for Justice." In David A. Smith and József Böröcz (eds.) *A New World Order? Global Transformations in the Late Twentieth Century.* Westport, Conn.: Praeger.

Sklair, Leslie (1991). *The Sociology of the Global System.* Brighton: Harvester Wheatsheaf.

Tomlinson, John (1991). *Cultural Imperialism.* London: Pinter Publishers Ltd.

Young, Iris Marion (1990). *Justice and the Politics of Difference.* Princeton, N.J.: Princeton University Press.

Zachariah, Matthew (1992). Letter to the editor. *Comparative Education Review,* vol. 36, no. 4.

Part I

Problems and Issues

Education for Development and Social Justice in the Third World

M.K. Bacchus

Introduction

The overall purpose of this chapter is to examine the contribution that education can make or has made to "development" in Third World countries. The concept of "development" as it is used here includes economic, social, and political development—an intrinsic element of which is social justice for all sectors of the population. The topic suggests two major foci—whether social justice is reflected in the distribution of educational opportunities in these societies and whether the type of education that is provided helps or can help to ensure that social justice for all citizens would become and remain a key consideration of the State.

Social Justice and Greater Equality among Nations

"Development," as manifested in greater social justice among the population, needs to be directly linked with a concurrent movement toward greater equality. Commenting on this issue, Galbraith suggested that there is a need for greater social justice as a prerequisite for sustained development because "Man is not so constituted that he will bend his best energies for the enrichment of some one else. As literacy is economically efficient, so is social justice" (1964, pp. 6–16).

But any discussion about greater equality in the economically less developed countries (the LDCs) needs to be situated within the wider context of a system of global social justice. Underdevelopment and inequality in the poorer countries cannot be ascribed simply to structural features or to the values, traditions, and beliefs of their population. It is partly a product of the international economic system, control over which is virtually in the hands of a small group

of rich nations. This inter-relationship between the economic/po-
litical power of the industrialized countries and the poverty of the
developing countries has been vividly described by Willy Brandt who
in 1986 noted that, "Every minute of every day the nations of the
world are spending around two million dollars on armaments and
other military expenditure. And every minute, some thirty children
aged five or six are dying because they do not have enough to eat, or
there is no clean water for them, and because they are denied any
kind of medical care" (1986, p. 15). His overall conclusion was that
the arms race, led mainly by the rich industrialized countries, was
inhibiting international efforts to improve the basic living standards
of the poor in the Third World.

To overcome this, global inequality efforts need to be made to
put an end to the dependency relationship that currently exists between the economically developed and the developing countries.
Viewed from this perspective, global inequality that helps to determine the foundation of economic life in the poorer countries becomes largely a political problem. Its reduction would permit a removal of the obstacles that, at the moment, arbitrarily allow one
group of people to impose their will over another, thereby reducing
the ability of those being dominated to choose and pursue their own
goals in life, with some realistic hope of success. However, any proposed step in this direction needs to start with an understanding of
the sources of such inequality.

Sources of Global Inequality
The current economic and political domination of the world order
by the richer countries has its roots in the industrialization of Europe that began in the nineteenth century. The industrial revolution
led to a "race for colonies" among Western societies seeking new
markets for their manufactured goods and additional sources of raw
materials. Colonial policy was therefore largely the "daughter of industrialization." A major outcome of colonization was "a long history of the subjugation" that transformed the social, political, and
economic structures of the colonized societies (Weisskopf, 1972, p.
45).

In addition, the concentration of economic power in the more
industrialized countries made it possible for them to shape the struc-

ture of the "world system" to serve their own interests, which contributed to the growing economic disparities between them and the poorer nations, especially after the 1850s (Patel, 1964, pp. 121–131). Colonialism thus led to the development of a world order that was based on a dominant/submissive relationship between the nations involved. This permitted the establishment of a world economy that allowed the dominant powers to pursue their own interests, irrespective of the consequences to the dominated.

Developments after the Second World War

After the Second World War, there emerged a number of new nation-states among the developing countries. But despite their achievement of "flag independence," the economic polarization between them and the more affluent countries continued. For example, while the difference in per capita incomes between the rich and the poor nations was around 1:2 at the beginning of the nineteenth century, the ratio had reached about 1:23 in 1950 and 1:40 by the 1970s. This situation has continued to decline further since then and by the year 2000, it is estimated that the developing countries that will then be inhabited by about 78% of the world's population will have only about 18% of the world's GNP (Kahn and Weiner, in Bell, 1969, pp. 84–86.). Incidentally, these estimates were based on the assumption of a 5.75–6.5% increase in GNP per annum among the developing countries between 1985 and 2000, which now seems quite unlikely.

This widening income gap between the poor and the rich countries has been occurring despite the official development assistance that the latter was providing. In fact, the level of this aid, which has been declining over the past years was very limited, both in terms of its real value and as a percentage of GNP of the major aid donors. The official development assistance was 0.52% of the GNP of the major donor countries in 1962, but this figure fell to 0.34% a decade later. The developed countries, as a group, have reduced the share of their gross national product devoted to aid every single year between 1962 and 1973—except in 1967 and 1973. By 1981 it was only 0.35% of their GNP, a figure that was far from the target of 0.7% suggested by the United Nations. Further, while there has been a recent tendency to shift more aid to the poorest of the developing countries, in 1980 they received on a per capita basis less than half the aid provided to middle income developing countries.

In addition, the aim of the richer countries in providing aid is not always or even primarily to raise the levels of living among the poor. Howard Ellis (1959) noted that of the $60 billion expended by the U. S. Government on foreign aid between 1945 and 1959, not more than 5% went as economic aid to the developing countries—an average of $3.00 per capita spread over twelve years. Military and defense support have been and still remain a dominant focus of the aid that some countries like the United States provide.

Admittedly, the new products introduced in the enclave sectors of the various colonial economies often became their main source of export earnings. But, because the industries were often foreign owned, the profits that could have been used for further local investment were exported to the metropole. The foreign entrepreneurs were less willing to reinvest their profits in the colonies from which they were obtained. In addition, the terms of trade that were largely influenced by the metropolitan countries were moving against the exports from the developing countries. For example, between the 1950s and the 1970s the non-oil-producing Third World countries had increased the volume of their exports by over 30%, while their revenues had risen by only 4% over the same period.

Further, the economically more developed countries spend large sums subsidizing their own primary producers thereby placing great price hurdles that the poorer countries have to face in trying to penetrate the markets of the richer countries. These countries also put up high tariff walls against the manufactured goods from the poorer countries (Ul Haq et al., 1977, p. 20). In the early 1960s, the recommendation by GATT was for a standstill on further trade barriers against the LDCs, and a gradual reduction in existing ones. A nonreciprocal reduction in trade barriers was also authorized in favor of the poorest countries. But these recommendations were ignored by the industrialized nations. At the same time, "a new international textiles agreement was approved" by which the economically more developed countries were permitted to discriminate against low-income countries, and "a new instrument of protectionist policy was introduced—the 'voluntary' export restraint, in which poor countries were induced, through threats of import quotas, to restrain their own exports" (Helleiner, 1976, p. 5). This attitude of the richer countries toward imported manufactured products from the developing countries has not substantially changed since. Hence, the long-term benefits of local economic growth often went to the metropolitan countries, contributing to the increasing income gap between these countries, both in relative and in absolute terms.

Finally, the richer countries utilize an inordinate amount of the world's resources, thereby enhancing their own economic growth in relation to and sometimes at the expense of the poorer countries. For example, the ten major industrial countries utilize over 75% of the world's energy resources, with the United States alone being responsible for consuming about of half of this amount (Tinbergen et al., 1977, p. 222). One outcome of this is the high price that developing countries have to pay for energy, which they can ill afford. In other words, as Professor Birch from the University of Sydney pointed out, one-third of the world became rich by continuing to use more than two-thirds of the world's available resources (in Tinbergen et al., 1977, pp. 220–227).

Redressing This Global Imbalance

The question that arises is, Can anything be done to ensure a fairer distribution of the world's wealth among its population? and if so, What role, if any, can education play in helping to readjust such growing economic, social, and political imbalances?

Judging from current international trends one has to admit that the possibility of achieving any marked reduction in the economic gap between these two groups of countries, which, "from an ethical . . . point of view . . ." is highly unlikely (Bhagwati, 1972, p. 9). There are a number of reasons for this conclusion. For example, in April 1974, the Sixth Special Session of the United Nations General Assembly made certain decisions—and these were nonbinding—that reflected the need for a more equitable distribution of the world's wealth to ensure the continued social and economic development of poor countries. But despite this, little progress has since been made with these measures.

The richer nations do not see any moral basis for a redistribution of the world resources and are usually not willing to make any temporary sacrifices, even when, as the Brandt Report pointed out, it is in their own interest to do so. Robert McNamara, a former president of the World Bank, having eventually recognized that the gains accruing to the global economy over the recent past had not been fairly distributed among nations or among population groups within nations, suggested that this pattern of development was unacceptable. However, in advocating some steps that might be taken he went on to ignore the importance of the existing global inequalities in influencing the maldistribution of the benefits from current development efforts. He therefore argued that we should not "waste our time" trying to place the blame for this situation on the economically developed countries "or worse, wear ourselves out in fruitless confrontation between rich and poor countries." Instead, we should concentrate our attention on reducing the marked income inequalities in the developing countries without paralyzing the incentive that they provide to increase productivity (McNamara cited in Chaliand, 1977, 13).

In 1984, when the World Bank tried to increase the amount of its interest-free loan to the poorest developing countries, or at least to make sure that the real value of the amount available for such loans was not reduced, the United States, which is economically and militarily the most powerful nation, unilaterally blocked these efforts and refused to make any compromise, despite the pressures from other nations. The result was that, as Brandt pointed out, in real terms there was less money available during the three-year period (1985–1987) than the preceding three years for such "soft loans." In terms of purchasing power, the amount provided was just over half of the sum previously available while the population that was eligible for these loans had practically doubled during that time (Brandt, 1986, p. 126).

On the other hand, with an increase in direct private investment in the developing countries by U.S. companies and private citizens, it was noted that the Reagan Administration became more heavily engaged in a systematic effort to "shape the world" in ways that would be most beneficial to these business interests. This has been a primary motivating force behind various instances of U.S. intervention in the developing countries in recent years (see McMahan, 1984).

In terms of human rights and democracy in the developing countries, Chomsky noted the commitment of the U.S. Government to it could mostly be regarded as rhetoric, directly contrary to the actual policies that it has pursued. It has often allied itself with reactionary ruling and military elites in the Third World whose role was to contain popular efforts to bring about change in the local political systems and extend democracy to the masses (Chomsky and Herman, 1979). In addition, the richer countries, and the United States in particular, have increasingly attempted to shift their support from multilateral organizations to those over which they have a greater degree of control, particularly their own bilateral organizations and even the World Bank, the IMF, and the OECD. The objective was to strengthen further their position of dominance over Third World countries.

These types of action have led some international development specialists to conclude that there is little chance of achieving greater equity in the distribution of the world's wealth. Birch (in Tinbergen et al., 1977, p. 226) noted that the economic gap between the developed and the developing countries is widening and

cannot be closed within the existing structures of international politics and economics. The present structures have brought us to a crisis which can only lead to deepening dimensions. Goods go to those who can afford to pay for them, and these are not usually those who need them most.

Possible Role of Education in Reducing Global Inequality

Nevertheless, many educators and others have not lost all hope in the possible contribution that education can make toward redressing some of this global imbalance. For example, the Brandt Report suggested that the provision of a broader education that would help people acquire a greater awareness of the interdependence among the nations of the world has been valuable in winning the support of some governments for increasing their aid to the poorer countries. As the report pointed out, "It is no accident that those countries in the North which score high in official development assistance also provide an outward looking education to their people and particularly to their younger generation" (Brandt, 1980, p. 259).

This more universalistic view of humanity implied in such "outward looking" education has always been shared by educators who have often tried to pass it on to their students and hence, to the future citizens of a country. But most governments have tended to be very narrow and nationalistic in their views about the appropriate education for their citizenry.

However, more recently, there has also been a shift in their outlook, as can be seen in the broadening of the content of the curriculum of schools in many countries, especially in the subject area usually referred to as "Social Studies." This was largely the outcome of a popular concern about the conditions that affect life on planet Earth—concern with such issues as the growing threat to the environment that is resulting from the often indiscriminate use and misuse of the world's natural resources, the lack of regard for other living species on earth, the gradual destruction of the ozone layer, and even the threat of nuclear destruction. The inhabitants of the world are gradually coming to realize that ultimately the survival of planet Earth itself depends on mutual understanding and cooperation among different nations.

Mutual Self-Interest versus Moral Consideration in Redressing Global Inequality

One useful strategy used to create a global concern among the world's population for the quality of life on earth was based largely on mutual self-interest. Such thinking dominated the report of the Brandt Commission, which suggested that the richer nations of the North should take steps to help alleviate poverty in the Third World—the South—out of enlightened self-interest. As the Commission (Brandt, 1980, p. 33) argued:

The achievement of economic growth in one country depends increasingly on the performance of others. The South cannot grow adequately without the North. The North cannot prosper or improve its situation unless there is greater progress in the South.

But while self-interest can be an important lever for action it is not a sufficient one when we are concerned with social justice for all and are considering the plight of the poorest inhabitants of this planet.

Douglas Roche (1977), a former Canadian Ambassador for Chairman of the United Nations Committee on Disarmament suggested that:

if there is any final proof of the inhumanity of the growth ethic that has dominated the life of the industrialized nations of the West, it is the fact that one billion men, women, and children in the thirty-five least developed nations are deprived of the basics of life while the affluent nations pile up their riches. . . . It is a scandal beyond belief. And our insensitivity is the greatest scandal of all.

The Brandt Report also suggested that we need to develop a sense of commitment to and solidarity with the less fortunate individuals throughout the world in our efforts to ensure social justice for all. Any educational program aimed at achieving this goal should therefore, in Pearson's words, also rest on the strong moral premise "that it is only right for those who have, to share with those who have not." This was one of the reasons why he recommended that "official development assistance should be raised to 0.70 per cent of donor GNP by 1975 and in no case later than 1980" (cited in Roche, 1977, p. 20).

Therefore, as educators, we have an obligation—even a moral obligation—to expose our students to these realities, such as the increasing destitution that now faces almost one billion individuals in the world and whose numbers are increasing annually. They should be made aware that this situation is inextricably linked not only with what is happening in the developing countries, but also with what is taking place in the world around them, especially in the economically more developed countries—events over which they often have no control. The objective would be to increase the sensitivity of the global population to the problems faced by all poor and marginalized peoples and provide them not only with an economic, but also a moral basis for action, to help alleviate these conditions.

Increasing Inequality in the Developing Countries

But even if these actions led to some modest redistribution of the world's resources between the economically more developed and the developing countries, a matter of continuing concern must be whether the broad masses of the people in the LDCs will benefit from this redistribution. In the developing countries themselves, there are even more marked inequalities in wealth among the population than in the richer countries and this gap is also widening. On the average, the top 5% of the population in the LDCs receive about 30% of the total national income as compared with 20% among the richer countries. In 1980, the poorest 20% of the population in Brazil received on an average only 2%, while the richest 20% received 67% of the country's income. In Malaysia the corresponding figures were 3% among the poorest 20% of the population and 57% among the richest 20%; in India the comparable figures were 7% for the poorest 20% and 49% for the richest 20% (see Griffin and Khan, 1982, pp. 236–251).

From 1950 up to about 1980, the developing countries on the whole have experienced a fairly substantial level of economic growth. During these years, their GDP increased at approximately 5.3% per annum, and, despite the fact that their population at least doubled during this period, their per capita incomes rose at about 2.3% per annum—a rate of growth that was said to have been unprecedented in world history. Yet, at the end of this period there was evidence that the overall economic growth did not affect a substantial section of their population.

For example, the "green revolution" has mainly profited the rich land owners, particularly in countries like India and the Philippines, since they were the ones in the best financial position to make the necessary investment to enhance crop production. Drawing from the research evidence from ten empirical studies undertaken to assess income trends in seven Asian countries, Griffin and Khan (1982, pp. 236–251) concluded that "development of the type experienced by the majority of Third World countries in the last quarter century has meant, for very large numbers of people, increased impoverishment." In most of the countries covered by their study, "the most outstanding facts to be noted are the worsening distribution of income and the declining real income of the rural poor." This decline has been occurring "even during periods of relatively rapid agricultural growth."

Export earnings in most developing countries are highly concentrated in a few commodities. This makes them extremely vulnerable to price changes that are usually dictated by the markets of the richer countries and over which the developing countries often have little or no control. They also depend heavily on inflow of foreign capital and this tends to be reflected in a large part of their economies being under foreign ownership, resulting in a steady outflow of income from foreign investment. This form of dependent capitalism makes sustainable development in these countries difficult. When restrictions are imposed on the export of profits, foreign investments in these countries tend to fall off, with a negative effect on their rate of economic growth.

It is estimated that between 20% and 50% of the population of many LDCs are still suffering from malnutrition. The UN figure was about 415 million in the 1970s, but other agencies put the number living in absolute poverty at about 1 billion in the 1980s. This suggests that about 40% of the population of the LDCs who are currently living "beneath any reasonable definition of human decency" are malnourished, disease ridden, and often illiterate (Hayter, 1981, p. 18). In some Third World countries, one child out of four dies before he/she reaches four years of age and in 1980 about 15 million children under the age of five years were reported to have died of hunger. Finally, about 600 million of them were reported to have been illiterate. Therefore, for these individuals the hopes that a faster economic growth rate would have benefited the masses of the people were not fulfilled and the increase in wealth that occurred was distributed very unequally among the population, with the poorest having increased their real income very marginally, if at all. In some countries, their standard of living has even been declining.

The growth rate experienced during the pre-1980 period has not continued for most developing countries—the major exception being some countries in South East Asia. This has resulted in a worsening of the position of the poorest sectors of the population in these countries. Up to 1988, it was still being noted that although rapid economic growth "has taken place over the past several decades in some Third World countries many others remain largely untouched by this process; the majority of the population remains illiterate and lives in abject poverty, especially in the rural areas. The overwhelming size of the rural population, its agrarian base," the heavy reliance by some countries on "food aid and the fact that such a large percentage lives below or at the poverty line, make it essential that development efforts be focused on the rural poor" (Barkat-e-Khuda and Vlassof, 1988, 1).

It was clear that economic growth and development are not synonymous. Improvement in the level of a country's GNP does not necessarily improve the living conditions of the poorest sections of the society. Therefore, it has been suggested that there is growing need to reconcile "the imperative of justice with the necessity of growth," a change that "might indeed constitute the greatest challenge of world poverty" (Loup, 1983, p. xv). This desire for increased economic productivity and output cannot be pursued without efforts to enhance social justice for all, if the stability of the State is not to be endangered.

From the information presented so far, it is clear that the poorer sections of the population in the developing countries have often gained little or nothing from the economic growth that their countries have experienced. In many cases the poor have become poorer, their share of the national income has decreased and rural poverty has increased. This type of lopsided development was experienced by many developing countries. Commenting specifically on the economic miracle that Brazil was said to have experienced some years ago, Furtado (1964, p. 32) observed:

We know that this development of which we are so proud has brought no change at all in the living conditions of three-fourths of the country's population. Its main feature has been a growing concentration of income both socially and geographically. The large mass of people who toil in the fields and constitute the majority of the Brazilian population have reaped no benefit (from this development). Worse than that, the masses have witnessed a relative decline in their standard of living as compared to those engaged in commerce and other services. As for individual workers . . . they have grown both in absolute and relative terms, without having improved their standard of living to any extent. They, too, have suffered a relative worsening of their economic position as compared to higher income groups employed in urban services. . . . Large amounts of wealth have been transferred to a few hands.

Similar outcomes of development efforts have been experienced in other LDCs. The situation of their very poor, especially in the rural areas, is worsening both in absolute and in relative terms, mainly because income and wealth distribution between the developed and developing countries and within the developing countries themselves is becoming more unequal. A key factor contributing to this is the very hierarchical and autocratic nature of the social systems of developing countries.

The Political Elite and Development

The system of stratification in most LDCs has proven to be one of the main barriers to a more equitable distribution of the fruits of development. Poor countries are typically characterized by a fairly rigid stratificatory system in which power is heavily concentrated in the hands of a small group of elites, either indigenous or foreigners who have established themselves locally. They include landowners, well-educated westernized professionals, senior bureaucrats, military officers, and some local entrepreneurs. This class of relatively wealthy individuals, with habits often characterized by higher spending and conspicuous consumption, generally recognize that there is a great similarity in their interests. They have, therefore, often come together collectively, at least in some loose but effective arrangement, to maintain their dominance in these societies. Sometimes they even form a fairly cohesive group—almost comprising a ruling class.

While the State can be an important instrument in facilitating a redistribution of incomes and wealth in these countries, the elites try to ensure that this does not happen by taking control of the State machinery. The result is that the State becomes primarily responsive to the interests of the members of this group. These politically dominant groups sometimes set up a democratic facade behind which they manipulate the affairs of the State, not in the interest of the masses, but of themselves. In this context, the State itself has often become a key obstacle to the achievement of greater equality and social justice in the LDCs.

Can the Increasing Inequalities within the LDCs Be Reversed?

The present and increasing inequality in the distribution of incomes and wealth is therefore a key aspect of life and an important feature of underdevelopment in Third World countries. There is, therefore, an urgent need to reverse this trend as a condition for speeding up their development. An earlier view, which was shared by some economists, was that there was an unavoidable conflict between economic growth and equality. It was therefore argued that poor countries had to concentrate their efforts on increasing production and had to put social justice and a more equitable distribution of the fruits of their development on the "back burner" until these countries had considerably increased the overall GNP. While this wealth was accumulating, the citizens had to pay the price of a more inegalitarian society.

The idea that production must take precedence over distribution was only challenged later when it become obvious that production and distribution were interdependent and had to move concurrently with each other. As Myrdal (1970) put it, greater equality in underdeveloped countries is a precondition for enhanced economic growth and, therefore, for "lifting" a society out of poverty. In the 1960s, the Economic Commission for Asia and the Far East (1968) pointed out that the lack of support for distributional aspects of a development policy provided a convenient excuse for the dominant groups in these societies to maintain the political and social status quo. The article went on to suggest that, judging from actual experience:

large and growing income disparities have not proved conducive to brisk economic performance and a strong thrust of development. It seems more likely . . . that heavy income concentration has often impeded healthy economic expansion by acting as a powerful disincentive (both material and psychological) to public participation in development. (1968, p. 58)

In the study of rural poverty in Asian countries referred to above, it was noted that many of the basic resources needed for development were at hand, foremost among them being the "intelligence, ingenuity, and effort of the labour force itself." But, "the exploitation and inequality to which the majority of the rural population is subjected is demoralizing, engenders resentment, and stifles initiative and creativity. The effect is not only to lower current output below its potential, but to reduce the capacity and willingness of the population to innovate" (Griffin and Khan, 1982, p. 241).

In trying to reverse this increasing inequality in these countries, major issues of concern have included the questions of who is in power? and in whose interests are development decisions made? In most cases, as indicated above, political and even economic power have been monopolized by cliques who, often with the assistance of the civil service and the military, directly or indirectly control the operation of the State machinery. To add insult to injury, they also loudly claim that they speak for the people in whose interest they are acting. In fact, as one development specialist observed, "the masses of people" in the developing countries have tended to be "the object of politics but hardly anywhere its subject" (Myrdal, 1970, p. 63). The "public opinion" to which reference is often made, is usually the view of the more articulate members of the upper and middle echelons of these societies. Therefore, the challenge that faces any attempt at increasing social justice in the LDCs, especially in terms of the distribution of the fruits of development, is to find ways and means of giving different forms of power—not only political, but also economic—to the ordinary people.

Hla Myint noted that LDCs tend to focus attention on the development of manufacturing as a key element in their efforts to achieve economic growth. But, as he pointed out, they tend to ignore the lack of an effective institutional framework that is necessary to support any ongoing development. This includes a "supporting political, social, and institutional framework" that gives growth "an ongoing character" (Myint, 1965, pp. 252–259). Similar sentiments were expressed by Paul Prebisch (1967) who indicated the need for profound changes in the economic, social, and political structure of Latin America for continuing economic growth to take place. In commenting specifically on the implementation of the Alliance for Progress Programme in 1967, he asked why people in that region should have to renounce their political freedom to reach higher targets of economic growth. He then went on to suggest the integration, in a single and coherent system of ideas, of the concepts of economic development and social justice, and of active democracy and personal dignity, with all their inherent prerogatives.

Galbraith, too, pointed out that economic and social progress in a society are dependent on political stability, which in turn helps economic and social progress. But this, in itself, rests on the greater participation of people in the decisions that affect their own lives. He therefore argued that there can be no advance in a society if the masses are not allowed to participate in determining their own political future, which implies a more "actively democratic" State. Political scientists such as Colin Leys also hint at the possibility of a positive correlation between the degree of democracy and a country's level of economic development. However, it is recognized that, while short-term economic gains are possible in more autocratic political systems, these are not likely to be lasting.

Furtado, drawing from the Latin American experience, comments on the importance of changes in the basic structure of these societies if they are to avoid the emergence of one of the major hindrances to self-sustaining development, that is, dictatorial regimes. He therefore emphasized the need for "principled political action" if a more equitable form of development is to occur. Commenting on the situation in Latin America also, Edmundo Flores noted that the most striking development need in these societies is for economic, social, and political change. He suggested that any rapid and sustained development will depend upon, among other things, meaningful land reform. But this will require drastic changes in the domestic balance of power and the political dynamics in these societies in general. Such changes would release the creative abilities and energies among the great mass of the population that have long been suppressed. Therefore, structural changes, especially in the political systems of Third World societies, are seen as a necessary precondition for an equitable and more lasting development.

The main point advanced by these different development specialists is essentially that the concentration of political power in the hands of a few members of the local political and economic oligarchy has been a major factor in stifling sustainable development in the Third World. For development of a more lasting nature to take place, there is need for an "active democracy" that will also make the realization of human rights for all members of the society possible. Conversely, greater equality among the population in these countries is also crucial for their maintenance of a stable democracy.

Furtado suggested that public opinion in these societies should be able to organize itself so that it can be expressed forthrightly, thereby starting a frank debate about what the population in general and the masses in particular expect from their government. This will help to ensure that a program emerges that will serve as the basis for strengthening and renewing the nature of popular representation. But, the proposal put forward below extends somewhat beyond this, to the direct involvement of the populace in decisions that are likely to shape their lives and the conditions of their existence.

Education for Development and Social Justice

The question that now arises is whether the provision of more educational opportunities or a different type of education might help to achieve concurrently both the goals of economic development and greater social justice for the population in the developing countries. Most educators consider a positive linear relationship between education and economic development to be axiomatic—with more education increasing qualitatively the stock of human capital, raising the level of cognitive skills of the workforce, and thereby increasing productivity and improving the rate of economic growth. For example, the Kothari Commission (Government of India, 1966) on education in India was convinced that it was education that determines the level of prosperity, welfare, and security of a people.

This point pertaining to the contribution of education to economic growth was initially advocated by the human capital theorists such as Schultz (1959) and others who tried to explain the rate of economic growth in the United States largely in terms of that country's rapid accumulation of better-educated workers. Later, Psacharopoulos of the World Bank also noted that returns on education were "well above the 10% normally used as a criterion for accepting an investment project" (1983, p. 11). Development economists therefore often suggested that many LDCs were allocating too little of their resources to education and concluded that the shortage of high-quality human capital was a key impediment to their rate of economic growth (Harbison and Myers, 1964).

The Unequal Impact of Education in Developing Countries

But while in general such a conclusion might be correct, it needs to be treated with some of degree of caution or even scepticism when applied to particular situations. In fact, the relationship between education and development is much more complex than is implied by this view. To illustrate this point, one might note that during the two decades between 1960 and 1980, primary, secondary, and tertiary enrollments in the developing countries rose by 142%, 358%, and 523%, respectively, and between 1960 and 1974 the LDCs increased the proportion of their national budgets on education from 11.7% to 15.1% (Coombs, 1985, p. 142). However, during the same period, unemployment in many of these countries rose, the number of malnourished and illiterate persons increased, inequalities in income distribution widened, and the number of those living below the level of bare subsistence multiplied.

In addition, despite the increased provision of educational facilities and the efforts made by some developing countries to universalize primary education, there is still only a very small proportion of individuals from the lower social strata who have been able to obtain a higher level of education, which is usually a prerequisite for access to the higher-income jobs. For example, Farrell and Schiefelbein (1985, pp. 490–506), in a long-term follow-up study of Education and Status Attainment in Chile, noted in 1985 that,

there is almost absolute inter-generational status inheritance at the very extremes of the system. All the children of the small upper class of 1960 retain their position, and all the agricultural labouring positions in the late 1970s are occupied by children of the same stratum.

From this and other studies, it is clear that for the poorer sections of these societies there still exist formidable obstacles to equality of job opportunity which result in "a tremendous waste of human abilities, vital energies, and initiative" (Coombs, 1985, p. 48).

In particular, the contribution of education to the improvement of life in the poorer rural communities seems even more doubtful and suggests that, in addition to education, other input variables are necessary to facilitate their economic and social development. In a fairly in-depth study of the contribution of formal education to the development of disadvantaged rural areas in Sri Lanka, Baker (1984) concludes that schools can and do "serve to enhance the development of individuals providing them with literacy, numeracy, and varied kinds of general knowledge, relevant or less relevant to their daily lives." But her findings also showed

that (such) successes are small. There is very little empirical evidence to link formal schooling in disadvantaged areas with community development in the sense of increased agrarian output, improved health, nutrition and housing, more equitable access to land and water, creation of new employment, or other such indicators. . . . In a setting where economic development has scarcely commenced, the village school cannot serve as a primary motor for advancement (p. 314).

Increasing Inequalities within the Developing Countries

After the developing countries had achieved their independence, they responded positively to the growing popular demand for more education and, as mentioned earlier, this resulted in the relatively massive expansion of educational facilities that occurred between 1960 and 1980. With the opening up of the higher echelons of their occupational structures to locals, following the withdrawal of expatriate staff, education provided substantial opportunities for upward mobility, especially for those who were able to obtain secondary and tertiary education.

But these countries then began to experience economic difficulties that resulted in a slowing down of the absorptive capacity of their labor markets, particularly for individuals with higher-level education and training. They also experienced financial problems in funding these services, especially since the 1980s. This resulted in a reduction of their previous rate of educational expansion and, in many cases, in the financial provision made for education. The outcome was often a lowering of the quality of education that their schools and other educational institutions were able to offer and increasing unemployment among the educated, even those with a tertiary education.

With their shrinking budgetary resources, these countries tried to grapple with the popular demand for more education in various ways, such as the privatization or increased privatization of schools and by encouraging communities to finance their own self-help schools as in the case of the Harambee Schools of Kenya. They have also tried to obtain more aid from the economically more developed countries or loans from the lending agencies, such as the World Bank, in order to meet their still growing demand for education. But with the current debt crisis and the decline in official development assistance, these solutions were not very effective. With the demand for education increasing, the governments of many LDCs became interested in educational services that were less expensive or were considered to have a more immediate economic payoff. Hence, greater emphasis began to be placed on nonformal education, distance education, education of women and girls, vocational education, and, in some cases, even universal elementary education.

But increased dependence on community financing of education has adversely affected educational opportunities in the poorer areas that can ill afford to raise the necessary funds to ensure that their children are provided with the necessary educational facilities required for high-quality education. In addition, with the slowing down of the economies of most developing countries and the reduction in the number of new jobs becoming available on the labor market, especially in the public sector, it is increasingly the children of the elites, including the political elites, who are often given preference in the selection of recruits to the better-paying positions on the job market.

In review, judging from the experience of individuals working in the LDCs, reports on educational projects, and research findings, it was the more depressed areas in these countries and the poorest sections of their population that benefited least from the economic and social benefits of education. This fact reminds us that a simple increase in the number of schools and greater access to them do not automatically result in increased social and economic prosperity for those living in the poorest sectors of these societies. There are obviously many reasons why this has been so.

It is quite clear that the objective of achieving a more equitable distribution of the fruits of education is not achieved simply by passing on new skills and knowledge to a larger number of students. The relevance or usefulness of the knowledge passed on in helping the students improve the quality of their lives, bearing in mind the resources that they have available, needs to be reexamined. Some of the educational programs that have been and are being offered are still in many ways, irrelevant to the needs and resources, especially of the poorer sections of these societies. One reason is that the education provided is not very useful in increasing the level of productivity in the large traditional sector of these societies. This is because it often does not take into consideration the other factors of production that are available and affordable to those in this larger sector in most developing countries. In other words, those providing the education have failed to recognize the fact that the usefulness of knowledge and skills imparted to individuals cannot be separated from the context in which it is to be used.

In addition to the seeming irrelevance of the education that is usually offered and the ineffectiveness of the instructional strategies that are often used, there are also problems presented by some of the structural constraints operating in the LDCs themselves and in their relationship with the economically more developed countries. These factors, which have been previously mentioned, also play a role in preventing education that is provided from making its maximum impact on the development of these societies. But, despite the local and international hurdles that interfere with efforts to improve the work of the schools in the LDCs, attempts need to be made to initiate ways and means by which what goes on in schools in these countries can more effectively contribute to national development.

It has been suggested above that an "active" democratic system of government will contribute to economic development by releasing the creative energies of all sectors of the population, enhancing the responsibility of individuals for their own futures, and deepening their participation in making decisions that are likely to affect their own lives. For this to happen, the educational programs and instructional strategies used in schools and other educational institutions must help to develop the necessary skills, capabilities, and attitudes in the population. The education should be the type that encourages enterprise and innovation, helping the students to overcome some traditional values and beliefs that might have a negative influence on the changes necessary for development. Therefore, what is needed is an education that not only provides certain necessary job skills, but also the normative support for progressive changes that are likely to foster development. It is only when the population as a whole has an important say in determining its nation's development strategies and is in a position to influence the distribution of the benefits of development, that one is likely to see educational programs contributing more effectively to an enhancement of economic growth and greater social justice for all citizens in the country. But the question that arises is how can education help to achieve this goal?

An Education for Development

The education currently provided in most developing countries has, as in the colonial days, continued to reflect the concerns and interests of the ruling elites. As these countries experience economic difficulties, those who control the State machinery try to use the school system to bolster their legitimacy as political leaders. When this fails, as sometimes happens with students in secondary schools and universities, the elites frequently resort to the use of the physical control mechanisms of the State to maintain power. But this, in turn, presents problems for achieving genuine and sustainable economic growth and a more just and equitable distribution of the benefits of development. More creative solutions, therefore, must be found and schools need to search for programs and strategies that might help to make a more effective contribution to the achievement of this "actively democratic" state that is needed in these countries. One way in which the educational system of the LDCs can play an important role in economic development is by attempting to empower the masses—thereby laying a foundation that is likely to ensure that the outcomes of the nation's development efforts will be used in the interests of all—and not only of the elites.

Here, it might be useful to remind ourselves of the fact that development in most Third World countries has, so far, resulted in increasing social divisions and marginalization of substantial sections of the population while their dominant groups have continued to be the main beneficiaries of their often elitist educational systems. The current situation should therefore present a challenge for the educators in these countries to develop counter-hegemonic educational strategies that will prepare students with the knowledge, skills, attitudes, and dispositions that can help to redirect the course of these developments in favor of the economically more disadvantaged groups.

The suggestion here is that a start along these lines might be made by examining the weakness of the very knowledge systems and the instructional strategies used by educational institutions in these countries. Habermas has drawn attention to the three basic knowledge interests that he suggests ought to guide the concerns of all educators (see Bacchus, 1992, p. 107). They are empirical-analytical; social, historical, or hermeneutic; and critical emancipatory knowledge interests. So far, the education offered in the ldcs has focused mainly on the first two areas, that is, empirical analytical and to a lesser extent historical or social science and virtually neglected the third area—critical emancipatory knowledge. But even with this major limitation, educational institutions in the LDCs have not done a very good job. Research evidence from the international studies on educational achievement indicates that, in the LDCs, students' performance in science still leaves much to be desired. In the area of the social sciences, the knowledge transmitted to students aimed at increasing their understanding of social events in their societies often has its roots in the experiences and research done in the metropolitan countries. Hence, this knowledge is usually quite inappropriate in helping them increase their understanding of the structure and dynamics of their own realities.

Importance of Critical Emancipatory Knowledge

The major objective of critical emancipatory knowledge is to help develop in individuals a greater and more perceptive understanding of the phenomena that surround them and sharpen their awareness of the relationships of dominance and submission that affect their lives. Hence, critical emancipatory knowledge aims at increasing people's consciousness of their own reality and, where necessary, making them better prepared to transform that reality.

Some would argue that the inculcation of critical emancipatory knowledge in students is a political act and therefore schools, as "neutral" institutions, should not be involved in it. This ignores the fact that education is itself a political act that attempts not only to produce skills for the economy, but also to legitimize the existing social order. The goals toward which educational specialists work and which they have often helped to define, are also political in nature—whether these deal with more efficient means of selecting students for secondary schools or with setting curriculum goals for the various subjects offered in the timetable.

As educators begin to realize the importance of a critical emancipatory knowledge interest in their work, this should lead them to be concerned with such questions as, How can education help to raise the sensitivity or consciousness of students and later the population in general to the realities of their own social existence? and How can it contribute to helping the population play a more effective role in the social transformation of their own societies as a first step toward improving the levels of living of the population as a whole and not only the more privileged sections? and How can teachers and others involved in the educational process help to overcome the barriers that interfere with the emancipatory possibilities of education? These types of questions are also likely to increase the concern of educators for such issues as, In what ways have the internal social, economic, and political structures of their societies been exerting a negative influence on the contribution that education has been making to development and what might be done to change this situation? How can they help to convert a so-called silent majority into a vocal one that will get deaf governments to really listen more responsively to them and act on their suggestions? One still finds that much of the efforts of those involved in education in the LDCs have tended to ignore questions such as these because they have neglected to consider the emancipatory possibilities of education. Instead, they have spent most of their time grappling with the more technical and sometimes peripheral issues in education.

As previously indicated, schools try to impose a knowledge system and an understanding of reality that support the interests of the ruling groups. This process is often carried out in what Freire (1972) describes as the "banking" mode and this is done through "a dominating social grammar" that regulates both what is to be taught in schools and how it is to be taught. In addition, formal schooling has been an instrument to assist the elites in their efforts to disparage and regard as inferior the knowledge, culture, and traditions of the masses. Therefore, total dependence on the two main knowledge systems that currently dominate the work of most educational institutions in the developing countries, limits the possibility of developing critical teaching and therefore reduces the emancipatory possibilities of education.

A change would also have to be made in the pattern of instruction currently used in the schools, through the development of a more active intervention by teachers in the way they teach. Teachers must be helped to become "transformative intellectuals," to use Giroux's phrase. As such, they would be in a better position to focus their instructional strategies on developing a sense of "citizenship and the politics of possibility." This is a concept of schooling in which classrooms are seen as active sites of public intervention and of intellectual and social struggle aimed at eventually preparing students to participate more fully in making decisions that would affect their own lives and those of other sections of the population. Students need to be taught to question the basic assumptions and precepts of their societies, rather than just adapting to them, and this process must be conducted in such a way that both teachers and their students will begin to redefine reality in their own terms and from their own experiences, grounded in the view that the standpoint of the victims of any society ought to always provide the starting point for a critique of that society (Giroux, 1989).

Therefore, a beginning needs to be made by getting teachers to no longer take as "given" all the knowledge that has been traditionally transmitted to students in school. Rather, much of the knowledge, especially in the social sciences should be treated as problematic, partly because, as was previously indicated, much of it is based on an interpretation of reality that serves the interests of the dominant groups and, as a result, reinforces the existing social relationships in a society. Therefore, both teachers and students must recognize the fact that various forms of knowledge currently passed on in schools tend to distort and produce a certain perception of social reality that influences the shape of their lives and eventually those of the population at large.

In review, one notes that the development of this critical emancipatory knowledge, as suggested above, depends both on the content of the knowledge that schools attempt to pass on and on the teaching methodology used. Even basic literacy, as Gramsci and others

noted, can be used to develop forms of counter-hegemonic education, a point that has been demonstrated by Freire in his adult education efforts. But, for this to happen, attention needs to be directed
at the development not only of reading skills, but also of a greater
social self-awareness among learners, including an awareness of the
underlying factors that perpetuate the relationships of dominance
and submission between various groups in their societies. Even literacy, it has been suggested, has to be viewed as a social construction
that is ". . . implicated in organizing one's view of the past, the present,
and the future" (Giroux, 1989, p. 152). Therefore, ignorance should
not be treated simply as the absence of knowledge, but as a condition from which a more incisive perception of reality can be developed in the population by means of what Simon refers to as "transformative pedagogy."

This view that much social science knowledge is socially constructed reality will provide students "with the opportunity" as Giroux
points out, "to give meaning and expression to their own needs and
voices as part of a project of self and social empowerment" (1989, p.
153). In other words, through a critical emancipatory approach to
teaching, students will learn to question more effectively the knowledge claims that the dominant groups often present as the obvious
and only legitimate basis of social relationships and life in society.

Therefore, if education is to better serve the interests of the masses,
it should not only enable the students to understand more fully the
scientific, political, economic, and cultural forces that directly influence their lives, but should also teach them how they might acquire
greater control of these forces and thereby be prepared to play a more
direct role in determining the outcomes of their own lives.

In summary, schools should not be involved in teaching only
the traditional academic subjects from the fields of the natural, physical, and social sciences, but should also, through the use of a "critical
pedagogy," create conditions that will prepare students to challenge
the reality presented by these areas of knowledge. This would be
part of a process of empowering students to become morally and
politically active individuals who would eventually be contributing
to the achievement of a more just and equitable society—locally,
nationally, and internationally.

Giroux makes a similar point defining empowerment, which he

sees as an outcome of effective schooling. This, as he pointed out, is "the process whereby students acquire the means to critically appropriate knowledge existing outside their immediate experience in order to broaden their understanding of themselves and the world around them and grasp the possibilities for transforming the taken-for-granted assumptions about the way we live" (1989, p. 153). The effect of such an approach on the students will be to prepare them not only to understand, but eventually also to transform the elitist political structure and dynamics of their societies, which are a hindrance to genuine and self-sustained development. This would help to ensure that political power is shared by all and that there will be active popular involvement in the making of decisions that are likely to affect the lives and living conditions of the citizenry in general.

As far as teachers are concerned, it is being suggested here that the overall aim should be to enable them to develop what is referred to as a more "active pedagogy" that starts with the view that education has a broader moral purpose, which is to help students play a more active role in overcoming injustice, inequality, and domination in their societies. To do this, it must begin by taking as objects of analysis and inquiry the knowledge, the experiences, the understandings, the needs, the expectations, and the problems of the students themselves as the points of commencement of their education. These should be brought into an interface and an exchange with the knowledge that schools have traditionally attempted to pass on to their students. Such an approach will provide students with the ability to question critically their own background experiences and traditional understandings of reality. It should also help them to acquire a deeper understanding of the dominant culture and this would better prepare them to transform it, so as to serve the interests of the population at large. It is this vision of the emancipatory possibilities of education that those involved in education for development in the Third World countries need to rekindle, if they hope to increase its effectiveness in contributing to the genuine development of these societies. So that, while some of the present educational policies and programs of most developing countries are likely to help raise the standards of living of at least some sectors of their population, they are really "Band-Aid" solutions to the problem of trying to ensure economic growth with social justice for all. However, given that schools in these countries are here to stay and will continue to increase their enrollments, a step that might be taken is to try to improve the effectiveness of their instructional programs. By "effectiveness," one is referring here to the value of the skills, knowledge, attitudes, and dispositions that teachers attempt to inculcate in their pupils and that might eventually help them to improve their quality of life. This would point to the need for educators to reexamine the nature of the curriculum and the instructional strategies that schools in the developing countries use. In these efforts, they should see how far both the stated and the hidden curriculum might be revamped to increase the contribution that can be made to the personal, social, and economic development of the students, especially of the poorer sections in these societies, and, at the same time, equip them to contribute even more effectively to the genuine development of their societies. This is why the inclusion of a critical emancipatory dimension in education in the developing countries is so important.

References

Bacchus, M.K. (1992). "Education in the Third World." In R.J. Burns and A.R. Welch (eds.) *Contemporary Perspectives in Comparative Education*. New York: Garland.

Baker, Victoria J. (1984). *The Blackboard Jungle: Formal Education in Disadvantaged Areas; A Sri Lankan Case*. Delft, Netherlands: Eburon Publishers.

Barkat-e-Khuda, and Carol Vlassof (1988). "Introduction." In *The Impact of Modernization on Development and Economic Behaviour*. Ottawa: IDRC.

Bell, D. (ed.) (1969). *Toward the Year 2000: Work in Progress*. Boston: Beacon Press.

Bhagwati, Jagdish (1972). "Introduction." In *Economics and World Order from 1970s to 1990s*. New York: Macmillan.

Brandt, Willy (Chairman) (1980). *North-South: A Programme for Survival (The Report of the Independent Commission on International Development Issues)*. (The Brandt Report) London: Pan Books.

———— (1986). *World Armament and World Hunger: A Call for Action*. London: Victor Gollancz Ltd.

Chaliand, Gerard (1977). *Revolution in the Third World: Myths and Prospects*. New York: Viking.

Chomsky, N., and E.S. Herman (1979). *The Washington Connection and Third World Fascism. The Political Economy of Human Rights, Vol.1*. Nottingham: Spokesman.

Coombs, P.H. (1985). *The World Crisis in Education*. New York: Oxford University Press.

Economic Commission for Asia and the Far East (1968). "Recent Social Trends and Developments in Asia." *Economic Bulletin for Asia and the Far East*, vol. xix, no. 1.

Ellis, H.S. (1959). "A Perspective on US Foreign Aid." In P. Zook (ed.) *Economic Development and International Trade: A Perspective*. Dallas: Southern Methodist University Press.

Farrell, J.P., and Schiefelbein, E. (1985). "Education and Status Attainment in Chile."

Comparative Education Review, vol. 29, no. 4.

Freire, Paulo (1972). *Pedagogy of the Oppressed.* Harmondsworth: Penguin.

Furtado, Celso (1964). "Brazil: What Kind of Revolution?" In Laura Randall (ed.) *Economic Development: Evolution or Revolution.* Lexington, Mass.: D.C. Heath and Co.

Galbraith, J.K. (1964). *Economic Development in Perspective.* Cambridge, Mass.: Harvard University Press.

Giroux, Henry A. (1989). *Schooling for Democracy.* London: Routledge.

Government of India, Ministry of Education (1966). *Report of the Education Commission 1964–1968* (The Kothari Commission). New Delhi.

Griffin, Keith, and A.R. Khan (1982). "Poverty in the Third World: Ugly Facts and Fancy Models." In H. Alavi and T. Shanin (eds.) *Introduction to the Sociology of Developing Societies.* London: Macmillan.

Harbison, F., and C.A. Myers. (1964). *Education, Manpower and Economic Growth: Strategies of Human Resource Development.* New York: McGraw-Hill.

Hayter, T. (1981). *The Creation of World Poverty.* London: Pluto Press.

Helleiner, G.K. (1976). "Introduction." In *A World Divided: The Less Developed Countries in the International Economy.* New York: Cambridge University Press.

Loup, Jacques (1983). *Can the Third World Survive?* Baltimore: Johns Hopkins University Press.

McMahan, Jeff (1984). *Reagan and the World: Imperial Policy in the New Cold War.* London: Pluto Press.

Myint, Hla (1965). "Social Flexibility, Social Distance and Economic Growth." *International Social Science Journal*, vol. xvii, no.2.

Myrdal, Gunnar (1970). *The Challenge of World Poverty: A World Anti-Poverty Program in Outline.* New York: Random House.

Patel, S.J. (1964). "The Economic Distance Between Nations: Its Origin, Measurement and Outlook." *The Economic Journal*, March.

Prebisch, Paul (1967). "Economic Aspects of the Alliance for Progress." In S. Tangri and Peter Gray (eds.) *Capital Accumulation and Economic Development.* Boston: D.C. Heath and Co.

Psacharopoulos, George (1983). "Education as an Investment." In A. Habte, G. Psacharopoulos, and S.P. Heyneman. *Education and Investment: Views from the World Bank.* Washington: The World Bank.

Roche, Douglas (1977). *Justice Not Charity: A New Global Ethic for Canada.* Toronto: McClelland and Stewart Ltd.

Schultz, T.W. (1959). "Investment in Man: An Economic View." *Social Science Review*, vol. xxxiii, no. 2.

Tinbergen, J., et al. (1977). "Rich Against Poor Nations." In *Political Economy of Development.* Sydney: Australian Broadcasting Commission.

Ul Haq, Mahbud, et al. (1977). "The New International Economic Order." In *Political Economy of Development.* Sydney: Australian Broadcasting Commission.

Weisskopf, Thomas E. (1972). "Capitalism, Underdevelopment and the Future of the Poor Countries." In J. Bhagwati (ed.) *Economics and World Order from 1970s to 1990s.* New York: Macmillan.

Education, Global Fordism,[1] and the Demise of Social Justice in the Third World

John Martino

Ironically the richest most capitalised country in the world is actually being financed by the poor countries through the creation of international monetary reserves. Economic logic as well as humane concerns should lead the richer and more capitalised countries to help economic development in the poorer countries. This is piously stressed again and again in United Nations resolutions. But the United States is doing the exact opposite; it is having itself financed by poorer countries, even the poorest countries.

Paul Vallely, Bad Samaritans: First World Ethics and Third World Debt

Introduction

The problem of how to pay off the Third World's massive debt, while at the same time maintaining some type of commitment to social justice goals, has been solved. The notion of social justice has been all but abandoned. This essay will highlight how the majority of Third World nations have, in the area of education, abandoned a commitment to social justice. It will also analyze the shift in funding from the provision of basic education programs to tertiary education programs that benefit the children of the elite and middle-classes (UNICEF, 1992, p. 31).

A major aim of this chapter is to show that the cutbacks engendered by the demands of the international financial institutions have not been equally shared among all classes in the developing nations. For the purposes of this chapter, I will focus on the ramifications of structural adjustment[2] for the provision of schooling and other basic social services in the developing nations. Programs of structural adjustment have been used as a mechanism with which this shift in

emphasis has been achieved. Under the guise of meeting the demands of the international financial institutions, existing levels of
injustice have been exacerbated.

Background

In the heady days of the postwar liberation movements, social justice, in the forms of socialist redistribution, development, and ex-
propriation was a dominant idea. African nations, such as Tanzania
under Julius Nyrere, took an independent and socialist development
path. In the case of Tanzania during the 1970s, it adopted a form of
socialism based on familyhood called *ujamaa;* the ideology provided
the basis for substantial agricultural reform. Nyrere argued that the
basis of the ideology of *ujamaa* would be the belief in ". . . putting
one's trust in one's own efforts" (Tetzlaff, 1991, p. 161). *Ujamaa*
aimed at achieving development that was not subject to dependence
on foreign money, a policy that has been an abject failure. Due to a
combination of external factors, in particular the decline in demand
for Tanzania's agricultural produce, Tanzania has become one of the
largest debtor nations and is subject to an IMF and World Bank
program of structural adjustment (Cheru, 1989, pp. 82–93; Tetzlaff,
1991, pp. 161–162).

In Latin America the Chilean socialist government of Salvador
Allende had been elected to government on a platform of socialist
policies, and a firm commitment to the achievement of social justice. Chile was not permitted the same latitude as Tanzania; its attempts to achieve social justice were subjected to external programs
of covert action culminating in the removal of Allende in a bloody
military coup in 1973 (Crough and Wheelwright, 1982, pp. 72–
73). Following the demise of the Allende government, Chile was
also subjected to an IMF and World Bank program of structural
adjustment. In both cases alternative models to capitalist development were overturned, and replaced with market-oriented models
and governments that would follow through with the IMF and World
Bank programs of structural adjustment.

The revolutions of 1989 in Eastern Europe also played their
part in removing alternative development models. With the collapse
of communism, the majority of Third World nations that had once
adopted the Soviet model, have now decided to follow the Western

development path and have moved to orient their social system toward a market-based social system. With the demise of existing socialism, any alternative social system to capitalism has evaporated. In this context the attempt by many developing nations to create a more equitable and just society has been left by the wayside.

Following decolonization, education in the newly emergent nations was regarded as a mechanism with which to enhance the process of development. As the great Indian nationalist leader Jawaharlal Nehru pointed out in 1949:

Ultimately the greatness of the nation depends on the number of first-rate people it produces in all fields of activity. For this certain innate qualities are needed as everybody cannot be an Einstein. . . . It is necessary to raise the general standard and give every person an opportunity to develop his potentialities. (Nehru, 1990, p. 83)

Nehru and the Indian nationalist movement saw education as providing the means whereby a postcolonial India could develop to its full potential.

The younger generation is our future hope. On them depends the progress of the country. The way their faculties are developed and minds moulded will make or mar India's destiny. Hence the need to give top priority to the educational needs of the growing generation. (Nehru, 1987, p. 407)

The high hopes of nationalist leaders such as Nehru, that schooling would act as a catalyst to the creation of a fair and just society, have in recent years been abandoned. The nature of education in the Third World has changed from a force for the uplifting of the masses, as reflected in the egalitarian aims of men such as Nehru, to a system that benefits the children of the ruling elite and the middle class.

The priorities for developing nations have changed from meeting some type of social justice agenda, to debt servicing as they borrow massively in an effort to develop a Fordist regime of accumulation within the global capitalist system. The massive foreign debt burden has deformed the modernization process in the developing nations. The goals of freedom and equity that were at the forefront of the rhetoric of the postwar liberation movements have been supplanted by the demands of participating more vigorously in the global market.

Fordism and the Third World

Advanced industrialized capitalist nations are investing greater sums of money on education as they reform their education and training programs in an effort to meet the requirements of the new, more flexible systems of production demanded by the global market under the post-Fordist regime of accumulation. At the same time, the Third World is grappling with how to bring about a functional Fordist[3] regime of accumulation.

Essentially, Fordism is a system of production based on Taylorist principles and the use of a conveyor belt; it was first used by Henry Ford in his Detroit factory (Mathews, 1989, pp. 24–28). This process created the first effective means of mass producing standardized consumer goods; in Ford's case it was the Model T Ford motor car. This was the dawn of the system of mass production.

In 1910, Henry Ford instituted the line production system for maximum production economy in his Highland Park, Michigan, plant. The innovation, though in many ways unsophisticated, and hardly educated as to its own implications, was the beginning of a momentous transformation in America's capacity to produce. In quantitative terms, the change was staggering. On the 1910 line, the time required to assemble a chassis was twelve hours and twenty-eight minutes. By spring of 1914, the Highland Park plant was turning out over 1,000 vehicles a day, and the average labor time for assembling a chassis had dropped to one hour and thirty-three minutes. (Ewen, 1977, p. 23)

Intimately linked with this productive process was the development of a Fordist regime of accumulation (Aglietta, 1987; Lipietz, 1987). Fordist productive processes, based on Taylorist scientific principles, created a system for the mass production of consumer goods. However, the ability to mass produce consumer goods is not enough to develop a functioning regime of accumulation; coupled with mass production, Fordism required a system of mass consumption (Ewen, 1977, pp. 23–27; Aglietta, 1987; Lipietz,

1987). This is dependent upon a system of regulation whereby, in the context of the Fordist economy, regulation refers to more than just the regulation of the labor process, or the principal sectors of growth in an economy, to move beyond the strictly economic to include both political and cultural considerations. It involves the policy interventions made by national governments in their attempt to balance mass production and mass consumption, and thus underpin long-term growth. In advanced industrialized/capitalist nations such as Germany and Australia, this has meant a kind of social contract being entered into by organized labor, organized capital, and the State, to provide social services, high wages, and a growing standard of living.

In the context of the Third World, it has been argued that since decolonization the ruling elites have been attempting to develop Fordist regimes of accumulation. This involves the creation of effective internal markets with a degree of mass-purchasing power. The Third World (with the exception of certain Latin American nations) has failed to develop a true Fordist regime of accumulation (Hein and Mutter, 1991).

Hein and Mutter argue that the reasons for this lay in the lack of a number of

preconditions for a sweeping process of Fordist modernization—the industrial base, the social and material infrastructure, and a growth in agricultural productivity, such as that which occurred in Europe in the lead-up to the industrial revolution—did not exist in the Third World. Nevertheless, in some countries the rapidly increasing income of the upper middle classes, which contrasted with the falling real income of the lower classes in towns and on the land, created the basis for a "peripheral-Fordist" accumulation model: the very classes which accounted for the bulk of effective demand were able to increase their incomes, whilst those whose low incomes did not permit them to demand luxury goods or consumer durables to any great extent sustained losses. (Hein and Mutter, 1991, p. 100)

Peripheral Fordism is based on a deformed regime of accumulation; it has neither the economic nor cultural infrastructure necessary to establish the type of social contract between organized labor and the capitalist classes that lay at the heart of Fordism proper. In contrast to this deformed model of Fordism, the economic power-houses of Japan and the Asian tigers have been highly successful in their efforts to move into a Fordist regime of accumulation, and in the case of nations such as South Korea and Taiwan they are moving beyond the Fordist model of capitalism, into post-Fordism. Where does this leave the Third World? During the 1970s and 1980s, they borrowed massively in an effort to follow the Asian tigers into the First World, a policy that has left these nations all but destitute. The immediate consequences of this growth in indebtedness has been a reorientation of government policy. It would appear that in the push to develop a Fordist regime of accumulation under the conditions of market society and global capitalism, issues of social justice have been ignored.

The rhetoric and ideology of the market (in the form of the ideas of the Chicago school)[4] have permeated both the discourse and prac-tice of government policies, leading to a further deterioration in the living conditions of ordinary people in developing nations. Under the influence of Western financial institutions, such as the IMF and the World Bank, the development ideology embodied in the trickle down and human capital[5] theories, so popular in the 1950s and 1960s, has given way to structural adjustment and the wholesale reduction of government services in an effort to repay the burgeoning debt bur-den. Over the past decade or more, governmental attempts to satisfy the "debt squads"[6] have led to a decline in the provision of basic levels of social and educational programs for the mass of the population. The immediate beneficiaries of this decline in the provision of pro-grams for the majority of the population have been the middle classes.

Although the results of the process—increasing social and regional polar-ization and the pauperization of large sections of the population—were not quite what the modernization ideologues had expected, they were nevertheless in no way inconsistent with the interests of those leading forces within society (transnational concerns, the bureaucracies, the middle classes, and the bourgeoisie in the countries of the Third World) which supported the modernization strategy. The propagation of the American way of life, the interests of transnational concerns in expanding the mar-kets for the standardized products which they had developed for the mass consumer-goods market of the industrialized world, and social conditions in the somewhat more advanced countries of Latin America, all came together in the process of the internationalization of domestic markets. (Hein and Mutter, 1991, p. 100)

In effect this meant the growth in demand for luxury goods by the small segment of the population, the elites, who have the income to do more than dream of the American way of life. This craving to be Western led to the creation of peripheral Fordism in which a regime of accumulation has ultimately benefited only a tiny portion of the population. The embracing of the American way of life by important segments of the population of the Third World and the subsequent internationalization of domestic markets led to their full integration into the global capitalist market. This was achieved at a massive cost in human life and misery.

Paying for the American Way of Life: The Effects of IMF and World Bank Programs of Structural Adjustment

During the 1970s, the World Bank outlined the role it saw education playing in the process of Third World modernization. World Bank educational policy asserted that in the developing nations:

There should be at least a minimum basic education for all, available as fully and as soon as resources permit. . . . Further education and training beyond the basic level should be provided selectively to improve, both quantitatively and qualitatively, the knowledge and skills necessary for the performance of economic, social, and other roles. . . . A national education system should be viewed as a comprehensive system of learning, embracing formal, non-formal and informal education, all working with maximum possible internal and external efficiency. . . . In the interests of both increased productivity and social equity, educational opportunities should be equalised as fully as possible. (World Bank, 1974, pp. 6–7)

The 1980s was a decade in which aims such as those espoused by the World Bank were all but abandoned in the Third World. During that period the primary objective of the IMF and World Bank was to regulate Third World debt, and ensure that the debtor nations repaid their loans. When Third World nations ran into problems in meeting their debt burden the IMF and World Bank would force them to engage in programs of structural adjustment. This type of

crisis management leads regularly to economic overkill for debtor economies: the GNP declines, the volume of imports has to be cut, and investment falls. The principal victims of failed adjustment policies are the members of the lower strata. For the majority of the population the so-called elimination of inefficiency in the public sector and the introduction of market-oriented prices policies mean, invariably, mass redundancies, the withdrawal of subsidies on basic foodstuffs and public transport, and cuts in public health services and education. (Chahoud, 1991, p. 34)

The end result of such government cutbacks in the Third World is the deterioration in the living standards of the already desperately poor. The thinking behind these programs of structural adjustment is that if the Third World can get the prices right, by cutting expenditure and reducing internal tariffs, these nations will become globally competitive. However, such thinking ignores the structural problems faced by the developing nations. Their lack of infrastructure, roads, ports, railways, as well as their lack of industries specializing in the production of primary goods, warehousing facilities, and so forth, means that it is near impossible for them to create the type of economically rational internal market that the IMF and World Bank demand. As Green (1989, p. 33) explains:

The challenge to Fund and Bank stabilisation/adjustment programs is often put in a form that suggests that the programs themselves raise inequality, poverty, and vulnerability and do so with deliberate intent. The last is not the case—the Bank and especially the Fund do often find the poor and vulnerable to be invisible and/or design programs without actually checking their social impact, but malicious aforethought is simply not evident. Indeed they genuinely (if often naively or erroneously) believe that a stronger economy is a necessary (quite possibly true) and virtually a sufficient (frequently false) condition for enhancing the welfare of the poor and reducing their vulnerability.

There is a two-sided dilemma here. On the one hand, how to fund social justice programs in the developing nations when they are all but suffocating under the weight of their indebtedness? And on the other, is the idea of social justice really an issue when developing nations subscribe to the laisse-faire philosophy of Milton Friedman and the Chicago school? This misanthropic philosophy is based on the notion that the weak retard the prosperity of the strong, and that to assist the weak is to handicap the natural functioning of market forces.

In the developing nations these dilemmas have been partially resolved to the extent that funding has been shifted from basic literacy programs to the provision of elite education. Basic literacy is not a high priority, however, the provision of tertiary education and the production of graduates is a high priority. The problem of paying for social justice in Third World education has been solved; social justice is no longer a major priority.

Education and the Demise of Social Justice in the Third World

The United Nations Children's Fund (UNICEF) has been documenting the deterioration in the provision of basic levels of education in the developing world in a series of annual reports on the condition of the world's children. According to the authors of the UNICEF report *The State of the World's Children:*

Despite decades of research findings which regularly demonstrate that investment in primary education yields significantly higher returns in both social progress and economic growth, government spending in almost all developing countries is heavily biased towards higher education for the few rather than basic education for the many. (UNICEF, 1992, p. 31)

This UNICEF report highlights the extent to which a great number of developing nations have shifted resources from basic education to the financing of higher education at levels that are quite disproportionate to the amount spent on basic education. According to UNICEF, this leads to

*the result that up to half of all children fail to complete four years in
primary school while secondary and tertiary education absorbs an ex-
aggerated share of the budget in order to produce many more of the
graduates than the economy can usefully absorb. (1992, pp. 31–32)*

The outcome of this reorientation of Third World education
systems, so that funding and resources shift to the provision of higher
education, has been that education services the needs of national
elites, rather than the whole of the population. It is these groups
who complete primary and secondary schooling and then move on
to University. The UNICEF (1992, p. 32) report asserts that

*in Chile, the Dominican Republic, and Uruguay, for example, more
than 50% of all government spending on higher education is devoted to
the children of families who belong to the richest 20% of the population.
In India, 50% of all government spending on education is used to sub-
sidize the best educated 10%.*

Not only do the poor miss out on a basic and minimum level of
education, in many developing nations resources are being siphoned
off in order to educate the children of the rich. These figures speak
for themselves; social justice in nations such as Chile and India has
long disappeared from the government agenda.

The beneficiaries of this reorientation in the provision of education in the Third World are not only the children of the elite and
the middle class; the First World gains a great deal from this distortion of Third World systems of education. I am referring to the old
cliché of being a "brain drain." First World industries, universities,
and government agencies are able to entice the best of the elite,
tertiary-trained Third World scientists and intellectuals to migrate
or stay on after graduation. Gerald Kruijer, for instance, points out
that:

*Between 1961 and 1972, some 300,000 highly skilled workers left the
underdeveloped for the developed countries. Most of them went to the
United States (90,000), Great Britain (84,000) and Canada (56,000).
The largest number of immigrants came from Asia (more than 50%),
above all from the Philippines and India. Most of these were engineers*

(25%) followed by doctors and surgeons (20%) and scientists (10%). . . . Had the West had to pay for this brain drain there would, according to an UNCTAD report, have been a 50% reduction in the foreign debt of the Third World in 1972. (1987, p. 105)

Although these are not the most recent figures, they do indicate the existence of a pattern, a pattern which can only have been exacerbated by the economic collapse of most Third World economies in the 1970s and the 1980s.

Conclusion

Considering the systemic constraints of debt management and the need to participate in the global economy, as well as the evaporation of any viable alternative to capitalist models, could we expect the Third World to maintain its postcolonial commitment to social justice? It would require visionary governments of an altogether more radical political complexion than those that currently exist in the Third World to try and maintain the kind of commitment to social justice that leaders such as Nehru once espoused.

Ironically, UNICEF still uses the rhetoric of social justice, as the following passage illustrates:

For reasons of both justice and efficiency, the overall effect of educational expenditure should be to redistribute incomes and equalize opportunities. In most developing countries today, its effect is almost the opposite. (UNICEF, 1992, p. 32)

However, one needs to ask, is it possible to work toward a more just society, through institutions such as education, when the demands of the global market are so all pervading? The reality of life in the Third World belies the rhetoric of the United Nations and its agencies; in the end, the "dead hand of the market" carries more weight.

Notes

1.   The notion of "global Fordism" is derived from the work of Alain Lipietz (1987), who has attempted to apply the ideas of the "French regulation" school (Aglietta 1987) to the problem of development in the Third World.

2.   The structural adjustment program was a facility; ". . . established by the IMF in March 1986 in order to help low-income developing nations with balance of payments difficulties" (Altvater et al., 1991, p. 258). The immediate conse-

quence of these programs has been a slashing of social and economic projects by developing nations in an effort to meet IMF budget targets (Chahoud, 1991, pp. 33–35; van der Hoeven, 1989).

3. The Italian Marxist scholar Antonio Gramsci coined the term "Fordism" earlier this century. Gramsci described it as an:

American phenomenon, which is also the biggest collective effort to date to create, with unprecedented speed, and with a consciousness of purpose unmatched in history, a new type of worker and of man. . . . The expression "consciousness of purpose" might appear humorous to say the least to anyone who recalls Taylor's phrase about the "trained gorilla"! Taylor is in fact expressing with brutal cynicism the purpose of American society—developing in the worker to the highest degree automatic and mechanical attitudes, breaking up the old psycho-physical nexus of qualified professional work, which demands a certain active participation of intelligence, fantasy and initiative on the part of the worker, and reducing productive operations exclusively to the mechanical, physical aspect. (Gramsci, 1988, pp. 290)

4. The principal figure and ideologue of the Chicago school is the economist Milton Friedman; during the 1970s he acted as an advisor to such Third World governments as the military junta in Chile. At that time he advocated "neo-liberal" orthodoxy based on the principle of the value of an unfettered market. His most important works include: Friedman, M. (1962) *Capitalism and Freedom*; Friedman, M. and Friedman, R. (1980) *Free to Choose*.

5. See: Theodore W. Shultz (1961) "Investment in Human Capital," for a classic formulation of the idea. Human capital theory, in one form or another, has been one of the dominant ideas in educational policy both in the advanced and the developing nations since the 1960s.

6. This is a term coined by Sue Branford and Bernardo Kucinski (1988) to describe the role played by U.S. banks in the development process, in their book *The Debt Squads: the U.S., the Banks, and Latin America.*

References

Aglietta, M. (1987). *A Theory of Capitalist Regulation: The US Experience.* D. Fernbach, trans. London: Verso.

Altvater, E., et al. (eds.) (1991). *The Poverty of Nations: A Guide to the Debt Crisis from Argentina to Zaire.* T. Bond, trans. London: Zed Books.

Branford, S., and B. Kucinski (1988). *The Debt Squads: The U.S., the Banks, and Latin America.* London: Zed Books.

Chahoud, T. (1991). "The Changing Roles of the IMF and the World Bank." In E. Altvater et al. (eds.) *The Poverty of Nations: A Guide to the Debt Crisis from Argentina to Zaire.* T. Bond, trans. London: Zed Books.

Cheru, F. (1989). "The Role of the IMF and World Bank in the Agrarian Crisis of the Sudan and Tanzania: Sovereignty vs Control." In B. Onimode (ed.) *The IMF, the World Bank and the African Debt: Vol. 2, The Social and Political Impact.* London: Zed Books.

Crough, G. and T. Wheelwright (1982). *Australia: A Client State.* Ringwood, Australia: Penguin.

Ewen, S. (1977). *Captains of Consciousness.* New York: McGraw-Hill.

Friedman, M. (1962). *Capitalism and Freedom.* Chicago: University of Chicago Press.

Friedman, M., and R. Friedman (1980). *Free to Choose.* London: Secker and Warburg.

Gramsci, A. (1988). "Americanism and Fordism." In D. Forgacs (ed.) *A Gramsci Reader—Selected Writings 1916–1935.* London: Lawrence and Wisehart.

Green, R. (1989). "The Broken Pot: The Social Fabric, Economic Disaster, and Adjustment in Africa." In B. Onimode (ed.) *The IMF, the World Bank and the African*

Debt: Vol. 2, The Social and Political Impact. London: Zed Books.

Hein, W., and T. Mutter (1991). "The Debate on Development Policy." In E. Altvater et al. (eds.) *The Poverty of Nations: A Guide to the Debt Crisis from Argentina to Zaire.* T. Bond, trans. London: Zed Books.

Kruijer, G. (1987). *Third World Problems and Solutions.* A Pomerans, trans. Atlantic Highlands, N. J.: Humanities Press International.

Lipietz, A. (1987). *Mirages and Miracles: The Crises of Global Fordism.* D. Macey, trans. London: Verso.

Mathews, J. (1989). *Age of Democracy: The Politics of Post-Fordism.* Melbourne: Oxford University Press.

Nehru, J. (1984–1990). *Selected Works of Jawaharlal Nehru.* Ed. by S. Gopal, Vol. 2–10. New Delhi: Jawaharlal Nehru Memorial Fund and Oxford University Press.

Shultz, T.W. (1961). "Investment in Human Capital." In *The American Economic Review,* vol. 51, March, no. 1.

Tetzlaff, R. (1991). "LDCs (Least Developed Countries): The Fourth World in the Debt Trap." In E. Altvater et al. (eds.). *The Poverty of Nations: A Guide to the Debt Crisis from Argentina to Zaire.* T. Bond, trans. London: Zed Books.

United Nations Childrens Fund (UNICEF) (1992). *The State of the World's Children 1992.* Oxford: Oxford University Press.

Vallely, P. (1990). *Bad Samaritans: First World Ethics and Third World Debt.* London: Hodder and Stoughton.

van der Hoeven, R. (1989). "External Shocks, Adjustment, and Income." In Weeks, J. (ed.) *Debt Disaster.* New York: New York University Press.

World Bank (1974). *Education Sector Policy Paper.* Washington, D.C.: World Bank.

Metaphors of Educational Development

An Analysis of Information Flow between Cultures

Christine Fox

Introduction

The language of social justice in education is the language of ethics. We believe it is only right and good that all members of a society have a chance to "develop" and "grow" through some kind of education or training. Such a system also assumes that individuals' formal or informal education will assist them to become more valuable members of society, perhaps more productive and responsible, more capable and knowledgeable, in the public and private spheres.

What images do we conjure up with the words "development" and "growth"? Are they the same images as those produced by the words "equity" or "social justice"? In many cases, the images are quite clearly in opposition. For what is right and good for the individual may not appear right and good for the country's economy or society's overall needs and vice versa. Choices have to be made. For example, is social justice better served by training a few doctors or is it better served by educating all mothers and mothers to be? Is it equitable that schools in remote areas provide the same education as city schools? Should one language be taught to everyone for equity's sake, regardless of the student's mother tongue?

An equitable system implies social justice for everyone, no matter who they are, or what their individual aptitudes or cultural backgrounds might be. Yet equity remains a contentious sphere of critical debate. Third World governments make multiple decisions about social justice issues, based on perceived political, economic, and social needs. Even after these decisions have been made, they cannot be implemented unless there are sufficient resources, human and material, to turn policy into practice. In most Third World countries, educational needs far outstrip the budgetary possibilities. Literary rates are still well below 50% in many countries, especially in rural areas. School enrollments have by no means reached the goal of universal primary education, let alone secondary. Health education has not resolved the problems of unclean water, lack of sanitation facilities, and high infant mortality rates.

In many cases, therefore, Third World governments will seek funding and resources for their educational programs from international agencies and from government and nongovernment bodies of more industrialized countries. Outside "donors" may well initiate the ideas for projects that they are prepared to fund, and they may set criteria that must be met before funds are forthcoming. Depending on the percentage of the budget that comes from such funding, and the state of the art in educational development, the input from outside may have a very significant influence that is felt at every level of education, from the classroom and the community to the Cabinet and Treasury.

Equity is served not only by the government's ideology and policy and its commitment to particular educational programs, but also by its international relationships. Important agreements are made about educational policy and programs through multilateral (international agencies) and bilateral (between two countries) contracts. The question that must be examined, then, is how these international relationships can serve to enhance equity, and how they can be instruments of further injustice and domination by the powerful.

The potential for matters of equity to be overlooked because of political and economic expediency is undeniable. However, instead of viewing the situation as a political–economic question, it should be seen as a particular form of *intercultural communication.* By taking a critical view of intercultural communication, it will be shown that each situation has the potential for being a real dialogue where First and Third World representatives sit down together to work out the most equitable way of enhancing educational opportunity. On the other hand, each situation may also exhibit a strategic manipulation of power, where genuine dialogue does not take place.

It has often been contended that Third World countries have had to combat dependency toward First World countries because of the exploitative practices of the capitalist First World (Frank, 1971;

Carnoy, 1974; Larrain, 1989). It has also been contended that much of the so-called assistance given to Third World countries has been inappropriate in that it has assumed, incorrectly, that the only form of development possible was some form of technological industrialization and modernization, using a rational planning model of what development should be. Many of these images of development, modernization, and rational planning are contained in the language used by educational planners engaged in intercultural communication. We generally describe our ideas in the form of *metaphor*. Intercultural communication can well be described as an exchange of meaning through metaphor. An analysis of the metaphors we use reveals many of our secrets of communication—of what we believe, how we think, and how we see others. By exploring the texts of educational contracts, and of communication events between cultures, we can explore contrasts of just and unjust actions, and of genuine collaboration compared with exploitation.

Colonial Days and the Metaphors Used by Colonizers
In the colonial days of many Third World countries, the colonizers were driven not by the modern sense of social justice toward all the colonized, but by a desire to govern efficiently, to "civilize the natives," and to appear to be humane to people whom they often depicted either as childlike or savage. In the Pacific Island context in the 1920s, a typical European view of the islanders was expressed by a New Zealand colonial administrator, Sir George Richardson (1926) about the inhabitants of Western Samoa. He was advocating a small amount of education for some of the Samoans. He said that a Samoan's education

absolutely ends on the day he leaves school. If he does not go to school he will only return to his village and become absorbed in village life with its primitive customs. The European boy, after leaving school, is daily learning and acquiring knowledge from his ever-progressing environment or by further instruction at technical schools or other institutions. . . . (Correspondence of Sir George Richardson, January 1926, Fiji)

Richardson went on to explain that only about 10% of school

leavers were required to serve with the various missions or in the government service, and therefore it "would be wrong and create a social evil, and retard the development of Samoan lands if every boy were educated to the highest standards required by the few. . . ." (Sir George Richardson, January 1926, Fiji). Richardson was influenced by an earlier report by a New Zealand government official, William Bird (1920), who had reported:

For the great majority of the Samoan children a very simple scheme of education such as that prescribed in the village schools of the various missionary bodies is probably all that is required. . . . A child should be taught to read in Samoan in less than a year, and his whole education so far as the vernacular goes should not require more than two or three years. . . .

We tend to make judgments about other cultures based on the extent or limitations of our own awareness of cultural background. It is easy now to interpret these colonial texts as "misplaced," because of our present knowledge of Samoan people and their history. We can understand Bird's and Richardson's comments because the text is filtered through our understanding of the inherent racism of colonial practice. We can "hear" the metaphors Richardson employs about Samoan life when he uses the word "absorbed" (in village life)— soaked up like a sponge, or swallowed up and assimilated. This contrasts with the words he uses for European life as "ever-progressing," or moving forward, getting somewhere, traveling on. Similarly, Bird portrays a sense of the inferiority, or lack of complexity in the Samoan language and lifestyle when he uses words like "simple" and "probably all that is required."

The discrepancies between what the colonial administrators saw as Samoan cultural simplicity and the reality of Samoan cultural complexity created one of the many distortions in communication between colonizer and colonized, distortions that were typical of the colonial era. Communication was therefore not authentic. No genuine agreements could take place unless they were in some way strategic commands, or a manipulation of the dominant over the dominated.

Metaphors used by the colonizers prior to the 1950s tended to be spatially oriented, referring to whole cultures rather than individuals. Cultures were seen as higher or lower than others, or going forward or backward. The process of "civilizing" was seen as "lifting" a culture to the level of the better, or European, culture—but, of course, not quite reaching the same heights. As Tejaswini Niranjana comments, historians of the nineteenth century, such as Macaulay and Trevelyan, felt that the writings from the Orient were "worse than useless" (Niranjana, 1992, p. 31). Metaphor was thus used in language to distort and misrepresent, not only the lives and environment of the people described, but as well the relationships between the so-called "civilized" world of Europe and the "backward" world beyond Europe.

The experiences of Europeans encountering new cultures naturally lent themselves to metaphorical description. Europeans were viewed as gods, strange birds, barbarians, and so on. Europeans saw "natives" as savage, animals not altogether human, or as children as yet unformed, still "enveloped" or wrapped up as opposed to developed or unfolded. Europeans saw their language, customs, and religion as sitting on a higher plane, and the "other" as uncivilized or lower, waiting to be lifted up.

Arndt (1987) noted that Louis XIV laid down a royal decree that the natives of Africa were to be converted to Catholicism so they could be considered "citizens and natural Frenchmen," a mission born of the conviction that French culture "represented the acme of human achievement and a priceless gift to all who could be helped to share it" (Arndt, 1987, p. 24). Arndt compared the prevailing French attitude with that of T.B. Macaulay whom he quotes as saying:

To have found a great people sunk in the lowest depths of slavery and superstition, to have so ruled them as to have made them desirous and capable of all the privileges of citizens, would indeed be a title to glory all our own. (Arndt, 1987, p. 25)

The nineteenth century saw a new interest in the idea of "material progress" and connected such progress with notions of civilization. James Mill talked of the "low state of civilization" in India. Regarding both India and China, he commented that ". . . both nations are to nearly an equal degree tainted with the vices of insincerity; dissembling, treacherous, mendacious, to an excess which surpasses even the usual measure of uncultivated society. . . . Both are cowardly and unfeeling . . . and disgustingly unclean in their persons and houses" (J. Mill [1820], *The History of British India,* bk. 2, p. 88, quoted in Larrain, 1989, p. 25). Malthus gave his view of South American Indians as lazy and needing to be motivated to create new wants and tastes before they could improve. J.S. Mill agreed with Malthus that the people were weak in motivation and therefore backward. They were lacking in the "right attitudes" and were also "immature" and needed colonial rule (in Larrain, 1989, p. 27).

Much of the development literature in the later twentieth century is based on Marxist or neo-Marxist interpretations of development and modernization. Yet Larrain maintains that Marx's views on the colonial question and on "development" evolved and changed, and that as his understanding of colonialism grew, his belief in the necessity of colonial rule diminished. His moral repudiation of the excesses of colonialism were at first coupled with the theoretical justification of its mission (Larrain, 1989, p. 49). Later, he voiced doubts as to whether colonialism was not actually hindering industrialization in the colonies. He began to see that material progress was not necessarily dependent upon destroying the precapitalist culture, except in terms of the colonizing country. "By ruining handcraft production in other countries, machinery forcibly converts them into fields for the supply of its raw material. . . ." (from *Capital* [1974 edition], vol. 1, p. 424, quoted in Larrain, 1989, p. 49). Nevertheless, it should be remembered that Marx's references to precapitalist societies were not in terms used by neo-Marxists of "underdevelopment," which is a concept originating in the post-1945 era. Marx instead talked about "backward" countries, a common Eurocentric viewpoint voiced by economists, historians, and politicians alike. Marx and Engels spoke contemptuously of several non-European societies, and did not attempt to analyze non-European societies in terms of internal social or political conditions.

The metaphors of going backwards, of being lower, or inferior, of being outside, the child, and so on continued throughout the nineteenth century. Hegel, for example, described South American nations as "physically and psychically powerless . . . inhabited by individuals whose inferiority was manifest, who lived like children . . . in a world outside the true theatre of History" (in Larrain, 1989, p. 58). Edward Said captures a similar sense of "otherness" in his definitive work on Orientalism, that is, Western conceptions in history of the so-called Orient (Said, 1978, 1983; and see Spivak, 1987).

From early colonialism, European ideology moved to a more belligerent imperialist approach that saw the more liberal ideology of early capitalism transformed into political struggle for power and the conquest of finance capital (Larrain, 1989, p. 64). Critics of imperialism saw the European policy of the time as "parasitic." Holson claimed that the economies of Europe were trying to "fasten economic suckers into foreign bodies so as to drain them of their wealth in order to support domestic luxury" (Larrain, 1989, p. 68, quoting Holson). Opponents of imperialism from within the British Empire also condemned the situation. At the turn of the century, Dadabhai Naoroji stated with regard to British policies toward India that British policy was

the pitiless eating of India's substance in India, and the further pitiless drain to England, in short, it is the pitiless perversion of economic laws by the sad bleeding to which India is subjected, that is destroying India, (Naoroji, 1901, 1962, p. 191)

The metaphors are clear: The imperial animal is devouring the prey, bleeding the prey to death.

Although Larrain makes a cogent case for the Eurocentrism of the pre-twentieth-century economists, he then falls into the same trap himself in his observations about Australia and North America. First, he bemoans the lack of analysis of internal social and political conditions of non-European nations. While he notes that Paul Baran was really the first economist to put into doubt the homogeneous conception of world capitalism and the homogeneous nature of "backward" countries, he then goes on to say:

In those areas like Australia, North America, etc., European settlers entered more or less complete societal vacuums and succeeded in establishing indigenous societies of their own. It was different elsewhere where they faced established societies with rich and ancient cultures. (Larrain, 1989, p. 81, emphasis added)

The vacuum metaphor recurs in the literature on Third World societies, much as teachers used to believe they were filling empty vessels—children's minds—with knowledge.

The whole idea of the evolution of society along European lines presupposes some kind of superiority of European culture as being the "most advanced." This idea stems from Marx's original belief that it was enough to investigate the "inevitable" overthrow of capitalism of England by the proletariat because all other industrialized countries would naturally follow suit. He later revised his view and realized that each society had its own internal "evolution." Nevertheless, the assumption of superiority has worked its way into sociological and psychological theory far beyond the intentions of its economic–industrial origins. Thus we have the erroneous examples of psychologists "proving" that blacks were less intelligent than whites (Jensen, 1969), or of political leaders during Hitler's regime claiming that Jews were inferior to the Aryan race, and similarly, of psychologist philosophers stating that male adolescents achieve higher moral development than females (Köhlberg, 1981; Gilligan, 1982). In more recent times, it has been the economic theorists who have tended to represent the neocolonialist expectation of modernization through dependence on the First World for finance and technological assistance in order to bring about some form of industrialization.

The Power of Metaphor in Communication
Of all the different mechanisms we use to make ourselves understood, metaphor is probably the most powerful.[1] Metaphor "serves as a device for reorganizing our perceptual and/or conceptual structure" (Johnson, 1981, p. 31). Max Black emphasizes that metaphor must not be construed as an ornamental substitute for plain thought. Rather, metaphor has the power "to bring two separate domains into cognitive and emotional relation by using language directly appropriate to the one as a lens for seeing the other" (Madison, 1988, p. 189). In this way metaphor acts as a bridge to allow access to common meanings. Ricoeur's notion of metaphor is similar:

Metaphors . . . can tell us something about the really important things human beings are concerned with, "things" such as the self, or the soul, human freedom, Being, God and so on. (Madison, 1988, p. 85)

In intercultural communication, the use of metaphor for everyday occurrences can alert those from other cultures to differences that might exist about the interpretation of a seemingly common idea. For example, in the English language people are often referred to metaphorically by the name of an animal. We call someone a snake, a dog, a pig, a tiger, a cat, or a butterfly. Each of these metaphors conjures up an idea of a characteristic of that person. In some other cultures, the idea of attributing permanent characteristics to a person is not part of the culture and therefore these words would not mean the same. In some African societies, you may call a person a witch when they are acting in the capacity of a witch. That same person is not always characterized as a witch; it is only so when they are carrying out those specific functions.

The place of metaphor as a cultural linguistic reality is central to the discussion of the filtering function of metaphor. No analysis of intercultural communication would be complete without looking at the power of metaphor as a filter (which can both clarify and distort) as integral to the study of utterances. Geertz (1973, pp. 210–211) makes this point strongly:

In metaphor one has, of course, a stratification of meaning, in which an incongruity of sense on one level produces an influx of significance on another. . . . The power of metaphor derives precisely from the interplay between the discordant meanings it symbolically coerces into a unitary conceptual framework and from the degree to which that coercion is successful in overcoming the psychic resistance such semantic tension inevitably generates in anyone in a position to perceive it. When it works, a metaphor transforms a false identification . . . into an apt analogy: when it misfires, it is a mere extravagance.

Lakoff and Johnson note that "the most fundamental values in a culture will be coherent with the metaphorical structure of the most fundamental concepts in the culture" (Lakoff and Johnson, 1980, p. 22). Of course, the most obvious, negative connotations through metaphor interculturally are those relating to the idea that white is good and black is bad or evil. Three examples from their work are illustrative. The first is the idea that some cultural values in Western society are coherent with up–down spatialization metaphors (p. 22). It is usually anticipated that up is toward good and that down is toward bad. Similarly, they reason that cultural values generally accept more as good and "up," while less is bad and "down"; bigger is better and smaller is bad. Yet in other societies, cultural values may not tally with these metaphorical constructions. However, successful cultural filtering becomes possible when the metaphor is recognized and values are inferred, allowing the communication to proceed with a clearer awareness of what the speaker believes to be good.

A second example is the concept in English that "argument is war" (Lakoff and Johnson, 1980, p. 4). Western speakers may say phrases such as "Your claims are indefensible," or "he attacked every weak point in my argument," or "his criticisms were right on target" (p. 4). A hearer of these metaphors will quickly understand the direction in which the speaker is heading, and will gain an awareness of the tensions and contradictions of arguments. I suggest here that a speaker in another culture can see argument in other terms, perhaps as a more persuasive process, perhaps in terms of a person at sea catching someone or saving someone. I have heard comments similar to "she drew a net [of understanding] about us" or "she played out the line" as a way of attempting to convince another of their point of view. In this way the assumptions and values become clearer, so that a reinterpretation of normative validity is possible, so leading the speakers to a newly created intercultural communicative context. Both participants would now be aware that a difference of opinion had occurred, but within their own understanding of normative rightness.

It becomes clear, then, the extent to which metaphor functions as a filter in everyday communication. Its significance in intercultural communication lies especially in the use of filter to achieve a commonality of meaning that could perhaps have been lost through a lack of expository clarification of meaning in a situation where cultural interpretations differ (Fox, 1992). A study of metaphor is perhaps the master key by which we can unlock meaning. As most of what we say stems from metaphorical language, and as the references we use depend on our cultural and social learning, it is here that differences in meaning can be clarified and that new truth can be discovered. Metaphor is not only an expression of our individual viewpoints, a codified expression of our ontological understanding, but it is also an expression of systemic organization, a codified interpretation of power, bureaucracy, and the economic order.

Educational Development and Social Justice: Metaphors of Linear Growth

As we know, most formal education of the Western mode was instigated by colonial powers from Europe. As Colin Hindson notes in his dissertation on education and development in the South Pacific: "The developing countries placed a great deal of trust in the formal Western-oriented rational planning process as they sought economic and educational direction" (1988, p. 26). Hindson's view is that this rational paradigm did not work in the Third World.

Watson (1985) provides a detailed account of the differences in approach by colonial governments to provide education for "development," where European ideas on education were either transferred with few changes to another cultural context, or else adapted to suit local needs. Heyneman (1985) used the terms "equivalency" and "adaptationist" to describe these two models. The British Colonial Office of the 1920s, as discussed above, tried to adapt their African programs to what they saw as suited to the "mentality, aptitudes, occupation, and traditions of the various peoples" (Crossley and Weeks, 1986, p. 420), which in effect were seen as "lower" than the European and suited mainly to manual tasks.

In the decades that followed, a dual system of educational practice tended to emerge in colonial education systems, whereby a few residents of the non-European culture were "permitted" to study academic subjects in elite schools as training for a few white collar positions, and a slightly larger number attended village-based schools that were based on a "practical" curriculum. Either way, the dual system was imposed rather than negotiated. When negotiations between the colonizers and the colonized did take place as a lead-up to independence, the support for academic types of education by the colonized populations was overwhelming.

The 1950s and 1960s saw a rise in the belief that education could be a catalyst for economic growth and development in the Western rational style. "Dimly lurking behind the new progressive colonialism was the acknowledged likelihood that sometime in the later years of the century the British colonial dependencies might aspire to self-government, even to full independence" (Castle, 1972, p. 5).

Yet, educators were not prepared for a change in outlook from their comfortable understandings about education from a European perspective. Beeby, in his introduction to his now classic work on the quality of education in developing countries said:

It was scarcely to be expected that our philosophies of education would be adequate to cover the problems of the Belgian Congo which became a sovereign state with some 26 college graduates, or of Libya . . . which had about 10 percent of adults with schooling of any kind when it achieved independence in 1951. (Beeby, 1966, p. 1)

As Fägerlind and Saha (1983) note, the educational policy making of the time was heavily influenced by notions of structural functionalism and the evolution of modernization through the imposition of Western structures and Western education.

The 1960s and 1970s were periods of rapid growth in education systems, based on earlier manpower planning models (e.g., Harbison and Myers, 1964). These rational plans failed to achieve their objectives in country after country, and in the 1970s the attempted expansion upward into secondary education was replaced with an emphasis on "basic education" (ILO, 1976). Zachariah (1985), who has analyzed the metaphors of the role of education in the Third World, stated that the 1960s period demonstrated a false assumption, which was

a resurgent belief in inevitable, linear *human progress . . . supported by another belief that* rational *human beings would be able to come to agreement about the nature of a society's problems and the measures necessary to deal with them and co-operate in implementing such measures. (1985, p. 3, emphasis added)*

The development metaphors of growth, of plants being nourished, of rising economies, and so on was translated in educational policy into human capital theory and modernization; that is, from the traditional self-sufficiency model to the rational economic sector planning model (Anderson, 1967). In 1976, Ronald Dore wrote a stinging critique of this model in *The Diploma Disease* (Dore, 1976). He says in his preface, "Nowadays we are supposed to smile at the naive optimism of the Victorians who believed so unquestioningly in the inevitability of 'progress'" (Dore, 1976, p. ix). He then goes on to show how desperately wrong the economic planners were being in the Third World in the 1960s, and how strangely educators have followed a quantitative input–output model of education and the gaining of skilled graduates trained for particular occupations, many of which did not exist in the countries he discusses, namely Sri Lanka, Kenya, China, Tanzania, and Cuba.

The 1970s saw the beginnings of a strong critique of educational policy, in the form of proponents of the dependency theory and cultural imperialism as discussed in earlier sections of this chapter. Chief among the critics were educators such as Illich (1973), Freire (1972), Carnoy (1974), and others. Their work concerning the Third World was similar to the rise of critical theorists of European and American education, including Apple (1979), Bourdieu and Passeron (1977), Bowles and Gintis (1976), and others.

Paulo Freire was perhaps one of the most influential writers in the Third World. His *Pedagogy of the Oppressed* (1972), based on his work on literacy in Brazil, was widely read in Latin America as well as later in Europe. For example, the ideas contained in Freire's work closely approximated those of educational theorists in Peru who drew up the 1970 Education Reform Act, one of the first radical reforms in the developing world that was not based on social reproductionist models (Fox, 1977).

Watson (1985), among others, has noted that in spite of a move to make educational models increasingly relevant to the cultures and contexts of the different national groups, there is still a dominance of European influence and the problem of unequal control of resources. From the point of view of dominance of language and cultural ideas, he notes that "many still use international languages, foreign textbooks, foreign-set examinations, employ expatriate staff. . . . The process is bound to perpetuate dependency" (Watson, 1985, p. 84). Maglen has noted similar influences in the South Pacific, including the increasing awareness that educational development seems to be assisting the "donor" countries' economies more than it is assisting appropriate improvement in the quality of educational services in the Third World countries themselves (Maglen, 1990). Hindson has elaborated on the tensions that arise between consultant and Third World educator in their programs of attempted solutions to educational problems (Hindson, 1988). These tensions are evidence of the miscommunication and systemic distortion in attempted intercultural communicative action.[2]

Much of current educational development assistance continues to be planned by international and First World agencies along rational, technical lines. The metaphors of development are not based on notions of social justice, but on economic, structural images of building models, drawing analogies to the formulation of ground plans, making a blueprint for program implementation, delivery of materials, the sending "in" of a "team," the tight time line, inputs and outputs, product flow, monitoring, and so on. There is a sense of internal consistency within a predetermined, prewrapped "package," which often fails to match the requirements of the ongoing social processes of educational development in a changing society. The language used by consultants "in the field" is often particularly distorting, since they move within the "packaged" time frame, speaking of strategic planning and delivery, while their counterparts move within the more fluid and broader cultural framework of their ongoing educational context, speaking of people's lives (Fox, 1992).

The essence of *authentic* intercultural communication lies in accepting equal validity for all participants that what they are saying is true and a sincere representation of what is socially acceptable. Participants coming from different cultural backgrounds will make judgements that concur with their own validity criteria. We may then be in a situation where validity claims are not acceptable to both cultures. A denial of the validity claims of one culture by another will create far-reaching communication problems and may form the basis of systematic distortions in what people think is happening. Often, by analyzing the actual texts of intercultural communication, we can discern the differences in points of view.

A Metaphor of Social Justice in Educational Development

Helu-Thaman (1992) sees educational development in terms of the

Tongan *kakala* flower, a metaphor for learning symbolized by the three processes of gathering (of knowledge), making (of a "product"), and giving (of knowledge, skills, and values) motivated by respect. This is not a strategic focus, nor a linear focus, but a social, equitable, and respectful focus. Helu-Thaman explained her metaphor in this way:

Kakala *simply means fragrant flowers. But* kakala *also has an interesting origin. For Tongans,* kakala *does not mean just fragrant flowers, but also fragrant fruits, leaves and wood which have mythical or legendary origins.... When* kakala *are strung or woven together into garlands, the end products are ranked. The different ways of stringing* kakala *and the patterns used have been standardised and have remained almost unchanged over the years. There exists a full and sophisticated vocabulary as well as an elaborate etiquette associated with* kakala.

The relevance of the metaphor of kakala *to ... teacher education ... may be reflected through the three main processes associated with it: namely* toli, tui *and* luva. *The first of these is ... the gathering of fragrant flowers/leaves etc. This process demands not only knowledge of the materials with which to fashion the* kakala *but also skill in how to obtain these.... The second aspect ... relates to the actual making of the garland.... The method used ... often depends on a variety of considerations including the desired type, the occasion ... as well as considerations of the maker, bearer or wearer of the* kakala. *The final process is the giving (away) of the* kakala *by the wearer or bearer, to somebody else, for* kakala *is never retained or kept indefinitely by the wearer; it is always given away.*

In Tongan tradition ... kakala *takes on an added significance— as a symbol of respect, as well as* ofa *(compassion or love); for the recognition of the beauty and power in the creator of love.*

... we need to share our cultural knowledge with those who come to help us but who may not yet know us, so that they too would better understand the contexts in which we work and which give us sustenance....

> *for we cannot let our silences*
> *again keep us apart....*

Conclusion

Development has been variously defined in terms of evolution, modernization, economic growth, material progress, and maturity. Until recently it has been generally referred to as a positive change, using words metaphorically connected to what is seen as positive— up, high, rising, forward, growing, moving toward, unwrapping, and so on. Moreover, the development metaphor is generally used in reference to the contemporary relationship between the industrialized world and the countries of the so-called Third World. In the last decade, the metaphor of unrestricted growth has been challenged in the industrialized countries, with arguments for limits to growth (Trainer, 1985).

While metaphor is a filter through which a new concept can be digested from different points of view, it also serves to distort meaning when the metaphor is used, or misconstrued to create inappropriate and misleadingly negative images. Thus, the development metaphor in reverse—when used to contrast a situation negatively in its "undeveloped" context—implies low, downward, backward, stagnant, behind, primitive, unformed, immature, childlike, unevolved. These generalizations about non-European contexts have influenced intercultural communication deeply, and negatively. Any assumption that so starkly distinguishes one society from another by using images that vividly depict positive and negative in such a general way can only serve to create inequality, to allow for unequal power relations.

The potential for systemically distorted communication between educators in the First and Third worlds is based on the social and political construction of the notion of "development" and the structural inequalities that development policies have exacerbated. The notion is metaphorically formed, ideologically based, strategically constructed, and economically implemented.

It is somewhat surprising, but highly instructive, that the notion of development has continued to be used in reference to contemporary Third World societies in much the same way that nineteenth century sociologists referred to the barely known and as yet not understood non-European societies of the day. First, the problems of interpretation of development lie in the long-held assumption that the process of modernization is evolutionary and linear, and proceeds for all cultures along predetermined lines. Such an assumption does not tally with historical evidence, as can be seen through the different processes of change undergone in every continent and island. Second, it is assumed that the process is inevitable, and is universally applicable even if it occurs at different moments in history and at different rates. Third, development is assessed in relation to contemporary industrialized countries, rather than in relation to the internal historical perspective of the country concerned. Fourth, development is seen not from the point of view of the lifestyle or values of the inhabitants of Third World countries, but in terms of the relationship of economic, technological, and industrial "relative progress" between Third World countries and more industrialized countries. Last, it is mistakenly assumed by development theorists that there is some kind of homogeneity among Third World cultures as compared to so-called First World cultures. The power of metaphorical interpretation continues to dominate policy and development initiatives to the detriment of policies for social justice. Only by breaking those silences between cultures and creating genuine dialogue will development assistance be able to contribute to social justice in the Third World.

Notes

1. In-depth discussions on the role of metaphor in communications are extensive. I have benefited greatly from discussions and arguments in, for instance, Capra, 1988; Johnson, 1981; Black, 1962; Austin, 1975; Levinson, 1983; Cooper, 1986.
2. Third World educators are tending to extend the metaphors of Naoroji's feral animal devouring the intestines of the colonized world to see First World educators, human resources managers, and so on as predators (Larrain, 1989). Such expressions as *pirates* (Baba 1990), *sharks, vultures,* or *piranhas* have been used (personal comment).

References

Anderson, C.A. (1967). *The Social Context of Educational Planning.* Paris: Unesco: IIEP.

Apple, M. (1979). *Ideology and Curriculum.* London: Routledge.

Arndt, H.W. (1987). *Economic Development: The History of an Idea.* Chicago: University of Chicago Press.

Austin, J.L. (1975). *How to Do Things With Words.* Cambridge, Mass: Harvard University Press.

Baba, T. (1990). "Australian Aid in the Pacific." *Current Affairs Bulletin,* March.

Beeby, C.E. (1966). *The Quality of Education in Developing Countries.* Cambridge, Mass.: Harvard University Press.

Bird, William (1920). Correspondence to Secretary of External Affairs, New Zealand Department of External Affairs, Series 13, 31/3/20, Wellington.

Black, M. (1962). *Models and Metaphors.* Ithaca: Cornell University Press.

Bourdieu, P., and J. Passeron (1977). *Reproduction in Education, Society and Culture.* London: Sage.

Bowles, S., and H. Gintis (1976). *Schooling in Capitalist America.* New York: Basic Books.

Capra, F. (1988). *Uncommon Wisdom.* Glasgow: Fontana.

Carnoy, M. (1974). *Education as Cultural Imperialism.* New York: McKay.

Castle, E.B. (1972). *Education for Self-Help: New Strategies for Developing Countries.* London: Oxford University Press.

Cooper, D.E. (1986). *Metaphor.* Oxford: Basil Blackwell.

Crossley, M., and S. Weeks (1986). "Curriculum as an International Commodity: Dilemmas of Relevance and Change." In R. Gillespie and C. Collins (eds.) *Education as an International Commodity.* Brisbane: ANZCIES.

Dore, R. (1976). *The Diploma Disease: Education, Qualification and Development.* London: George Allen and Unwin.

Fägerlind, I. and L. Saha (1983). *Education and National Development: A Comparative Perspective.* Oxford: Pergamon.

Fox, C. (1977). *Teacher Education and Educational Reform in Peru.* Unpublished M.A. thesis, University of London.

———— (1992). *A Critical Analysis of Intercultural Communication: Towards a New Theory.* Unpublished Ms., University of Sydney.

Frank, A.G. (1971). *Capitalism and Underdevelopment in Latin America.* Harmondsworth: Penguin Books.

Freire, Paulo (1972). *Pedagogy of the Oppressed.* Harmondsworth: Penguin.

Geertz, Clifford (1973). *The Interpretation of Cultures.* New York: Basic Books.

Gilligan, Carol (1982). *In a Different Voice: Psychological Theory and Women's Development.* Cambridge, Mass: Harvard University Press.

Harbison, F.H. and C.A. Myers (1964). *Education, Manpower and Economic Growth. Strategies of Human Resources Development.* New York: McGraw Hill.

Helu-Thaman, K. (1992). *Looking Towards the Source: A Consideration of Cultural Context in Teacher Education in Pacific Island Countries.* Keynote address to the international teacher education forward planning meeting, June. Suva, Fiji: Institute of Education, University of the South Pacific.

Heyneman, S. (1985). "Research on Education in Developing Countries." *International Journal of Education Development,* vol. 4, no. 4.

Hindson (1988). *The Education Debate in the South Pacific During the 1970s with Particular Reference to Fiji and Kiribati.* Ph.D. thesis, School of Education, Flinders University of South Australia.

Illich, I. (1973). *Celebration of Awareness.* Harmondsworth: Penguin.

International Labour Office (1976). *Employment, Growth and Basic Needs: A One World Problem.* Geneva: International Labour Office.

Jensen, A.R. (1969). "How Much Can We Boost IQ and Scholastic Achievement?" *Harvard Education Review,* vol. 39.

Johnson, M. (ed.) (1981). *Philosophical Perspectives on Metaphor.* Minneapolis: University of Minnesota Press.

Köhlberg, L. (1981). *The Philosophy of Moral Development.* San Francisco: Harper and Row.

Lakoff, George, and Mark Johnson (1980). *Metaphors We Live By.* Chicago: University of Chicago Press.

Larrain, J. (1989). *Theories of Development: Capitalism, Colonialism, Dependency.* Cambridge, UK: Polity.

Levinson, S. (1983). *Pragmatics.* Cambridge, U.K.: Cambridge University Press.

Madison, G.B. (1988). *The Hermeneutics of Postmodernity: Figures and Themes.* Bloomington: Indiana University Press.

Maglen, L. (1990). "The Impact of Bilateral Aid on Educational Development: The Case of Australia and the South Pacific." *Comparative Education,* vol. 26, no. 1.

Naoroji, D. (1901,1962). *Poverty and Un-British Rule in India.* New Delhi: Government of India.

Niranjana, T. (1992). *Siting Translation.* Berkeley: University of California Press.

Richardson, Sir George (1926). *Private Correspondence,* Series 1/33/1, Department of External Affairs, Wellington.

Said, Edward (1978). *Orientalism: Western Conceptions of the Orient.* Harmondsworth: Penguin.

———— (1983). *The World, the Text and the Critic.* Cambridge, Mass.: Harvard University Press.

Spivak, G. (1987). *In Other Words: Essays in Cultural Politics.* New York: Methuen.

Trainer, T. (1985). *Abandon Affluence!* London: Zed Books.

Watson, K. (1985). "Dependence or Independence in International Education?" *International Journal of Educational Development,* vol. 5, no. 2.

Zachariah, Matthew (1985). "Lumps of Clay and Growing Plants: Dominant Metaphors of the Role of Education in the Third World, 1950–1980." *Comparative Education Review,* vol. 29, no. 1.

Education and National Unity
Toward the Sociocultural Integration of Ethnic Minorities

Ibrahim Alladin

Introduction

Since formal colonial rule ended, many developing countries have been preoccupied with forging cohesive and stable societies from the legacy of ethnic, cultural, linguistic, and religious divisions that they inherited from the colonial rulers. A variety of approaches for sociocultural integration of minorities have been tried. Some approaches have sought to preserve a certain degree of local communal values to achieve unity. Others call for cultural pluralism in an attempt to attain socioeconomic parity among ethnic groups. Yet others argue that equity and social justice are essential ingredients of any approach, for equity is an important factor that can contribute to unity and cohesion in a multiethnic society. But these approaches have certain weaknesses that will be examined here. What this paper proposes is an approach in which the sociocultural integration of ethnic minorities forms an integral part of the overall development strategy of the society. It will be argued that problems of "underdevelopment" will persist as long as minorities remain marginalized.

Ethnicity and Multicultures: A Theoretical Analysis

The term ethnicity, as employed in sociology and social anthropology, is not easy to define as it used in a number of social contexts. As a theoretical concept, "ethnicity" remains quite vague. Sociologists, for example, have take different positions with respect to what is race and ethnicity. These positions represent theoretical orientations that focus on different aspects of intergroup relations. The way race and ethnicity are defined has a bearing on explanations and analysis. Furthermore, the theoretical status accorded to ethnicity has influenced the political focus in the development of the public policy on multiculturalism.

Sociologists have generally focused on the question of subjective identity as a basis for their definition of ethnicity and race. Ethnicity, is therefore, ascribed or given at birth. An important aspect of an ethnic group is that its members share a sense of peoplehood or identity based in part on descent, language, religion, tradition, and other common experiences (Weber, 1968, pp. 385–398). According to this view, ethnic identity provides a basis for members of an ethnic group to develop closures or boundaries, within which ethnic institutions, neighborhoods, beliefs, and cultures are developed and maintained.

Studies on ethnicity have indicated that the most often mentioned attributes of ethnicity are ancestry, culture, religion, race, and language (Isajiw, 1974; Li, 1988). Driedger (1978) identified six factors of ethnic identification that form the components of an ethnic community. These factors are identification with an ecological territory, an ethnic culture, ethnic institutions, historical symbols, an ideology, and charismatic leadership. Rosen (1959) argues that an individual may identify himself or herself with others on three levels. First, one may identify oneself with some important person in one's life, for example, a parent or friend (that is, significant other). Second, one may identify oneself with a group from which one draws one's values, for example, family or coworkers (that is, reference group). Third, one may identify oneself with a broad category of persons, for example, an ethnic group or occupational group (that is, a social category). It is on the third level that ethnic identification occurs.

Race and ethnicity can also be examined as a consequence of unequal relationships, produced and maintained by differential power between dominant and subordinate groups (Li, 1989). From this view, racial and ethnic groups are constructed on the basis of social relationships and are not based on genetic differences or primordial features. The focus is on the institutional framework within which groups are defined as racial or ethnic and how social interactions are organized accordingly (Bolaria and Li, 1985). Physical and cultural traits are the basis of defining social groups only insofar as they are socially recognized as important. The dominant group has the power, and therefore capacity, to define socially what constitutes a subordinate group, using physical and social features.

What emerges from the literature on race and ethnicity is a confrontation between two powerful theoretical perspectives for the analysis of ethnic group relations. The theory of assimilation has dominated policies on multiculturalism since the Second World War. Only recently has it been challenged by theories of social pluralism.

The theory of assimilation or "the melting pot," basically Social Darwinist, essentially claims that the dominant group is socially superior. Milton Gordon's work, *Assimilation in American Life* (1964), was a pioneer work in the theory of assimilation. He posits four distinct types of assimilation. His variables are: cultural assimilation (adoption of dominant group culture, values, and lifestyle); structural assimilation (entrance into group institutions, clubs, and cliques); amalgamation (defined and measured by intermarriage rates); and identificationable assimilation (minority group members think of themselves as American, Canadian, Mexican, etc). In addition to these four types of assimilation, he argues that assimilation may be measured by the absence of three phenomena: prejudice, discrimination, and power or value conflicts between groups (Newman, 1978, p. 43).

The assimilationist and "melting pot" integrationist policies that emerged in North America were consistent with the liberal ideals identified by Smith. Smith argues that liberal theorists had generally taken the view that "as mankind moved from a primitive, tribal stage of social organization toward large-scale industrial societies, the various primordial ties of religion, language, ethnicity and race which divided it would gradually but inexorably lose their hold and disappear" (Smith, 1981, p. 2). With mass migration and with the expansion of industrial capitalism, it was expected that there would emerge a time when it would be necessary to organize production and trade on a global scale. The rational use of labor would mean that old cultural differences and political divisions would become increasingly irrelevant. The growth of mass tourism, the expansion in communication systems, and the standardization of mass culture would inevitably lead, according to the liberals, to a global cosmopolitan culture (Rizvi, 1986, p. 5). According to Smith, however, this foreshadowed dissolution of ethnicity has not occurred. Indeed, he maintains that modern history, if anything, has demonstrated that economic and industrial trends have tended to reinforce ethnic and cultural divisions.

Van den Berghe (1981) develops his analysis of race and ethnicity on the basis of his rejection of both the assimilationist ideology and what he refers to as the liberal tradition in race and ethnic relations. According to van den Berghe, this liberal tradition in ethnic and race relations is constituted by the following propositions:

1.   All humans are members of a single species, and there are no biologically meaningful subspecies within it. Races are social constructs corresponding to no biological reality.

2.   Differences between human populations are smaller than within them, and such differences as exist (for example, in IQ test performance) are largely, if not entirely, the product of the social environment.

3.   Racism and ethnocentrism are irrational, dysfunctional attitudes, if not downright aberrations, to which certain rigid, authoritarian types of personality are especially prone. Such attitudes must be combated through a social therapy promoting equal status contact between groups. (van den Berghe, 1981, pp. 2–3)

Van den Berghe contends that assimilationist and melting-pot ideologies are fundamentally misguided because they are based on the assumption that cultural diversity can be eradicated through the forces of urbanization, industrialization, and modernization. Cultural diversity is for van den Berghe a necessary condition of human evolution and adaptation. On the basis of this view, ethnicity, according to van den Berghe, has something to do with kinship, a deeply rooted biological affiliation, which is often referred to in the social science literature as primordialist. For van den Berghe, it is this kinship and biological affiliation that brings people together to acquire common cultural attributes like language, religion, rituals, and other customs, and that these are constitutive of ethnicity.

In a powerful critique of the primordial conception of ethnicity, Barth rejects the views that ethnic groups have a primordial quality, that is, the characteristic of being biologically self-perpetuating, and that they share fundamental cultural values, realized in overt unity in various cultural forms (Rizvi, 1986). In Barth's view, what is missing from the primordial view of ethnicity is any account of how individuals come together to see each other as sharing a common culture, and others as having a distinctively different culture. Barth accepts the view that the classification of persons and local groups as members of an ethnic group depends on their exhibiting the traits of a particular culture. But he denies the assumption that this is something that can only be "judged objectively by the ethnographic observer, in the culture-area tradition, regardless of the categories and prejudices of actors" (Barth, 1969, p. 12). For Barth, what is of crucial importance is the subjective interpretive dimension of ethnic classification. So, in contrast to van den Berghe analysis, Barth is concerned with the social processes by which groups identify themselves and maintain their difference from other groups. Barth explains these processes by reference to his concept of boundary maintenance (Rizvi, 1986).

Another version of assimilation theory, pluralism, stresses both the demise and persistence of ethnic cultures. In a culturally pluralistic society, ethnic groups are believed to share some aspects of a common culture and participate collectively in its economic and political life, while retaining their unique ethnic culture in their networks, residential enclaves, churches, and languages. The notion of cultural pluralism has led to the development of policies of multiculturalism that seek to encourage cultural diversity and promote racial and cultural harmony with the aim of reducing racial/ethnic discrimination. Cultural pluralism assumes that every individual and group desires to maintain a distinctive ethnic identity and heritage, and multiculturalism as a policy gives recognition to the fact that some individuals will find greater human affinity outside their ethnic group than within it. Furthermore, the voluntary nature of maintenance of ethnic ties, loyalties, and identities under the multicultural policy protects the individual rights of members to freely dissent or dissociate themselves from the collective values of their ethnic origin.

Critiques of pluralism argue that pluralists downplay the problem of ethnic and racial inequality, and that their view of a pluralistic society often assumes a basic equality for all groups (Li, 1988, p. 8). This same criticism can be applied to multicultural policies that often fail to combat racism and discriminatory practices in that they succeed only in managing race and ethnic relations within a state apparatus (Bolaria and Li, 1985).

The accounts of race and ethnicity indicate that there is an assumption that cultural traditions tend to be static unchanging phenomena, divorced from the broader social context in which they acquire meaning. In the analysis given above, ethnicity remains a key concept, but the questions of the dynamics of cultural change are either pushed aside as being irrelevant or simply ignored. In short, culture is reified (Rizvi, 1986). Reification occurs whenever culture is treated as though it is a thing unto itself, independent of other spheres of life. The reification of ethnic values has made a mystique of ethnicity, creating phenomena that do not lend themselves to rational explanation. This is particularly the case when ethnic groups are assumed to be endowed with a given set of cultural values that are taken to be unrelated to the material and political context in which they arise and acquire significance (Rizvi, 1986, p. 17).

Colonization and the Creation of Multiethnic Societies
The developing countries that were under colonial rule for a number of years went through a long and painful state of transformation. Colonialism has left a long-lasting legacy on the now independent states of the Third World. The impact has been felt in two ways: first, the creation of ethnic-regional inequalities that have become conflict-laden problems, and second, the lopsided development and the lack of opportunity for social mobility for the minorities. The existing structures were either destroyed or replaced by colonial institutions or institutions modeled upon those that existed in the "mother country." The new institutions that emerged served primarily the interests of the colonial rulers and the local bourgeoisie.

The Third World states comprise a heterogeneity of nations or peoples (Saram, 1991, p. 8). Initially, the colonial powers were able to establish artificial political boundaries that divided peoples into different regional groups and brought them under different political jurisdictions. For example, the creation of India, Pakistan, and Bangladesh has resulted in ongoing conflict. These three states, created after colonial rule formally ended, share a number of common elements, but they are divided on religious, regional, and political grounds. In some cases, groups were united for independence, but tribal and religious differences resulted as power became firmly entrenched in the hands of a minority elite or a dominant tribe. In these situations, there are tendencies to create regions or provinces with some autonomy to the ethnic population. These administrative structures are however, governed by a centrally controlled machinery. Frustrated by this type of arrangement, a second-wave of independence movements by the ethnic or minority groups was arisen. The ethnic minorities feel left out and they exist only outside the formal system. There is little encouragement for these groups to participate fully in the decision-making process.

Colonialism has created "a number of sub-societies each of which is an integrated entity with its own culture" (Smith, 1966, p. 49). In the former colonial societies argues Smith, "no peaceful change in the social system is possible because the sections have nothing in common except involvement in economic and political relations which are essentially antagonistic" (Smith, 1966, p. 49). Groups are invoked with so much difference that it becomes essential to maintain separate cultural systems. Singer and Areneta (1967) saw the cultural systems of the East Indians and the Negroes in Guyana as so exclusive that they found it necessary to invoke the theory of basic personality differences in order to account for the maintenance of their separate identities.

Education and National Unity

It is essentially claimed that the basis of the conflictual relationships in the developing societies rests on racial differences—with the races being composed of "institutionally diverse groups" that are incorporated differentially in terms of their status and power, with the same nation state. These discrete groups develop or maintain their own institutions that express their own cultural values, which helps to maintain a significant degree of segregation between them, even though they might inhabit a common geographical location (Bacchus, 1991, p. 98).

The value differences that exist between the diverse groups result in their developing and supporting different institutions. According to Depres (1975), some of these are "local institutions" that serve the specific needs of the particular racial groups, while others become "broker institutions" that link the local institutions to the national institutions. This linking process helps to reduce the possibility of interracial conflict. For example, in the United States differences between blacks and whites have resulted in the creation of a Black Caucus as a "local" institution within a national institution— a nationwide political party. Such "local" institutions aim at meeting the specific needs of a particular racial or minority group. These are then fed into the mainstream national institution that, whenever possible, takes the concerns of the different racial groups, enunciated through their "local" institutions, into consideration. In other words, argues Bacchus, some of these "local" institutions serve as "broker institutions," with the aim of linking the local institutions into the national ones. Similarly, local schools are usually considered as important broker institutions that link the different racial groups into the same labor market and develop in them a set of values and aspirations that is common to all the different groups in the society. However, the sharing of common occupations by diverse racial groups produces status and class divisions and hence, conflict.

The "entanglement" created brings these racial groups into competition for scarce resources, namely, political and economic resources. Because of the nature and distribution of political and economic power in the ex-colonies, the competition for such resources is often seen as equivalent to a zero-sum contest. The racial groups have little in common and they "enter into the domains of intergroup relations and individual transactions, imparting to both domains, a segmentary character" (Bacchus, 1991, p. 98). As a result, Depres posits the persistence of ethnic boundaries in a multiethnic society and conflict over continued competition for scarce resources, even though there might develop many forms of interethnic accommodation.

Racial conflict has prompted policies on unity and national integration in many countries. In Malaysia for example, the race riots in May 1969 clearly indicated the need to speed up the process of national integration. As a result, *Rukunnegara*, or the national ideology and the New Economic Order (NEP), were formulated. The *Rukunnegara* lays down the principles of belief in god, loyalty to king and country, upholding the constitution, rule of law and good behavior, and morality. The NEP drew attention to the socioeconomic foundations of national unity and argued that national unity is not possible where ethnic and racial conflict persists (Singh, 1991, p. 42). The aim was to propose a strategy that would lead to the removal of ethnic barriers and encourage economic participation.

In Malaysia, as in other plural societies, the educational system has taken a multicultural approach for achieving unity in diversity. In this process, education becomes the main broker institution that could break down communal and ethnic identities and replace them with a common national one. In Malaysia, schools are perceived as "the most powerful tools for peaceful persuasion fostering common ideals, common ambitions, and common loyalties" (Singh, 1991, p. 42). Core values are transmitted through a common curriculum. While there is an emphasis on unity, there is also a tendency to preserve some individual ethnic values and customs. Through such a policy, ethnic groups are provided the opportunity for upward social mobility. Recent studies indicate that educational attainment in Malaysia is a key factor for achieving social equality. Education therefore, becomes the principal avenue for reducing ethnic tension and promotes social equity and national integration.

It should be noted that in spite of Malaysia's efforts toward national integration, some elements of disunity have been observed. The support for national institutions has weakened at the expense of the support for local cultural institutions. According to Jasbir Singh (1991), the current policies have not gone far enough to forge national unity and to reduce dissent among the ethnic groups. In a situation where all ethnic groups are seen as competing in the same labor market and for scarce resources, educational policies do not necessarily facilitate social mobility for all groups. The Malaysian experience indicates that the social and economic underpinnings of the national educational policy govern ethnic relations.

The brokering function of schools can be considerably strained if equity is defined along ethnic lines rather than class and poverty lines. The Malaysian government has tried to achieve national unity and encourage social mobility among its ethnic population. A weakness of this approach is that in its effort toward the sociocultural integration of minorities, it has dichotomized the population between Malays and non-Malays, thus making the differences between these two groups more pronounced. This policy needs to be reassessed, for ethnicity has to take precedence over individual needs (Singh, 1991).

Equality and Social Justice for Minorities

Recent events suggest that there is greater need than ever to recognize the rights of minorities. There is a global movement toward freedom and social justice by groups that have been marginalized. While underdevelopment and inequality in developing countries are largely products of external factors, there are certain internal structures that have caused the marginalization of minority groups. The interethnic conflict very often takes on an internal dimension. Minorities have been isolated through a long history of subjugation from the mainstream society for economic and political reasons. Social justice for these groups is a requirement for the development of the society as a whole. Ethnic conflict and tribal disputes hinder development.

Societies in which ethnic conflict persists for a long period of time become segmented. A segmented society is one in which different ethnic or racial groups either want or are forced to live separately. An example of such a society is Sri Lanka. Segmented societies are not always successful in accommodating their various groups. For example, civil war breaks out, repression and even genocide are resorted to, societies are split up, or chronic political instability occurs (Rossides, 1990, p. 298). Economic and social development in a segmented society often benefits the ruling elite, while minorities are brutally dealt with by the repressive state apparatus.

In many societies, minority and tribal groups have been denied basic human rights: for example, the aboriginal peoples in North America and Australia, the Kurds in Iraq, the *mestizos* in Latin America, and the Palestinians, to name just a few. The separate existence of these groups from the mainstream has created a large gap between the dominant group and the subordinate one. The inequality that currently persists has made living conditions for the minority groups unbearable, so that they are forced to express their discontent, often through violent means. The violent clashes have allowed the state to become more repressive in dealing with the minority groups. The army now absorbs scarce resources at the expense of social programs. The inability of the state to deal effectively with the demands of minorities has brought misery to countries like Sri Lanka. The dominance of a religious or ethnic minority tends to exacerbate socioeconomic inequalities and to contribute to the establishment of an authoritarian regime, which may curtail political freedom and violate basic human rights in order to maintain power and dominance. Strong military forces are established and frequently used by the political elite to assure regime security and sustain authoritarian rule. Most military-dominated governments tend to suppress minorities, curtail political activities, and violate basic human rights (Pourgerami, 1991, p. 178). Any attempt to form greater social justice for the minorities would have to take into account the sources of inequality.

One useful strategy with which to redress the problems of ethnic inequality is to reverse conditions that already exist in most developing countries. The state should facilitate redistribution of resources and accommodate the needs of the minorities through a policy of mutual consent, rather than one of containment or appeasement. Without redistribution of resources, attempts toward sociocultural integration will not be fully realized.

A policy on redistribution requires some internal structural changes. The role of the state has to be redefined. The state and the political machinery cannot be coercive. Whether it is access to education or land, the dominant group should show a willingness on its part to deal with the minorities. Redistributive measures should be an integral part of an overall development strategy. Long-lasting economic and social development is often impossible in the case of prolonged hostility among local groups. The national development strategy requires changes in order to improve the quality of life of every citizen.

The immediate change that is required is to dismantle the authoritarian regimes that monopolize power by establishing a state-controlled political party system that closely checks the movement of minorities and minimizes their activities. Such arrangements will enable the political machinery to become more democratic. Constitutional democratic systems tend to be more peaceful than their coercive counterparts. Highly militarized autocratic political systems tend to induce more violence. Excessive internal conflicts tend to produce more aggression and coercion. Hence, a reversal of this policy is required that can quickly establish noncoercive governments. The objective of the state becomes that of ensuring political and civil liberties. The violence-prone tendencies of the regime will no longer be shared by all members of the society.

Redistributive policies have been tried in the 1970s, but little redistribution has taken place (Griffin and Khan, 1982). The economic growth that occurred benefited a segment of the population, without increasing the real income of the marginalized groups. The experiences of minorities in Brazil and Argentina indicate that their living standards have been declining. When economic growth stopped in the 1980s, the minority groups became the worst affected. The desire for increased economic growth cannot be pursued if the plight of the minorities is neglected. On the contrary, economic growth will ensue with the support of minorities, who, in some countries, occupy vast expanses of land. Agricultural development can alleviate rural poverty and reduce rural/urban migration. The lopsided development that occurred in many developing countries has brought little change in the lives of marginalized groups.

Redistribution refers to a process of generating equal opportunities to allow all members of the society to prosper. It consists of a long-term economic development strategy that leads to a growth of per capita real income for everyone, improvement in living conditions, and availability of goods. One of the ways this type of development can take place is through education. Education has been linked with economic growth and it is now an accepted assumption. One positive way education can play a more effective role is to liberate the marginalized groups. The function of education should be to go beyond what is generally proposed; it should lead to political emancipation. A formal structured type of education that is only accessible to a few would not benefit the more disadvantaged groups. The objective of an emancipatory type of education is to free individuals from their struggles and to make them politically more aware of their surroundings so that they can transform their reality.

In a plural society, minority groups cannot attain their goals through normal channels of educational achievement. They cannot compete in a system that does not favor them. If the goals of education are the same for everyone, that is to achieve upward social mobility, the ethnic origin of the applicant will become a decisive factor for the distribution of rewards. For example, in Malaysia, the Malay is more likely to be successful in the labor market than the non-Malay or in Fiji, a native Fijian will be more favored than a Fijian of

Indian origin. In both cases, the minority faces obstacles in spite of attending the same school. Because they could not attain upward mobility through education, the Chinese in Malaysia and the Indians in Fiji have substituted their goals for that of accumulation of wealth and independent self-improvement. But the minorities in Brazil or Argentina, especially the native population, cannot substitute their goals for historical reasons. They became marginalized through a long period of colonial rule. For them, common aspirations for social mobility through education do not exist. Social change for these groups will occur with political emancipation.

Education is a political act and it can transform the oppressive groups in society into active political participants. Education has a more liberating role for the minorities. Through basic literacy programs as demonstrated by Freire, a greater self-awareness among the adult learners is achieved. A critical education empowers the oppressed to understand more fully the forces that determine the outcomes of their existence. Freire (1989, p. 48) notes:

To acquire literacy is more than to psychologically and mechanically dominate reading and writing techniques. It is to dominate these techniques in terms of consciousness; to understand what one reads and to write what one understands; it is to communicate graphically. Acquiring literacy does not involve memorizing sentences, words, or syllables— lifeless objects unconnected to an existential universe—but rather an attitude of creation and re-creation, a self-transformation producing a stance of intervention in one's context.

At its most basic, literacy means being able to read and write and count. But it is not as simple as that. In certain societies, it has often meant being able to read and learn sacred texts. For Freire, literacy is part of the process by which illiterate people become aware of their personal situation—and learn to do something about improving it. Learning to read, write, and count are steps toward achieving political, economic, cultural, and human rights. This, in turn, enables people to read and play a role in making their world a better place to live. This is positive development. Although literacy may not be the great panacea that leads to prosperity, it could lead to change in the way power is distributed in society.

The process of transformation leads to greater consciousness for social justice and democratization. Democratization of the Third World must result in increased politico-economic participation of minorities in order to systematically reduce social inequality and to improve allocation and distributive mechanisms. As Pourgerami puts it, "Democracy enables people to take instrumental policy actions on their own behalf to eliminate inegalitarian social and economic arrangements" (Pourgerami, 1991, p. 8).

Conclusion

The above analysis indicates that policies on the sociocultural integration of minorities in developing countries have not achieved the desired outcome. Minorities have remained marginalized and their demands for greater social justice have not been fulfilled. There is a global attempt by minority groups to seek redress after a long history of subjugation. In many societies, ethnic conflict continues to dominate political life. A combination of an authoritarian regime and the oppression of the minorities have hindered economic and social development in developing countries. Conflict has a negative effect on development.

In order for positive development to take place, it is being suggested that a policy of redistribution can overcome the current ethnic tension in developing countries. Redistribution combined with a development strategy can moderate conflict and provide alternative economic opportunities to everyone. Economic development is less likely to take place in societies where an impoverished population confronts a small wealthy elite who control the means of production and distribution. Redistributive measures focus on direct living improvements in living standards of the marginalized, the poor, and the minorities. Redistribution without some structural changes of the current political order may not be possible.

Education has an important role to play in the alternative development strategy discussed. For the minorities, education is for greater political participation and social consciousness. Participatory, liberating education seeks to increase equality in the access to knowledge and to continue to transform society. Minorities can liberate themselves through this process. Once they are emancipated, they can play a more active role in the development of the society as a whole.

References

Alladin, Ibrahim M., and Kazim M. Bacchus (eds.) (1991). *Education, Politics and State in Multicultural Societies: An International Perspective*. Needham, Mass.: Ginn Press.

Bacchus, M.K. (1991). "Socio-cultural Integration Among Teachers in a Multicultural Society." In Ibrahim M. Alladin and Kazim M. Bacchus (eds.) *Education, Politics and State in Multicultural Societies: An International Perspective*. Needham, Mass.: Ginn Press.

Barth, F. (ed.) (1969). *Ethnic Groups and Boundaries: The Social Organization of Cultural Difference*. London: George Allen and Unwin.

Bolaria, Singh, and Li, Peter (1985). *Racial Oppression in Canada*. Toronto: Garamond Press.

Depres, Leo A. (1975). "Ethnicity and Resource Competition in Guyanese Society." In Leo A. Depres (ed.) *Ethnicity and Resource Competition in Plural Societies*. The Hague: Mouton Publishers.

Driedger, Leo (ed.) (1978). *The Canadian Ethnic Mosaic: A Quest for Identity*. Toronto: McClelland Stewart.

Freire, Paulo (1989). *Education for Critical Consciousness*. New York: The Continuum Publishing Company.

Gordon, Milton M. (1964). *Assimilation in American Life*. New York: Oxford University Press.

Griffin, Keith and A.R. Khan (1982). "Poverty in the Third World: Ugly Facts and Fancy Models." In H. Alavi and T. Shanin (eds.) *Introduction to the Sociology of Developing Societies*. London: Macmillan Press.

Isajiw, W. (1974). "Definitions of Ethnicity." *Ethnicity*, no.1.

Li, Peter. (1988). *The Chinese in Canada*. Oxford and Toronto: Oxford University Press.

——— (1989). *Ethnic Inequality in a Class Society*. Toronto: Wall and Thompson Inc.

Newman, William N. (1978). "Theoretical Perspectives for the Analysis of Social Pluralism." In Leo Driedger (ed.) *The Canadian Ethnic Mosaic: A Quest for Identity*. Toronto: Stewart McClelland.

Pourgerami, Abbas (1991). *Development and Democracy in the Third World*. Boulder, Colo.: Westview Press.

Rizvi, Fazal. (1986). *Ethnicity, Cass and Multicultural Education*. Geelong, Victoria: Deakin University Press.

Rosen, B.C. (1959). "Race, Ethnicity and Achievement Syndrome." *American Sociological Review* vol. 24, no. 1.

Rossides, Daniel W. (1990). *Comparative Societies: Social Types and Their Interrelations*. Englewood Cliffs, N.J.: Prentice-Hall.

Saram, P.A. (1991). "Multicultures and the State: A Theoretical Analysis." In Ibrahim, M. Alladin and Kazim M. Bacchus (eds.) *Education, Politics and State in Multicultural Societies: An International Perspective*. Needham, Mass.: Ginn Press.

Singer, Philip and Enrique Areneta (1967). "Hinduization and Creolization in Guyana: The Plural Society and Basic Personality." *Social and Economic Studies* vol.16, no.3 (September).

Singh, Jasbir Sarjit (1991). "Multicultural Education, Social Equity and National Unity in Malaysia." In Ibrahim M. Alladin and Kazim M. Bacchus (eds.) *Education, Politics and State in Multicultural Societies: An International Perspective*. Needham, Mass.: Ginn Press.

Smith, A.D. (1981). *The Ethnic Revival*. Cambridge: Cambridge University Press.

Smith, Raymond, T. (1966). "People and Change." In *New World: Guyana Independence Issue*. Georgetown: New World Group Associates.

van den Berghe, Pierre (1981). *The Ethnic Phenomenon*. New York: Elsevier.

Weber, Max (1968). *Economy and Society*. Ed. G. Roth and C. Wittich. New York: Bedminster Press.

Part II

Case Studies

Doing Justice
Education and Gender Relations in Africa

Lynn Davies[*]

Introduction

A review of a conference at the University of Natal in 1991 on "Women and Gender in Southern Africa" described how "We were all trapped in different languages—the language of academics, the language of slogans. People denied and discounted each other's realities" (Lund, 1991, p. 20). The theme of this chapter—and indeed of the book—raises immediate questions of the power to define. Before we can proceed to any discussion of the elements of social justice for, say, women, we have to ask, Who defines social justice? Who are they defining it for? Whose definitions carry the most weight?

The original title requested for my contribution was "Women, social justice, and education in Africa." This raised a number of immediate problems. First, there was the danger of a bourgeois white feminist attempting to define African women's problems for them. Second, there was the tension between "women" and "gender" as areas for action and debate. The shift from focusing on "women" as a victim minority group to focusing on gender relations as a determinant of social injustice has been a slow one, but a necessary corrective. Third, there was the temptation to rehearse the well-known dreary statistics of female underrepresentation in access to schooling, in outcomes of schooling, or in participation in professional and political decision making about education. These are generally followed by calls for government intervention, for women's mobilization, for "forward-looking strategies." I have yet to be convinced

* With the participation of Zola Conjwa, Sarah Karanja, Ramadhani Magoha, Changu Mannathoko, Khadija Mbarak, Elisha Mkomole, Pholoho Mochekele, Ignatius Mutungi, Sahr Ngegba, Barbara Udanoh-Nwadialo.

that presenting people with the facts changes very much. There are always explanations that will justify imbalances, and those explanations invariably and conveniently lie outside the people one is talking to. Ironically, the more educated people are, the more explanations are available (a theme to be returned to later). Policy makers will blame socialization; parents will blame the media; teachers will blame the government; everyone will finger this amorphous entity called "our culture."

In an attempt to address some of these problems, this chapter is based on the following assumptions. First, it is not sufficient, or indeed wise, to change women without also changing men. Hence there is an insistence on gender, not women. The aim is to explore how changes in gender relations (not just in women's achievements) can occur both in and through education. For this, we need to have proper indicators. While I have reservations about the managerial, technicist ideologies surrounding lists of competencies and performance indicators for individuals, I am convinced of the value of identifying institutional indicators for areas such as equality. I will look first at what I term "doubtful" indicators of justice, and then move to possibilities for more "real" indicators that there have been moves to gender justice.

Second, I will wherever possible try to use the interpretations of African writers (while conceding that such interpretations are also filtered through my Western selective consciousness). At the time of writing this chapter only two of the contributors to this book actually appeared to be living in the Third World; it would have been interesting to ask an African woman to write about social justice in education in the UK. I would want therefore to avoid the impression that there is automatically less gender justice in the Third World than the First, or that the North has nothing to learn from the South's initiatives.

Third, I tackle my doubts about whether books of readings ever make any practical inroads into the deep issues they address, by using the opportunity to generate some interventionist research that asks African teachers to identify indicators, examples, and personal strategies for gender justice in their lives and institutions. In line with the focus on gender and gender relations, the views of both women and men teachers are recorded. Justice, for me, is not the same as equality, although justice may incorporate aspects of equality; but it is important to know how the practitioners define it.

Finally therefore, my title, *doing* justice, reflects my concern that we all need to take responsibility for changing gender relations, and that individual stories are as important, if not more so, than grand policy initiatives. Betty Boothroyd, M.P. and Speaker of the UK House of Commons, once commented "after all, every male chauvinist is some woman's son." I will very briefly develop my interpretation of structuration theory, which brings back individual human agency into the "reproduction" of culture. Rather than relying on "outside" explanations for continuing injustice, one immediate translation of structuration theory is to ask, How will YOU raise your sons or daughters?

What Are the Indicators of "Justice"?
(a) "Doubtful" Indicators
Traditionally, the indicators of whether gender equality (and by implication, justice) was nearer to being achieved in education have been the statistics on boys' and girls' access to schooling, and their relative destinations after formal education. While the revelations of continued disparities have indeed galvanized policy makers into such affirmative action as quota systems or employment of more women teachers to encourage girls into schooling, there are problems of the reliance on sex-differentiated statistics as the sole indicators of (in)equality.

First, there is the question of what girls and boys are gaining access *to*. There is now a wealth of research on the hidden curriculum of schools all over the world that demonstrates that formal education is not a benign force, and may act to reproduce inequalities of gender, race, and social class rather than eliminate them. The "myth of equal opportunity" was well exploded by Imam (1987) for Nigeria, by showing, among other things, the concentration of women in "soft" and low-status subjects in the curriculum, and the links to "marriageability." A recent report on gender in Tanzania (SIDA, 1991) noted the typically "macho" substance of school relations, with punitive, militaristic regimes underpinning male domination of teaching and differential treatment of girls and women. The mur-

der of nineteen girls by their male peers in the dormitory of St.
Kizito school in Kenya is described in an article in *Southern Africa*
under the title "The Reality of Hating Women" (McFadden, 1991).
Equal access to a stereotypical curriculum and equal entitlement to
an inequitable and hostile set of gender relations in an institution
are not likely to challenge surrounding disparities in work and family, and may even compound them.

Second, the over-use of sex-differentiated "categories" continues
to imply that "boys" and "girls" are the names of two species, whose
traits are not primarily defined by the relations between them. It is
like having tables of how many giraffes and elephants there are in a
zoo. We could have positive action policies to increase the number of
elephants, but this would not alter in the slightest what it meant to be
a giraffe. Yet, gender for humans is a social construction. The very
definitions of masculinity are predicated on NOT being feminine,
and vice versa. Trying to alter concepts of what it is to be "female" or
"feminine" in any society (i.e., whether women are educated, articulate, assertive, paid, and respected) by definition alters what it means
to be "male" or "masculine." Any attempts to change one column in
the statistics without recognizing the sociopsychological impact on
the other column is doomed to failure. Quota systems using lower
pass marks for girls into secondary education, for example, may merely
confirm a belief by both sexes that women are substandard, and require "special" treatment (as Martin [1983] found for Zambia).

Third, the educational statistics can be used and manipulated
to demonstrate a false sense of progress (especially where the condition of women may have worsened overall). A good example of this
is quoted by Cutrufelli (1983). The official report from UNAZA,
the National University of Zaire, claimed a "remarkable increase in
the number of female students" as proved by the fact that in 1974
the female/male ratio was 1:13, and in 1975 it "appears" to have
become 1:10. The report goes on:

*Times have changed. . . . Thanks to our President, citizen Mobutu Sese
Seko, the education of women and the acknowledgment of their rights
have become a reality and can surely go down on record as one of the
achievements of the Second Republic. Of course, women's evolution is
still facing a few difficulties. . . .*

In "reality" the trend was toward the establishment of "women's professional training" centers and courses—equipping women for the usual ghettoes of "women's work"—in agriculture, sales, needlework, crochet, and typing (Cutrufelli, 1983). As well as the political manipulation of statistics I also find interesting the report's semantics around the "evolution" of women, as if they were primitive creatures. Do we talk of the "evolution" of men? Incremental differences in statistics can all too easily be interpreted as an inexorable trend toward equality. The regressions and the "backlash" effect of progress recently demonstrated by Faludi (1992) need equal attention if statistics are going to be used.

Of course, access statistics on their own are also dubious unless we look at drop-out rates. Teenage pregnancy is a concern in many African countries at present, compounded by the threat of AIDS. Rees (1991) reports a study in Transkei on pregnant rural schoolgirls that showed that in nearly all cases the pregnancy was unplanned. Most of the girls were misinformed about sexual development, conception, sexual relationships, and appropriate use of contraceptives. It would seem that the school had done little to educate teenagers on these central issues, in spite of the fact that an extensive study from a teenage clinic in Cape Town showed that 81% of girls attending for their first visit were sexually active. Even the term "drop-out rate" can be misleading, as it implies a voluntarism not accordant with the forced expulsion of pregnant schoolgirls (to be further discussed later).

Another doubtful indicator of progress is the lone woman in a position of power or influence. Education may well have helped such a woman, but if she has "pulled up the ladder behind her" there is no guarantee that she will use her position to improve women's position, and indeed her very presence may be counterproductive by lulling everyone into a false sense of security and progress. Women—and men—in Africa have frequently asked me about Margaret Thatcher, or spoken approvingly of this apparent symbol of social emancipation. This is called the "But What About" syndrome. Every time one expresses a concern about women being generally excluded from decision making, the counter is, "But what about Margaret Thatcher/Indira Ghandi/Corinne Acquino?" My own indicator would not be their simple presence, but what they had achieved in changing gender relations in a society. Had they fought for equal pay, altered inequitable marriage laws, brought in workplace nurseries, introduced more women into power and more men into domestic life? While I have spent much time collecting data on gender representation in educational management in Third World countries (Davies, 1986, 1987; Davies and Gunawardena, 1992), I acknowledge that the bare numbers of representation become possibly less indicative than what people actually do when they are in senior positions within education.

The impact of educated women in high-level government positions and of educated women's groups is described very positively for Tanzania (SIDA, 1991). However, Amadiume (1987, p. 197) writes of Nigeria:

The responsibility of educated elite women and organisations to their rural sisters was identified as providing information, education and leadership. In my opinion, any organisation committed to the achievement of economic and social justice for women must be guided by a socialist ideology. Such an organisation cannot, therefore, be an umbrella or a miscellaneous organisation representing women with conflicting and varied ideologies and orientations . . . [nor] working for or always with whatever government is in power. As we know, like male politicians, on the platform of umbrella organisations, many women have used the services and support of the majority of women, especially at the grassroots, to enhance their own political careers.

This quotation found strong agreement from Sarah Karanja with regard to Kenya. She cited the conflicting activities of the Maendeleo Ya Wanawake organization in pledging "loyalty" to the president, the government, and the ruling party. A prominent woman environmentalist who publicly opposed the government in its proposal to convert a public park into a private business project was condemned by the organization chairperson (with the Green Belt offices eventually closed by government); two main initiators of multiparties were similarly detained with the "blessings" of the women leaders.

This leads into the final doubtful indicator, which is public activity around "women's issues." There has certainly been a vast increase in the last two decades in conferences, planning meetings, workshops, and seminars on women, as well as in the number of large and small organizations promoting women. The difficulty is evaluating how far such activity actually creates change. Organizations and women's projects can perhaps be more easily assessed, and must provide accountability, but the public arena for discussion is more difficult to quantify. While a women's conference may raise awareness for the (perhaps mainly female) participants, they may still return to patriarchal setups at home, work, and in the union. As Driver (1991, p. 90) reports when discussing the ANC constitutional guidelines:

Political articulation has been male dominated because of the intricate combination of women's double roles as working mothers and their conventional reluctance to fight against or even speak of this difficulty, coupled, of course, with sharp resistance from men to political participation by women. In trade unions, even in the predominantly female Sactwu, for instance, women shopstewards sometimes have to fight at home with their husbands for the right to assume a political role.

The writer Boitumelo Mofokeng noted how politically vocal women are *redefined* by domesticity:

Outside, we stand up on platforms, but at home, some of us go back to the typical African tradition, we are submissive, passive, non-existent. I cannot relate to my husband or my brother the way I do to other men out there. (quoted in Driver, 1991)

We shall return to the difficulties of personally challenging "culture" when outlining structuration later. The point to be made here is the obvious one, that talk does not necessarily imply action, and public talk does not necessarily imply public action—it may even mask the absence of it. Hence the increase in the number of academic books and conferences about women and education are not a sound indicator of whether men have shifted ground or whether educational institutions lower down the hierarchy are actually educating about gender and sexual relations. A Kenyan women's magazine, *Viva*, claimed "Men in our society are probably the biggest obstacle to a successful family planning campaign . . . men do not want women to have the ability to control their reproductive functions" (quoted in Hartmann, 1987). The presence of a proper sex education program in a school that included considerations of rights to decide reproduction might be a better indicator of social justice than a university conference on "Women into the Year 2000."

(b) Indicators of Change through Education

To assess the possibilities of gender justice being achieved in or through education, we need specific examples rather than the rhetoric about what education should do. Long-term, the tracer studies are admittedly difficult to provide. Dirasse (1990, p. 57) writes of Botswana:

The education/training and employment linkage is indeed complex. The empirical evidence clearly shows gender-segmented patterns in labour force participation whereby women tend to be concentrated in the services sector and in secretarial and clerical occupations. A considerable number of studies on women's occupational status and participation in both the formal and informal sectors are widely available. However, analytic studies that directly trace and explicate the linkage between education and the gender segmented labour market are rare. For example, how do we explain the changes that took place in primary school teaching and clerical occupations that were predominantly reserved for males during colonial times in Botswana but are now a female preserve? . . . The outcome of non-formal education has been generally to keep women in the same service and domestic oriented sectors. However, it is also true that some of the innovative approaches in participatory training and training with production have been tried under the rubric of non-formal training.

Thus the cause-and-effect within education and employment is difficult to ascertain. Do women succeed in spite of or because of education? Are shifts in gender segmentation in the labor market more due to shifts in the economy than to an increase in trained females? There is little evidence generally that education *creates* employment, and even less about education independently acting to alter gender segmentation in work. At present, therefore, the "success stories" of education remain at the small scale, and the aim would be to collect enough of these to start finding generalizable patterns.

Differences between institutions provide one clue. In Tanzania, in contrast to the general lower achievement of girls and their experience of harassment and discrimination in school, Weruweru girls' boarding school had a high achievement record and a teaching staff committed to the denial of girls' inferiority in the classroom. In another, mixed, school, the women survived with the help of a transformative Headmaster who made a number of new rules to control male students and also provided the women with appropriate role models and encouragement (SIDA, 1991). The report also cites the general impact of education in imparting a "reading culture," whereby there is high demand by women for relevant books, pamphlets, and newspapers containing gender issues.

IWRAW (the International Women's Rights Action Watch) provides a constant set of useful potential examples in its own newsletter *The Women's Watch*. Public education columns in *Speak Out*, the quarterly magazine by the Women's Action group in Zimbabwe, cite current legal cases of inequities in land inheritance, or marriage/nationality laws, and through this public education in areas such as wife beating, women and AIDS, prostitution, and structural adjustment, provide levers for people to challenge inequities in their own lives (IWRAW, 1992, vol. 5, no. 3, p. 3). In Mali, a new project aims to counter the problems of cultural biases in favor of boys' education—keeping girls at home, lack of female teachers, and traveling distance to school—all of which hinder girls' educational attainment. Popular radio and TV shows convey messages about the importance of girls' schooling in an effort to change adult behavior (IWRAW 1992, vol. 5, no. 4 p. 3). It will be noted however, that both these examples are "education" outside the institutional system, and also not yet evaluated in terms of actual impact. In Botswana, a Girls and Science Roadshow took a science display all over the country, and a follow-up video did have both girls and boys saying that it had changed their perceptions of whether women could take jobs in scientific and engineering fields. In the absence of institutional monitoring, the personal accounts and stories are the best indicators of whether education can change lives. One of my favorites is Assitan Diallo from Mali:

Until I was 24 years old, I knew that female circumcision involved cutting, and I knew that it was painful, but that was it. Then there was a French lady teaching at my school, and she wanted to find out about female circumcision. She kept asking us questions. I was the only female in my whole class, so she harassed me with questions about female circumcision. Fortunately I had an old grandmother, she was 108 at that time. The older you get, the more democratic you get in our society. So when my teacher asked me a question, I would go back to my grandmother. I knew that if I went to my mother she would say "God, you are disgusting." So I would go to my grandmother . . . I made her talk about it and then would go back to my teacher. In the end my teacher said "You know so much about female circumcision, can't you write a book about it?" That's how I began. And as I read more, from doctors etc., I began to learn about its harmful aspects. (Gevins, 1987)

The powerful effect of a particular teacher is perhaps something experienced by all of us. In this example, the interesting feature is that the teacher did not appear to proselytize, to preach; she merely kept on asking questions. This leads at this point into a discussion of agency and the links with social structure.

Personal "Agency"

One of the theoretical and practical problems surrounding avenues for change is the relative impact and linkage of what are usually called "macro" and "micro" levels. The macro refers to large-scale systems, policies, structures; the micro to individual schools, people, daily interactions. Within sociology, the implied division between macro and micro means a tendency to focus more on one than the other, to attribute more causality either to large-scale forces (the economy, government, patriarchy, society) or to individual interpretation (how personal or institutional definitions of the situation condition our behavior). Clearly there have been many attempts to "reconcile" these two perspectives (and one which I have used has been the notion of the interplay between personal "scripts" for action and cultural "typescripts" attached to particular social groupings or positions (Davies, 1984, 1992). However, part of the problem has been the very construction of the idea of two "levels," the implication that there are "constraining" structures that act primarily in a one-way direction on individual action. Our only concern might be the "relative autonomy" we have to interpret and decide our behavior. Structuration theory (developed by Giddens, 1979, 1984) draws our attention, on the other hand, to the fact that "structures are both the medium and the outcome of social intercourse" (Giddens, 1979, p. 171). Structures refer to the "rules" and "resources" that individuals use to accomplish everyday social interaction. Gender "rules," for our concern, would refer to those sets of gender-appropriate behaviors drawn on by girls and boys in classrooms, and by their male and female teachers—often elsewhere termed "expectations." "Resources" refer to goods and services and the authoritative power to control these—the "capabilities of making things happen" (Giddens, 1981, p. 170). Gender-based or gender-differentiated resources would, in my interpretation, include the power of money/pay and of access to public politics; in schools, gender-based resources would include student access to teachers and control over classroom events and discourse.

The difference between this and more deterministic views of structure is the recognition that structures are dependent for their continuation on the actions of individual agents. Through our everyday language, discourse, conscious and unconscious "choices" of behavior, we constantly reproduce and consolidate the rules and resources attached to social positions. Every time we say "boys will be boys," every time we defer to a man in a meeting, we are not only infinitesimally consolidating the rules for ourselves, we are strengthening their power for others. Conversely, every time we act in a nonstereotypical way, every time we refuse to make tea, we are casting a minuscule doubt on the permanence and absolute totality of gender rules. This is not to claim more power than we have, and as Shilling (1992) points out, rules and resources can "stretch away" beyond the control of any individual actor or individual institution. A teacher can implement nonsexist practices, but this does not change overnight the sexist nature of an education system. However, our task in analysis and action is to discover how deeply embedded in time and space are what appear to be the major structural principles of a society and to remember that these structures cannot continue or exist without the continued reinforcement by individuals on a daily basis.

I have grossly oversimplified what can be a very intricate discussion—particularly in terms of explanations of how certain rules and resources appear more enduring than others, and the links between structures and systems. Shilling (1992) has an excellent and full account. However, the purpose of the introduction of structuration theory here is the reminder—for all of us—that justice or injustice is a practical achievement, not just a theoretical concept. Our task is not just to measure injustice, nor to call on others to rectify it, but to ascertain in each society how we as individual women and men within the institutions of education and family use, implicate and reproduce the rules that act to underpin unjust distribution of resources. Even those in oppressed positions have the power to influence events because of the "dialectic of control," the fact that power relations, like gender relations, are reciprocal and depend on the actions of both dominator and dominated (Giddens, 1979, p. 149). Again, this does not claim *equal* power of influence, but stresses *reciprocal* power. Because of the dependence of the powerful on the relatively powerless, there will always be spaces for resistance.

The Power of Asking Questions

Education is a prime arena for the discussion of doing justice, in that it is ideally the site for asking questions and insinuating resistance. Enquiring why a society operates in the way that it does ought to imply the possibility of difference. Like the teacher in the example given above about circumcision, the act of asking questions is possibly more powerful than preaching or providing answers on the need for change. Interventionist research can therefore be based on the principle of the chain of questions: a researcher asking a teacher to explain a social phenomenon and their role in it may empower that teacher to surface that question with their students or their own families, and those students with their peers or families. The Freierian principles of consciousness raising were often predicated on the asking of seemingly simple questions of the disempowered in order for them to realize their social position. I include here a very small example of opening up dialogue with a mixed group of (already powerful?) teachers from Africa, using the claim that this is a different, but equally effective, way of making change and surfacing the rules, from writing an article for passive reading. The group came from Tanzania, Kenya, Sierra Leone, Zanzibar, Nigeria, Lesotho, Namibia, and Botswana; questions were raised mainly in the form of discussion, but also using written reflections. They loaned me books and journals that they thought might help. Drafts of this chapter were also relayed to them for comment. Personal names are attributed— or not—as individuals wished.

I asked three questions—not just because I wanted their "views," but to see what happens as a result of asking those questions. The questions were:

1. How would you measure whether there was justice in gender relations in African schools?
2. Have you any examples of a change in gender relations which has been achieved in—or through—education?
3. What could you as an individual do in your everyday life to challenge any gender-based practices that lead to injustice?

The *indicators*, first, were perhaps predictable ones, and focused initially on equity rather than gender relations: female and male access to schools; equal provision of schools for girls and boys in single-sex systems; equal staying-on rates; equal access to all curriculum areas. However, the need to focus on gender rather than women was underscored by the differences among African countries. In East and Southern Africa the problem was of larger drop-out for girls; in Nigeria and Sierra Leone, more boys were perceived to drop out because of the lack of jobs for school graduates and the need for boys to go straight into whatever "business" they could find. The consensus therefore was that justice was the equal right to stay in school, whether for girls or boys.

Examples of *changes* in gender relations, however, started to reveal the dilemmas in differing definitions of "justice." Examples of women achieving high positions through their education led to a discussion of the relative benefits of single-sex and coeducational schools, particularly for women. A girls-only military college in Nigeria that encouraged the girls' aspirations was described: It made them "stretch out" like the boys almost physically when they returned to the school to visit. This was a further example of individual action modifying structures: The inception of the school was supported by an army general who had only daughters and wanted high achievement for his otherwise disadvantaged offspring. We did not discuss the fascinating blend of militarism and feminism that might have been a feature and would provide interesting research on the social "rules" in such an institution.

It was in the discussion of the links between school and family/marriage/morality that the greatest dilemmas or disagreements arose. There is variation among African countries in the policy on pregnant and/or married schoolgirls (and women teachers). There was agreement that expelling a pregnant schoolgirl, but not the schoolboy father, was unjust, but an expressed justification in terms of the greater embarrassment for the girl if she returned to that same school. Was justice achieved if she were allowed to continue in another school? The competing claims for equal rights and for "morality" emerged, with fear, especially from the men, that a "bad example" would be set if the school appeared to condone pregnancy by allowing the girl to remain in school. A further complication was raised by the example of parents being willing to look after the child, and managing to break the rules by unofficially gaining acceptance for their daughter in another school: Again, whose definition of justice should prevail, the school's or the parents'? A "success story" was related from Sierra Leone whereby parents resisted pressure for their daughter to abort her child, transferring her instead to another school, whereby she was able to complete her education and become a medical doctor. We see differing ways of using resources of power here, in that they were presumably influential parents: Is beating the system an example of justice being done or merely an illustration of the reproduction of unjust access to power?

Another argument was around the use of strategy. It was agreed that issues of teenage pregnancy and drop-out could be helped by sex education in the school. It was unjust that in Zanzibar, for example, men received sex education through the mosque, but women had no access to this. But it was acknowledged that there was parental resistance to overt sex education in schools, and implicitly that parents had rights over such curricular choices. Therefore at what age should sex education begin? Should it be done openly, or "smuggled in" through health education and the sickle cell program that educated on genetics? Zola, from Namibia, disagreed with the idea of confronting parents, whereby it would be possible to be labeled a "bad teacher" and lose one's job. That would be a different kind of injustice. The only agreement in the group was that parents needed to be educated, and teachers should encourage parental participation—as Barbara acknowledged:

I had a lesson from my experience here which I hope to take home. Parents participate here, even in curriculum and school development. In Nigeria we have a fault. We don't let the parents participate . . . to let them know what we are doing with the children.

However, the resistances within schools themselves, and teachers' and heads' interpretations of the weight of culture also caused conflict:

In my class, I told the boys to clean the floors . . . but a boy came the following day, my father said I shouldn't sweep the floor—his father was a member of the school committee. He took issue with the headmistress, and she said it was fair to make him sweep, it was common in the school, but she was afraid though. She told me to ignore him, and he was exempted from sweeping . . . I left that open for the day I will be in a responsible post . . . [Interview with Zola Conjwa]

Here we have an example of gender-based rules being initially challenged, but then both rules and resources being reproduced and reinforced through the actions of the headmistress. Yet, for the father, justice was done.

The invitation to reveal ways they themselves tried to achieve gender justice disclosed many such traps. Barbara said "you could start with cooperating with your own wife." Ignatius pointed out that if a man offered to participate in domestic life, he was criticized straightaway—by the wife—because of the fear of how the society would react. Sahr was more successful: He recounted how it was seen as funny for a man to have a basket on his arm—"especially if you are in a senior position"—but that he had started it, going to market with his little boy. One of the Tanzanian men, too, said:

What I am doing practically right now, in my family, I am bringing up boys and girls without segregation, all perform equal domestic duties. It's the upbringing . . . if we change the upbringing . . .

Sarah wrote in support:

In my own family of three sons and one daughter, household chores are shared regardless of gender in order to help remove the stigma so much rooted in our society of certain duties for boys and others for girls which to me has enhanced stereotypical tasks and roles to the detriment of gender justice.

There was agreement then in the group, and commitment too, that children should see parents in nonstereotypical roles—although no conviction that African men would ever be found washing their wives' underwear.

In schools, the role of teachers was clear. In Zanzibar, justice would be done when teachers stopped reminding girls that a woman's place was in the home. Instead, these African teachers would encourage the debate about gender issues; try to engage in self-development in order to act as a role model; show confidence and competence in everything; get the children to engage in nonstereotypical tasks and challenge biased divisions of labor; and discourage teacher language in schools that stereotypes female behavior. In the public arena they would "motivate every woman I come across to stand up for her rights"; encourage the government to put specific emphasis on females when a certain resolution on gender is established; train women to be aware of their rights; motivate women to upgrade themselves through mass media; and "get away with feminist concepts."

In this there appears to be a strong emphasis on the education of women; inevitably perhaps the thrust is toward female empowerment rather than male disempowerment. For Ignatius, there is a "need to get rid of concepts of masculinity and femininity—however educated a woman is she will still portray concepts of femininity." Sahr says that women should be "aware of their rights . . . the women themselves should be forward-looking."

The "women themselves" nonetheless recognize the "forked tongue" of education in all this: that education may be the key to breaking down gender divisions, but that "educated men are the worst: they call on the culture." For Barbara, the fact that her husband is doing a master's degree and she is "only" doing a bachelor's degree means that he expected her to go into the kitchen and cook. In spite of the calls for equal access, the group accept that there is no guarantee that simply educating everyone will create gender justice; it may merely provide new access into different discourses, new articulations and legitimations of existing inequalities. Education would have to be a specifically fair place in itself and actively promoting gender justice.

For them, education can nonetheless make inroads into social justice. In Tanzania, for example, the indicators are the introduction of UPE; day secondary schools expected by law to take 50% for each sex; opening up technical secondary schools and trade test centers for girls as well as boys; allowing women to join the university directly after high school; providing employment for a newly married female who has had to follow her husband; an increasing number of women as educational officers, ministerial directors, and district commissioners. In Lesotho, the indicators were similarly "women's voices being listened to," with increasing numbers of (qualified) female headteachers and Ministers.

Justice within institutions is when the school is able—in Sahr's phrase—to "relax cultural values" to enable participation in curriculum areas such as gardening (for girls) and needlework (for boys). Khadija relates: "My nephew came home and asked for cloth and a needle and his sisters said, 'They are going to make you girls!'—so this is an example of a success." In Namibia, when the school had a bazaar, the men teachers would come and help with the preparations, cooking, and serving; in Zanzibar, the boys volunteered to learn cooking for an exhibition. In Kenya, the introduction of home science for both sexes, and the training of male home science teachers had helped change the "long-held" attitude of domestic chores as women's responsibility.

The group were nonetheless far more comfortable with providing examples to demonstrate that in the main there was little gender justice in African life, whether talking of inheritance, chieftainship, family responsibilities, dress codes, domestic labor, career opportunities, pregnancy rights, posts of responsibility within education, or conversational rights. Translating all the "negative" indicators of existing injustices and putting them together with the "positive" indicators, the socially just school with regard to gender would:

- enroll equal numbers of females and males
- have equal staying-on rates
- avoid stereotypical books and tasks
- have equal access to curriculum areas
- respect similar human rights and dignity
- provide confidence for all
- permit pregnant girls to continue their education
- have sex education programs
- encourage future shared domestic responsibilities
- teach both sexes leadership
- have equal rights for women and men teachers
- give both unmarried and married women teachers maternity leave
- have equal representation in posts of responsibility
- have men being able to be told what to do by women
- have equal proportions of men and women teachers posted to rural areas
- encourage teachers to be involved in social mobilization in the community

Some of these could lead relatively easily to quantifiable "performance indicators" for the school or college; others require more qualitative information to assess progress. Yet, it is possible to draw up a workable institutional audit from these descriptors that would provide a more sophisticated, yet clearer picture than the traditional gender statistics. The task, of course, is not just to audit an institution, but to use the information-gathering process to create change.

Conclusion

This particular exercise has confirmed the need for more research—not so much raw data as both action research to create change and qualitative research to seek out models of resistance. Olekambaine (1991) recorded many researched examples of what she called "terrorist" pedagogy in Africa (rote learning, examination emphasis, control of knowledge by the teacher) as well as encouragement of girls in particular to be submissive, but noted that although exceptions among teachers and students exist, "forms of resistance and struggle are relatively poorly documented and need further research as well as encouragement" (p. 45). Mbilinyi (1991) commented for the SIDA report: "We were not able to identify any research which specifically studied how girls resisted negative stereotyping and other forms of discrimination" (p. 62). Of course, in line with the emphasis on gender in this chapter, the argument would also be for research on male resistance to masculinist stereotyping. As McFadden (1990, p. 3) points out, African women are tired of the constant stream of researchers, asking probing questions and promising what they can not deliver.

The need to focus equally on men, and the benefits of "mixed-sex" and participatory research were confirmed by the group evaluations. For one member, "seeing it written down—exactly what you say" made her realize how research was done and put together. A male perception was that ". . . the discussion was very useful because I got the views from the other side of the coin"; a female response was that "I personally feel that social transformation for all, that is, men and women alike, is the answer to the many gender issues confronting us today in Africa."

The notion of education as "transformation" is, of course, the key to placing gender relations in the context of development as a whole. In the end, we have to ask why we want to change gender relations in and out of school. In the interests of women, certainly; in the interests of many men, too; but in the long term, in the interests of economic and social progress. The unbalanced, competitive, militaristic, and masculinist nature of formal education is intricately linked to the unbalanced, competitive, militaristic, and masculinist modes of social operation that characterize African and Western countries alike. The Tanzanian report talks of "the competitive basis to classroom relations" as unfriendly to girls; I would assert that it is equally unfriendly to development.

International competition—in the form of nationalism—has come under scrutiny as a major challenge for women in Africa. There is a problem that participation in the liberation struggles of the region may define women mainly in reproductive roles as mothers for the nation and the youth (McFadden, 1990). The Organisation of Angolan Women argued for raising the scientific and literacy level of women, "educating them politically and ideologically to ensure that tomorrow they will be women dedicated to the cause of the revolution . . . enjoying their legitimate right to a freely consented motherhood" (1984, p. 33). While the president had admitted that "machismo still exists," the concentration from him and the OAW was on women's emancipation, not on male emancipation from that machismo and its effects. Instead there was an emphasis on participation in (competitive?) sport for both sexes (Organization of Angolan Women, 1984). The impetus of this chapter has been to conclude, however, that unless masculinity and gender relations are rigorously laid bare, women will continue to be seen as an "issue"; and the broad questions of the complete set of social and political relations of a country will not be fully challenged. International machismo masked as nationalism poses one of the greatest problems of all—for men and women.

We have seen that changing gender relations in and through education can provide greater social justice for participants. Its long-term measure, is, however, the extent to which such changes transform the definitions, the spending, the effort, and the importance attached to the achievement of "justice" throughout the society.

References

Amadiume, I. (1987). *Male Daughters, Female Husbands: Gender and Sex in an African Society*. London: Zed Books.

Cutrufelli, M. (1983). *Women of Africa: Roots of Oppression*. London: Zed Books.

Davies, L. (1984). *Pupil Power: Deviance and Gender in School*. Lewes: Falmer Press.

———— (1986). "Women, Educational Management and The Third World: A Comparative Framework for Analysis." *International Journal of Educational Development*, vol. 6, no.1.

———— (1987). "Research Dilemmas Concerning Gender and the Management of Education in Third World Countries." *Comparative Education*, vol. 23, no.1.

———— (1992). "School Power Cultures under Economic Constraint.." *Educational Review*, vol. 44, no. 2.

Davies, L., and C. Gunawardena (1992). *Women and Men in Educational Management: An International Inquiry*. International Institute for Educational Planning, Research Report No. 95. Paris: IIEP.

Dirasse, L. (1990). "Gender and Education: Selected Issues in Gender and Educational Research in the SADCC Region." In G. Mautle and F. Youngman (eds.) *Educational Research in the SADCC Region: Present and Future*. Gaborone: Botswana Educational Research Association.

Driver, D. (1991). "The ANC Constitutional Guidelines in Process: a Feminist Reading." In S. Bazilli (ed.) *Putting Women on the Agenda*. Johannesburg: Ravan Press.

Faludi, S. (1992). *Backlash: The Undeclared War against Women*. London: Chatto and Windus.

Gevins, A. (1987). "Tackling Tradition: African Women Speak Out against Female Circumcision." In M. Davies (ed.) *Third World, Second Sex, Vol 2*. London: Zed Press.

Giddens, A. (1979). *Central Problems in Social Theory, Action, Structure and Contradiction in Social Analysis*. London: Macmillan.

——— (1981). "Agency, Institution and Time-Space Analysis." In K. Knorr-Cetina and A. Cicourel (eds.) *Advances in Social Theory and Methodology*. London: Routledge and Kegan Paul.

——— (1984). *The Constitution of Society*. Cambridge, UK: Polity Press.

Hartmann, B. (1987). *Reproductive Rights and Wrongs: The Global Politics of Population Control and Contraceptive Choice*. New York: Harper and Row.

Imam, A. (1987). "The Myth of Equal Opportunity in Nigeria." In M. Davies (ed.) *Third World, Second Sex, Vol 2*. London: Zed Press.

IWRAW (The International Women's Rights Action Watch) (1992). *The Women's Watch*. (Newsletter), vol. 5, nos. 3 and 4.

Lund, F. (1991). "Impressions: Conference on "Women and Gender in Southern Africa." *AGENDA: A Journal about Women and Gender*, no.9.

McFadden, P. (1990). "The Condition of Women in Southern Africa: Challenges for the 1990s." *Southern Africa Political and Economic Monthly*, vol. 3, no.10.

——— (1991). "The Reality of Hating Women." *Southern Africa Political and Economic Monthly*, vol. 4, no.12.

Martin, V. (1983). *Gender Differentiation in Secondary Education in Zambia*. B. Phil. (Ed) dissertation, University of Birmingham.

Mbilinyi, M. (1991). "Secondary and Higher Education." In SIDA, *Education in Tanzania with a Gender Perspective*. Education Division Documents No. 53, Swedish International Development Authority.

Olekambaine, P. (1991). "Primary Education." In SIDA, *Education in Tanzania with a Gender Perspective*. Education Division Document No. 53, Swedish International Development Authority.

Organization of Angolan Women (1984). *Angolan Women Building the Future: From National Liberation to Women's Emancipation*. Marga Holness, trans. London: Zed Books.

Rees, H. (1991). "Women and Reproductive Rights." In S. Bazilli (ed.) *Putting Women on the Agenda*. Johannesburg: Ravan Press.

Shilling, C. (1992). "Reconceptualising Structure and Agency in the Sociology of Education: Structuration Theory and Schooling." *British Journal of Sociology of Education*, vol.13, no. 1.

SIDA (1991). *Education in Tanzania with a Gender Perspective*. Education Division Documents No. 53, Swedish International Development Authority.

Social Justice and the Micropolitics of Schooling in India

Ruchira Ganguly-Scrase

Introduction

Accounts of schooling of marginalized communities and groups in India are almost exclusively positivist in nature, and mainly provide statistical data on educational enrollment, completion, and literacy rates. With few exceptions (for instance, Newman, 1989; Thapan, 1991), ethnographic study of educational settings remains a neglected area of research. Indeed, as Newman (1989, p. vii) argues, despite the enormous number of theoretical and prescriptive studies, and exorbitant expenditure on resources, little is known about the working of educational processes at the micro level. More important, however, while documenting inequality is largely an exercise in statistical sophistication, equity in curriculum has more often than not implied the effacement of cultural difference altogether, and has thereby perpetuated a class and gender bias in both educational practice and content. For example, the government of India's aim of distributing justice through raising literacy levels and promoting the goals of "socialism, secularism, and democracy" outlined in the Constitution, also has the goal of achieving national cohesion. Implicit in the objective is the overriding concern that education should foster a unified national outlook regardless of class, gender, and caste.

In light of the above, this chapter has the twin aims of addressing the question of educational justice and inequality, first, in qualitative terms, by emphasizing ethnographic and historical approaches to the analysis of the education of marginal communities, and second, by emphasizing the legitimacy of the culture of subordinate classes that are often ignored in schools (by teachers and administrators). In particular, I focus on the lived experiences of school children from a leather-working community, the Rabi Das, in the town of Krishnagar in the state of West Bengal.[1]

Background

Originally from Bihar, the Rabi Das settled in Krishnagar approximately one hundred and fifty years ago and have been mainly engaged in tanning and shoemaking. Capitalist expansion of the Indian leather industry in the last decade has largely rendered the Rabi Das economically redundant. Previously segregated (due to their ritually polluting "untouchable" status) at the margins of Bengali society, the Rabi Das were drawn closer to the dominant culture of the Bengali *bhadralok* (respectable people) since the 1940s as a consequence of their association with Gandhian social reformers. The present Rabi Das identity is constructed to a great extent through their interaction with the *bhadralok* social reformers.

Since the Left Front government came to power in West Bengal almost two decades ago, a number of efforts have been made to redress the problems of educational inequality. Yet, it is the contempt and disdain of some *bhadralok* toward marginalized groups, such as the Rabi Das, that continue to plague educational reform. In order to conceptualize the significance of this cultural divide, it is necessary to explore the social relations that govern Bengali society. This will be followed by a discussion of the social reformers' role in implementing formal education among the Rabi Das.

Dominant Culture, Class, and Educational Inequality

The *bhadralok* are literally "respectable people." The opposite category is *chotolok* or "lowly people." In Bengal, this dichotomy is an important principle of social organization (Sinha and Bhattacharya, 1969) and is not coterminous with either caste or class (Mukherjee, 1975). Rather, it intersects with class divisions of contemporary India.

From their original position two centuries ago as a reasonably well-off, educated, and highly cultured status group, the *bhadralok* have become a heterogeneous group and often poor. Although economic power of the *bhadralok* has declined, they have maintained their ideological dominance in West Bengal. The main arenas in which *bhadralok* culture shapes and influences Bengali society are politics and ideology, the arts, and education (Scrase, 1993, pp. 25–37). In short, the dominant ideologies in West Bengal are the *bhadralok* ideologies.

The process by which the dominant classes and class fractions seek to universalize their cultural tastes, language, and bodily representations through a "legitimate culture" (see Bourdieu, 1984) is also visible in the overall behavior of the *bhadralok*.[2] Scrase (1993, pp. 59, 90–92) has introduced Bourdieu's notion of symbolic violence to explain partly the domination of *bhadralok* culture in Bengali society. His study demonstrates the way in which the ideological construction of knowledge through school textbooks has served to debase the cultures of the subaltern classes to the benefit of the *bhadralok* and the middle classes more generally. The latter's symbolic violence therefore operates to distance and denigrate subaltern cultures. This has happened to the Rabi Das culture as well.

In the context of schooling in this locality, teachers describe the Rabi Das and the other poor as bold and demanding, different from what they were previously. Initially, the teachers (who themselves came from poor economic circumstances) came into the community with the *bhadralok* ideology of having a moral obligation to help the lower classes. But as the stigma of untouchability of the Rabi Das has disappeared, so has the teachers' moral commitment to them. Furthermore, their present salaries, which are high compared with the incomes of the Rabi Das families, and the fact that they married well, has removed them economically, socially, and culturally from the Rabi Das. The main objective of the teachers who are in a state school system is to ensure the success of their charges in passing the required examinations. The Rabi Das do not understand why. They attribute the failure of their children to "the teachers' lack of concern." For their part, the teachers bemoan the disappearance of "simplicity and innocence," indicating a *bhadralok* nostalgia for past purity. In the educational sphere, this relationship epitomizes the *bhadralok* and *chotolok* dichotomy in the sense that educational inequality is a result of the cultural distance between dominant and dominated groups, not merely the outcome of a lack of economic capital.

Influence of *Bhadralok* Social Reformers

Untouchability had designated a separate physical space for the Rabi Das. From their settlement on the outskirts of the town in the latter half of the nineteenth century until the middle of the 1940s, their social contact with *bhadralok* Bengalis was minimal. However, in August 1944 the nationalist leader, Bijoylal Chattopadhyay, inspired by the Gandhian ideals of social reform, gathered a group of young volunteers to work in the enclave of the Rabi Das leather workers. The virtues of self-sacrifice, the eradication of inequality, and the bringing of enlightenment were at the core of the volunteers' objectives. In their own words, the aim was the "upliftment [*sic*] of the backward classes to our level." Bijoylal and his band of followers thus had the firm objectives of eradicating illiteracy, removing customs deemed to be socially dysfunctional—*(shamajik bisrinkhala*— literally socially enchaining), raising consciousness about health and fitness, and fostering economic advancement. Two of the workers, Debaprasad Chakrabarty and Aparajita Mukherjee, who were to have the greatest influence among the Rabi Das, later came to be fondly known by them as *Mashtermoshai* (respected teacher) and *Aparajitama* (respected mother).

The group's initial work involved the setting up of an adult education center. Their work among the Rabi Das shaped the growth of a spirit of individual mobility through education and certain Brahmanical ritual practices. In addition to the adult literacy and numeracy program, at night the students and volunteers followed the tradition of spinning. The school frequently served as a center for conducting *bhajans*, or devotional hymns. Initially, the women did not attend classes and began to participate only toward the end of the 1950s. Meanwhile, young men from surrounding areas were also keen to become literate—Muslim boys, a number of boys from the poor shopkeeper families, boys who worked in the day in a printing press, and so on. The school welcomed them as it had not been able to attract every boy from the enclave. Gradually, girls from other communities also joined the night school.

Educational Outcomes

Within a decade it became apparent that schooling was no longer a viable option for youth. They had to earn a living for their families and were encouraged to look for a job. Leather work was considered worthy since it was also a craft, a *shilpa*, and for Gandhians manual work formed an essential element of their moral philosophy. The government instituted some training schemes for leather work. At least twenty-three youths were enrolled in these programs. Some were absorbed into the large shoe-manufacturing sector, and others made attempts to start small businesses.

However, it was clear to the activists that the traditional occupation of shoemaking no longer brought sufficient rewards for the survival of all the Rabi Das families. Thus other avenues were suggested to the youth: white collar work, other forms of technical work, and so forth. *Mashtermoshai* went to extraordinary lengths to fight for the educational improvement of individual students, such as enrolling a student who had never had any formal schooling in class 10 at high school. Thus individual students pinned their hopes on *Mashtermoshai's* help: "Without him we would have been nothing," they say now.

The educational programs ran successfully until 1967. By then the social reformers had reached the stage where they felt that they could not shoulder the responsibility of the school by themselves. A regular, structured system of education had to be devised. They wanted to employ a "completely trustworthy person who was prepared to give up everything and work for nothing—like us." Such a person was never found.

Contributions were, however, raised to employ some needy *(abhabi)* young men to run the school for a while, and thus the night school ran for a further five years after 1967. A volunteer was paid a meager sum. An elderly attorney also helped out in the teaching. This was not in accordance with the reformers' desires, but was considered a stopgap measure. While *Mashtermoshai* completely withdrew from voluntary work to nurse his ailing father, Aparajita Devi recruited three women (three of the current teachers) to start a day school. For over two years, the women teachers worked without pay. These idealistic young women were marginally better off economically than the Rabi Das, but their poverty was genteel. Thus they aspired to help those "living in darkness" and their values were firmly embedded in the moralistic mental framework of the *bhadralok*. Aparajita Devi tried to lobby for a government-sponsored school and she was eventually successful in 1973.

Apart from their educational work, the social reformers[3] were also actively involved in other "constructive work," such as the provision of municipal roads, communal toilets, and, most important of all, housing. The volunteers were not only engaged in endless efforts to raise the standard of living in the Rabi Das locality, they sought to reshape comprehensively the Rabi Das community. There was a commonly held assumption that the Rabi Das lacked higher cultural values and led a chaotic way of life. Thus, the Gandhian reformers wished to bring about an urgent moral development and instill discipline and order in the lives of the Rabi Das. In many ways they also imposed their own Brahmanical Hinduism to the detriment of the Rabi Das's values and communal solidarity. Their project was motivated by their self-conceived moral obligation, rather than by the notion of enabling the Rabi Das to assume effective leadership for themselves. The project was paternalistic. The volunteers were moved by "an obligation of the privileged towards the less fortunate," but they defined the good in essentially *bhadralok* Hindu terms.

Despite this, the older Rabi Das appreciated the efforts of the reformers, and *Mashtermoshai* in particular. Indeed, they have not only genuine feelings of gratitude for their material achievements, but an unquestionable appreciation of his personal sincerity.[4] Curiously, in comparison, the current teachers who have been employed at the school for nearly two decades are regarded as self-seeking. No sense of gratitude is extended to them. Paradoxically, the feelings of gratitude toward the older Gandhian volunteers has made the Rabi Das rely on the former's sense of moral obligation. This was acceptable to both parties as long as the volunteers remained "self-sacrificing." The fact that teachers are paid salaries by the government binds them in a contractual relationship with the Rabi Das, rather than the preferred personalized patronage relations between the Gandhians and their wards.

Having outlined the particular milieu of the Rabi Das I shall now turn to a detailed discussion of schooling and my role as a teacher.

The School
School was a major part of children's lives. Though for many girls, it

was an escape from the drudgeries of work, the schooling experience for most girls and boys was a reinforcement of failure. The school caters to primary school students from classes I–IV. The children begin schooling around the age of four. The classes are composite, so that one room has children in preschool grade, class I, and class II. The other smaller section contains the senior students: classes III and IV. A teacher sits at the desk in front of the students, who sit on the floor in three to four rows. Apart from an old blackboard there is no other teaching aid, and all students except the preschoolers sit facing her desk. The preschool children do not have lessons, but do the same work as class I. Apart from dilapidated blackboards and desks, there are no other facilities. The walls are bare and unpainted, the playground has no grass, and the lavatory often gets blocked.

Children come to school piecemeal in the first half hour of the start of the day. Only a handful of children attend morning assembly. Each day the headmistress strives to get the children to stand in rows and makes only a partially successful attempt at getting them to recite nationalist songs and Hindu prayers. The atmosphere of the school is quite "informal" despite the rigidity of formal teaching method in the classroom. Children keep wandering in and out of the class in the first hour of schooling. Because the school is not heated in the winter months, some children have to be sent away because they are ill-clad and shivering. Often children come back with more clothing. The headmistress constantly chides the students about homework:

I told you to write things in your exercise books at home, but you don't listen. If you don't study you will be good for nothing. . . .

The children get bored and some do nothing. A rote-learning method is used to teach. The teacher writes the questions on the board and children copy. Then she provides the answers verbally and the children recite them aloud. The teacher remains behind her desk at all times. When the children go up to her to have their work corrected, she says, ". . . this is all wrong. Do it all over again." The children return to their place and try to learn from each other. The child who knows the answer tells the others. The information is shared. The bell rings and children close their books.

Ironically the Rabi Das parents say that the school is lax in discipline:

The teachers are too slack . . . they let the kids come in at all hours of the day. . . . If they had proper discipline, no child would be allowed in after the morning bell.

Comments such as these reflect the parents' views that schools should also be places of strict discipline and control. The older people especially lament the fact that the school does not counteract the influence of films because they hold that popular films are responsible for leading the children astray. Parents also accuse the teachers of "not teaching the children properly." They link the failure of their children in getting jobs to the poor abilities of the teachers. They also blame the current teachers for lack of commitment and for failing to inspire the children with Gandhian ideals. One of my informants who studied with *Mashtermoshai* in the late 1950s expressed it in this way:

It is true to say that the children today do not have the type of relationship we had with Mashtermoshai. *The school is not getting the type of training we had which enabled us to develop with self confidence. The children are not getting an adequate replacement for* Mashtermoshai. *He is old now. They are unable to have faith in themselves. The teachers of today cannot adjust themselves to our children.*

They simply treat it as any other job. The difference between then and now is that our teachers never thought of their work as a job.

Most Rabi Das held a negative view of the current school teachers, who they say are "stuck-up," "big-headed," and "think that they are better than us." Biren, one of the past pupils of the night school, now a man in his early forties, was furious at the teachers for not accepting *prasad* (divine offerings) at *Saraswati Puja* (celebration dedicated to the Goddess of Knowledge). Some Rabi Das complained to *Mashtermoshai* about it. He defended them by arguing that the teachers have *shashti* to perform at home.[5] The two Brahman women teachers were regarded by the Rabi Das as perpetuating untouchability. One of them (not from the original volunteer team of three women) used to enter the neighborhood with a handkerchief over her nose. She finally stopped doing so after the *para* boys wrote graffiti about it. The other woman was accused of being very insensitive. Biren once argued with me that a teacher in this school had to be more than a technician imparting literacy; she has to be "a social worker as well." He said that the teachers "were sowing the seeds of divisiveness and inculcating prejudice among pupils."

The teachers in the school are not ignorant of the children's needs. They are not totally removed from the children's everyday experience, but they firmly believe in ideologies of meritocracy embedded in government educational ideology in India. Although their salary and occupational status puts them above the Rabi Das, among the middle classes their status is low. In their own childhood, these women were indeed poor, as I have noted earlier. For example, one old Rabi Das woman described one of the present teachers—whom she had watched growing up—as "the snotty-nosed daughter of a half-starving Brahman." Ironically, their poverty was one of the reasons why the teachers were recruited when the school was initially started by the Gandhian reformers.

My Role As Teacher

As mentioned earlier (see note 1), I gained entry into the *para* (neighborhood) by becoming a voluntary primary school teacher in the school. From day one, my role of the "new school mistress" was clearly defined. It was through my legitimacy as a school teacher that I was able to carry out my fieldwork, particularly in terms of establishing close contact with children in the school and developing relationships with neighboring Bengali families who were highly differentiated.

The school building serves as both educational and community center. Yet, ironically, the much loved centerpiece of the community symbolizes both the former idealistic vision of an educated and respected community and the current, seemingly cynical attempt by the government to provide a resource that will provide only the lucky few with an escape from their economic misery and despair. Like the surrounding environment, the school appears to be in a permanent state of decay. One cannot deny the lively voices of inquisitive boys and girls eagerly ingesting new knowledge of their world, yet all around there remains a pall of cynicism about education, on the part of both teachers and parents. Indeed, as in most schools in India, the children soon have their minds attuned to the rigors of memorization, while the innocence of naive inquiry is slowly and perpetually dulled.

For anthropologists combining holistic community studies and working in schools presents special problems as they are faced with multiple layering of their selves. For me, complex relationships emerged from the roles permitted to me as a fieldworker and this in turn impacted on my strategies for gaining ethnographic data. My role of school teacher both permitted and prevented the use of certain methods. "Teacher" was the least complicated role for me, particularly in relation to inquiries about children. Yet, in the process of collecting data, there were competing demands placed on me, conflicts arose between me and the other teachers, and to a very limited extent between me and parents outside the neighborhood.

For instance, during my early months in the field, I was allowed to have a double period after lunch with my class. The class actually became quite popular, since I encouraged children to express themselves freely. This was frowned upon by some of the other teachers. As the class became noisy and boisterous, it was considered a discipline problem. My open-ended, unorthodox approaches to teaching were regarded as a threat by two of the senior teachers. The tension stemmed from my critical views on the requirements of the rigid practices of the formal schooling system. The main objective of the other teachers in this state-sponsored school was to get children through the formal education system by passing the required examinations. However, I found that not only was the failure rate high, but most children dropped out by the end of primary school and few reached higher education. Yet, the other teachers pursued unrealistic objectives and expectations because they believed that schooling provided upward social mobility to the poor. To me they seemed oblivious to the actual state of affairs in gaining a job in India—the endless exams and interviews, and the class and gender bias. In leveling criticism toward their attitudes, however, I did not imply that the simple application of a "relevant curriculum" would solve the problems. While I did not attempt to radicalize the curriculum, I did incorporate the radical pedagogic approaches (e.g. Freire, 1972) that are adopted by many nonformal schools in Bengal and which advocate that education should empower and raise consciousness of marginalized groups.[6] I developed my own teaching aids from available material and also followed curriculum materials designed for nonformal schools.

Radical departures from teaching the set syllabus led to my eventually being asked to give up my class; I could continue it, but only after school hours. This created a number of problems. Some children had to run errands or go to work. A few students not resident in the neighborhood had to leave straightaway so that their parents would not become worried; others who had nothing to eat all day were too hungry to stay. Yet others were forbidden to attend this "extra-curricular" class since their parents regarded my approach as nonacademic. As a female vegetable vendor bitterly complained to me, "I don't send my daughter to school so that she can just play and read story books. Why don't you teach her to do sums?"

Nevertheless, the popularity of the after-school classes and the enthusiasm of the children enabled the classes to continue. However, the composition of the classes changed. The new classes consisted of children who had left school and children attending other schools. Although having this wide variety of students enriched my students' experience of learning, for me several practical and methodological problems arose. First, I lost my "control group" because different children turned up each time. Second, my own school day became very long. I had lost the most mutually productive and suitable times of working in the school, which were the hours immediately after lunch. During this time most men came home to bathe, eat, and to nap before returning to work again. Most people were too busy to talk to an ever-inquisitive anthropologist. The strategy that I adopted was to reduce the number of hours I spent on the school premises. This had a negative impact on my relationship with the teachers. Withdrawal from participation in the overall program of the school was perceived as selfishness on my part, and I was seen as being interested only in "extracting information" from the children. It led to growing tension between me and the other teachers. Their cooperation declined, while many parents were openly displaying their dissatisfaction with the teachers in favor of my approach to teaching as well as my involvement in community life. This in turn intensified the teachers' hostility toward me, since I appeared to undermine their authority. Such a tense relationship made it awkward for me to ask the other teachers for further interviews or to follow up points of clarification.

In summing up so far, unlike the past, the Rabi Das now regard education ambivalently because few children have gone on to higher secondary school or college. Therefore, they see the teaching content, as well as the pedagogic practice more generally, as worthless. It has created a sense of alienation among students who are taught by uncritical, unimaginative teachers. Yet, teachers as a category cannot be blamed entirely because they have no control over the curriculum (Ganguly-Scrase and Scrase, 1990, pp. 128–29). Additionally, as my own experiences show, both the community and the formally trained teachers are generally hostile and suspicious of "radical," innovative, or informal approaches to schooling. Their response illustrates that, while educational success is largely a dream for most, schooling nevertheless symbolizes a significant, meritocratic path to success that should remain unchallenged (especially by young, women teachers!).

Children's Accounts of Their Daily Lives

In this final section, I focus specifically on children's own accounts of their daily lives. From the point of view of pedagogic practice, the significance of their accounts cannot be overstated. Not only are they an extremely valuable source, providing an accurate representation of working class childhood, the writings can be compiled to form "informal" textbooks. This would help toward overcoming the use of unfamiliar material that children of the laboring poor are forced to study. Further, texts produced by the children for children become a source of pride. I had utilized children's own stories to construct my accounts of their childhood experiences. In doing so, I also sought to reverse the anthropological tendency to present adult-centered accounts of childhood. The children wrote for me on the topic "My Story/Life/Work."

In recent years, children's own narratives have been used to investigate working-class childhood. Steedman (1982, p. 37) contends that from the viewpoint of the poor and the unimportant, children's texts are good evidence of what happens. She shows that children as young as eight and nine are able to capture in the act of writing the contradiction and ambiguities of social life. However, she warns that "as a way of abstracting meaning from the contradictory events of the real world children need to be operating at a minimum level of literacy competence" (Steedman, 1982, p. 28). To this warning, I add that there are inherent dangers in using any text that is written in the institutional context of the school, since there may be teacher bias. I have drawn from the writings of those older children whose texts were composed spontaneously,[7] without continuous assistance or approval from me.

The children also kept a diary of "What I Did Today." Taking this task very seriously, many students frequently recorded a list of their activities as part of "homework." Most wrote them routinely, including the not very revealing: "Now Miss has asked [us] to write down what we did today. After that we are going to do more work until the bell rings. The End." Each day the students spent the first ten minutes of class listing the events of the previous day. I also used these journals to construct tally sheets in order to discover the patterns of daily activities in the homes. Some of the major notions that emerged from children's writings were about neighborhood, community, family and gender relations, and work. Below I first present some examples of writings by Rabi Das children and then contrast them with the Bengali children's writings.

Rabi Das Children
Baby Das (girl aged 14):

I get up in the morning, do the beds
After sweeping the floor and washing my face
I go to the shops
When I return my mother makes tea
After drinking my tea I go to work
From work I go to the market
From the market I go to study
Mother works at home
Washes dishes cleans the floor

Cooks
Father is dead
I make every one's bed
I shop alone
I work in other people's houses

When I was young my father died
We are four sisters and one brother
Father married off one of my sisters
Now we three are left
Mother laboured very hard to bring us up
We have stepped out to work
Because we could not bear the suffering

My brother works in a shoe store
My eldest sister's name is Chaya Das
Middle sister's name is Chabi Das
Third sister's name is Kalpana Das
My name is Baby Das

When I get a headache
When I am late from work
I don't go to school
I can't come
Mother yells at me when I don't go to the market.

Sankar Das (boy aged 14):

I make my bed. Ours is a mud hut. I sweep the floors.
I look after my sister.
Father drives a rickshaw. Grandfather repairs shoes.
My grandmother's name is Mangala Dasi
I do the shopping at home, light the firewood stove.
I study
I sell lottery tickets sometimes
At the bus station
I get up at dawn
After washing my face I read

I drink tea
Mum goes to work I look after my sister
Mum comes I bathe
I comb my hair, dress
With my books I go to school
At lunch time I go home to eat
When the bell rings I come back
School finishes
I play
At night I sit down to study
I have my dinner and go to sleep

My name is Sankar Das
I am fourteen years old
My brothers and sisters mother and father grandmother
and grandfather are all here.

Protima Das (girl aged 10):

I stay in Hemanta Sarkar Lane, Chamar Para. I live in Ward 27, in Krishnagar. I live in our own house. We have a pucca *[cement] house. It has three rooms and one verandah. There are roof tiles on top of the large room and the two other rooms also have tiles. So does the verandah.*

Most people in our neighbourhood work with leather. That is why it is called chamar para. People in our surrounding locality say chamar para. *That is how we come to know that our neighbourhood is called Chamar Para. During festivals leaflets [advertising the location of deities on display] have got Chamar Para written on them. Some leaflets also have Gait Rd written on them.*

Our para has a mixture of kaccha [mud] and pucca [brick] houses. Pigs roam about in our para. So do ducks and chickens. There are Banyan and neem trees. There are Shojne *[drumstick] trees. Our para is full of life because there are lots of houses. We have three play yards.*

People in our neighbourhood frequently fight with each other over ducks chickens and goats. Sometimes these animals either throw things or they eat people's food. That is why fights break out.

In our para there are mostly people of our jat [caste]. There are 39 households belonging to our caste.

In our families it is the girls who do most of the work. When Bobby Didi goes to work, Sureshda and I do all the housework. Sureshda is very brainy. That is why he gets sick all the time. Sureshda is really nice. There is something wrong with his brain. The doctors can't work it out. They are going to take him to the hospital in Calcutta. Among the men no one but Sureshda does any housework. Elder brother works in a small workshop.

We know just about everybody in the neighbourhood. We visit them. Of course we fight as well. If their ducks and chickens destroy any of our things we never say anything. But if our ducks and chickens do anything they fight with us. We are very friendly with two families. Our neighbours are very helpful. If there is illness or danger they rush over. Our house caught fire once. At that time we were all sitting in the kitchen. We didn't see the fire. My [maternal] aunt's daughter was sitting on her doorstep and wondered why there were so many people in the street. Then she ran up to our house and saw the fire. She shouted that the house has caught fire. From our kitchen we saw the big room on fire. We started shouting. Our neighbours rushed in and poured water over the fire to put it out.

Bengali Children

I contrast below some typical narratives of Bengali children to show that working-class children share more common experiences than differences.

Balaram Paul (boy aged 10):

I am writing the story of my life. Once I visited a place. A friend there asked me who is in your family and what is your name. I said my name is Balaram Paul and I am ten years old. I live in Krishnagar in Nadia District. The house that I live in is in Ukil Para *(the lawyers' colony) and it is called the* Tribedi *house. My step mother put me to work there. The people there are OK. I have been there for two years. Because my mother died I have to stay in a non-kin's home to do my studies. I live there and I call the people there* Boroma *(big mother)* Dida *(maternal grandmother)* Boromama *(elder maternal uncle)* Chotomama *(younger maternal uncle)* Mamima *(maternal uncle's wife) and brother. I get up in the morning. Firstly I put water on the threshold.[8] I wash the front of the prayer room. I brush my teeth and wash my face and make the beds. I drink tea. I go to the market. Afterwards I stack the washed utensils. Then I go over to court. After returning home from the court I change my clothes wash my hands and feet and have something to eat. Then I keep the table lamp ready by wiping it clean and pouring oil in it. I light incense. I read. Then I massage the feet [of the master?] I watch TV after that. I eat and go to sleep.*

Kanchan Adhikari (boy aged 10):

I live in Khoro Para. There are four lanes in our para. Next to the road there are drains. Surrounding our home there are lots of houses. Next to the coconut tree is the Gyanananda Ashram. Every Sunday lots of devotees come. Prayers are held, there is music. I like our para very much.

Every year next to our house we have a feast. Lots of people attend; clothes are distributed. Every Sunday a lot of people come, there is music and singing. That is why I like it. I like our para and I like music.

In the month of magh *(January) I will have my* poite *(initiation). My third brother and I will have our thread ceremony together. We are* vaishnavs *that is why. When we have our initiation we have to go begging to seven people's house. My* bhikkhema's *house is in Chakdah. My third brother's* bhikkhema's *house is on the banks of the old Ganges. My* bhikkhema's *name is Radha. She is responsible for whatever is necessary for the initiation ceremony. When we have our* poite, *we have to shave the head, keep one strand of hair and pierce the ears.*

Neighborhood and Community

The problem in working with children is not only to avoid eliciting standard responses, but also to avoid promoting diversity. I use in my analysis issues that I believe emerged unintentionally. The following is an illustration of how model answers were avoided.

Rabi Das children easily distinguished between ascription by others who call them *chamars*[9] (which carries a derogatory connotation) and their own awareness of a community as "our *jat* (caste)." So I was curious that Protima noted that there were thirty-nine households compared to my own census of thirty-seven. At a later date, I asked her to identify the names of each household by listing either

the eldest person in authority or by the child in the family. This led
to all the children in the class talking about the number of families
they knew in the neighborhood. Everyone of the *Rabi Das* children
completed his/her list very quickly. Then, together they started com-
paring their answers and argued with each other as the numbers
varied between twenty-seven and thirty-seven. Those who wrote
down fewer names in their exercise books did not necessarily know
everyone, but they had either rushed their answers or had avoided
names difficult to spell. The Bengali children's response was a remarkable contrast: The maximum number of families any child knew
was six. Even to the children the close-knit network of the Rabi Das
households was obvious. They also knew some of the kinship bonds
that underlay these links. Though some Bengali children also had
relatives living in the vicinity and used fictive kinship to identify
neighbors, their limited contact with other families in their respec-
tive *paras* was obvious. It is likely that settlement in the areas surrounding their neighborhood is recent. There is less communality
among them. It is also likely that the Bengalis conceive of their *para*
as comprising individual households (and not as *jat*).

When asked to prepare this list one Rabi Das child asked me,
"Do you mean everyone in our *para* or just our *jat?*" This distinction
suggests a caste consciousness. Another Rabi Das boy included in
his list a recent Bihari schedule caste immigrant who had rented a
property. When the boy mentioned his name all the other children
protested saying, "Don't be so ignorant, he is a Bihari." The boy
however stood his ground by saying, "He speaks our language, he is
not a Bengali [and therefore he is one of us]." It seems that for most
children *"jat"* implied kinship, rather than caste. As one child put it,
"That Bihari fellow is not our *jat."* He and other children considered "The Bihari" to be quite different from "we [Rabi Das] Bengalis."
These conflicting ideas reflect the essential paradox of Rabi Das's
ethnicity and identity.

Rabi Das children's accounts of the solidarity in the community
often contradicted the adult's point of view. Though children wrote
about fights between adults over children's actions, children in general are cared for and fondled by adults and they play daily in each
other's compounds without interference from adults. Adults did not
make a secret of their dislike of neighbors. They constantly recalled

earlier conflicts and disputes. I did not once hear an unqualified statement such as that made by Protima about neighbors helping each other (despite the fact that Rabi Das do cooperate with each other). What is striking about the children's view is that they recognized the warmth and security of the neighborhood rather than the strife. Even those who wrote about fights did not speak in negative terms.

My own cross-cultural, adult, and middle-class assumptions about the dullness of the *para* resulting from deprived physical conditions was challenged by children's view of the *para* as being "full of life." Their reference to play yards is significant. The open spaces referred to were no more than small barren dusty patches, but children who mentioned them did so with pride. The yards were their special space where the children invented their own games and played among themselves and with children of other neighborhoods. I had observed that while playing there Bengali children often spoke the Bhojpuri dialect, the language of the Rabi Das.

Because I had noticed that the adults always talked about the fights without ever referring to their immediate causes (they mentioned fights only to rue the loss of solidarity), it struck me that unlike adults the children identified as the cause of fights the behavior of animals, that is, trivia. While the Rabi Das children discussed conflict in the community, Bengali children wrote about conflict in the family. They wrote about it matter-of-factly. For example, China wrote:

My father fought with my mother and left. We now stay with our [maternal] grandparents.

Sankari wrote:

My uncles [father's brothers] used to live together with us. Now they have separated.

In a more dramatic manner, nine-year-old Mitali (female) wrote:

When I was little, my [paternal] grandmother quarrelled with my mother and we separated. We rented a house. One or two months later my grand-

mother and aunt [father's sister] went to get my mother. They took a
rickshaw. When they saw mother, grandmother and aunt started crying.
That is why mother couldn't talk about the fight any more. Ma quickly
got changed and went home. She made tea for them. Then aunt went
back to her own house.

Auntie laughs a lot; father doesn't like that. He doesn't like so much
laughing. Grandmother still fights. When my little brother threw rice
all over she swore at him. She said it in front of father, so there was a
fight. Everyday she says these things whenever there is a fight. She said,
"I'm going to sell off all the pots and pans if you spend all the money. I'll
sell the house." Mum says when we get enough money we'll build a house.
Grandmother used to teach swear words to my little brother. She taught
us too. I said it the other day. Mum was so mad. Since then we don't
swear any more.

Work

Protima's accounts have been outlined above. Her work hours climbed
dramatically after two of her sisters were married off and left home.
Her play time had been cut short by this change. As soon as school
finishes, she is summoned by her mother to do some work. She
hurries her work and rushes out the door. Teachers in the school are
worried since she is a good pupil who is increasingly being denied
the chance to do any study. She was kept back in class IV by the
teachers because her handwriting needed improving. This suited her
mother well, as she could be kept close to home to fulfill all the
additional household tasks because of her two elder sisters' absence.
Protima is clearly disturbed by the increasing burden, and has be-
gun to recognize the gender differences in this responsibility. However, we can see that she consoles herself by saying that her brother
helps her out. He is the closest in age to her and there is a deep bond
between them. Suresh, in fact, is the ideal brother, soft-spoken and
always ready to assist. Suspected of having meningitis, he is often
kept back from school. As a result, he has become Protima's constant companion.

Though a number of children were in paid employment or had
to assist their families in various forms of unpaid labor, ideally the
Rabi Das child does not work. Parents used every excuse to keep
boys from work while they were at school. However, as we can see in

Sankar's case, outlined previously, the reality contradicts the ideal. Sankar's case may be unique because his father is "an outsider who is like a Bengali." Not associated with leather work, he drives a rickshaw. Sankar's father married into a Rabi Das family and set up house on a vacant plot (alongside other Bengali squatters). To have a son-in-law residing in the same neighborhood this way is highly unusual. Sankar's (aged fourteen) efforts to sell lottery tickets was a short-lived experience. There was tension between his parents and grandparents about Sankar's working. While his father is not adverse to Sankar earning a living, his mother is more ambivalent and wants her son to go further in education so that "he doesn't have to end up pulling rickshaws." The father wants Sankar to start his working life because "there is not much future for a rickshaw puller's son."

In general, there was much shame associated with male child labor, an outcome of the prevailing ideology of childhood as a period of protection. Thus only those who put children to work were seen as destitute or morally lacking. The Rabi Das children made no overt distinctions among themselves between those who worked and others who did not. But one incident involved two Bengali boys. When one boy was ridiculed by another for selling bits of firewood (which he had collected) in the market, he countered by saying "Well you work too; you go shopping." Whereupon the teaser said, "Yeah everyone shops, even your mother," implying that shopping was a different kind of work. It was a task befitting a person worthy of respect, such as one's mother, while selling was dishonorable. This remark was made by Kanchan who comes from a *vaishnavite* family, where the child is regarded as holy and is viewed as the child god, Krishna, and is therefore not put to labor. Collecting cowdung or picking out charcoal were undoubtedly lowly and shameful tasks for which Rabi Das children, particularly girls, were teased. When ridiculed these children fought back aggressively, sometimes denying that the work was regular, or by trying desperately to find something worse with which to accuse their opponents.

As the children grew up, their awareness of the limitations of their economic circumstances deepened. But so also did their knowledge of their mothers' sacrifices in attempting to provide for the family. It was this last which kept the shame and indignity of doing lowly outside work at bay. Baby's comments from her extract encapsulate this experience of childhood, "Mother laboured very hard to bring us up [that is why] we have stepped out to work because we could not bear [her] suffering." Similarly, nine-year-old Sri Krishno wrote:

I'll do what my mother tells me to. I'll go up to V or VI, then I'll stop. I'll work hard and look after my little brother. I hope to learn to make shoes.

Sri Krishno lived with his mother's natal family in the same compound, but in a room separate from the main house. I found out that soon his mother was going to construct a hut of their own on a separate plot. Sri Krishno had witnessed his father's brutality to her, a reason for his mother's separation. His father's failure to provide, the constant harassment, and the denigration of his mother by others instilled in him a sense of fierce loyalty to her and the need to look after his two-year-old brother, who nearly died of malnourishment while they lived with the father.

Baby's and Sri Krishno's eagerness to do all for their mother contrasts with the case of Balaram where the real mother (who was dead) is contrasted with the archetypal step-mother who puts him out to work: "My step mother put me to work there. . . . Because my mother died I have to stay in a stranger's home (*porer bari*) to do my studies." However, he had little to say about school, presumably the reason why he was living away from his family and working for his keep.

A Woman's Worth

Evidently, it is the mother's endless sacrifices that created a powerful bond between herself and her children. Beyond that girls rarely spoke positively about women in general. Their lives were viewed as essentially constricted with limited access to the outside world:

My elder sister never went to school. She just learnt to write her name at home. She doesn't know anything except to sign her name. My second sister after passing class four gave up her studies. Now she doesn't study anywhere. Her only work is to cook.

The ideological principle that operates here is that only through schooling could ignorant women gain entry into the wider power arenas. This also reinforces my earlier assertion that girls' aspirations to become school teachers were not merely to gain approval or to please the teacher. Bina's description of her sister's whole life, reduced to only knowing how to sign her name, highlights the powerful legitimacy of the school, as the formal objective disseminator of knowledge. Knowledge assimilated from life was rendered worthless; only textbook knowledge was considered legitimate.

Schooling and Future Aspirations

In their narratives nearly all the children wrote that they "sit down to study." I do not believe that this statement was made to please the teacher. Interaction with children and their families on a daily basis revealed that most children, whether they are coerced, or voluntarily pick up their books (like most school children in India), proceed through the ritualistic process of "doing study." Children attending school did sit down each night in their dimly lit crowded homes to do homework and to copy laboriously from their textbooks. Their parents constantly reminded them of their own unswerving faith in the value of education. However, more often than not the very people who told them to study hard sent their children on errands or asked them to mind a crying sibling or told them to hurry up and finish their homework.

From the accounts, one can see that, despite their longings, children's own aspirations are not as high as those of their parents or their teachers. Many boys said they liked to follow their father's trade, while the girls said that they would like to be teachers, but would end up married with children. Girls said that as teachers they "would get to read many books," an activity they immensely enjoyed. As the school had no library, I began bringing books from outside the curriculum. On each occasion the girls immediately flocked to the books. If I asked one of them to read aloud a story or an article in class, at the end of the lesson the girls wanted to read it by themselves. With one exception, boys rarely showed such interest. Some girls regularly borrowed books to take home. Along with the other teachers, I was idealized by girls who believed that unlike their own mothers we led "happy and clever lives." Most boys said that they aspired for *chakri* (salaried job). Thirteen year old Ajim Shekh said:

I have a wish—to have a bank chakri. I want to work in a bank. If I don't get work in a bank, I am going to get a peon's job at least. If I study up to VIII, I will definitely get a job as a peon. I know the bank manager. My father says whoever has a job as a peon, goes around in a motorcycle. If I don't get anything I'll go to Calcutta. My uncle [maternal aunt's husband] is there. He has a coal business. There is money in that. There is one thing that I'll never do that is pull a rickshaw, even as a last resort. It is demeaning to say, "please sir, this way sir, get in the rickshaw sir." People get sick all the time pulling rickshaws, especially TB. Being a coolie is better than being a rickshaw puller.

Children were also far more realistic than their parents and teachers about their future prospects. Despite their own hopes and dreams, they were not convinced by parents' and teachers' rhetoric. However, they were well aware of the prestige of white collar jobs, and knew that a level of education was needed for them. Ajim's father's comment about riding a motorcycle is reminiscent of the Bengali proverb "*lekha pora kore je gari ghora chore she*" (One who reads and writes gets to ride a coach). Boys, especially the Bengalis, also understood that Calcutta is the last hope of the poor, but even for that patronage relations are needed.

Conclusion

In the final analysis we may argue that despite the large body of work on educational inequality in India, ethnographic research is marked by its absence. If we are to address issues of social justice among powerless groups and communities, we need to go beyond statistical abstraction to indepth analysis of the lived experience of pupils/peoples. The ethnographic method is particularly suited to this approach since it enables us to explore the complexity of social relationships in schools and the specific communities under study.

Undoubtedly, educational inequalities in India can not easily be reversed without significant changes to bring about economic and social equity together with the implementation of realistic educational policies that address the needs and living conditions of marginalized groups like the Rabi Das. Nevertheless, as I have illustrated above, educational research at the micro level can help us to evaluate critical and reflexive approaches to pedagogic practice and avoid middle-class bias and prejudices. Ultimately, the legitimacy of different cultures goes some way toward meeting the goals of justice and equality in education.

Notes

1. Fieldwork carried out between December 1988 and April 1990. When living in the community, I worked as a voluntary teacher in the local primary school (for further details see Ganguly-Scrase, Ruchira, 1993).

2. Members of subordinate classes use the term *babus* rather than more "neutral" *bhadralok* to refer to the dominant classes. *Babu* has the connotation of being an employer or a master; thus from the point of view of subaltern groups, it characterizes the relationship of domination and subordination between the two classes. The meaning of *babu* varies from resistance to resigned acceptance.

3. The school teachers are not included in the general category of Gandhian social reformers.

4. The most pervasive Gandhian idea among the social reformers was the underlying "trusteeship." Lakha (1988, pp. 122–127) has demonstrated Gandhi's advocacy of the well-off having a duty to perform toward the poor in distributing benefits, often urging the industrial bourgeoisie to serve the workers in the manner of benevolent kings outlined in the *Ramayana* and the *Mahabharata*. Deriving this view from the Hindu philosophical text, the *Gita*, Gandhi argued,

   I understood more clearly in the light of the Gita teaching the implication of the word "trustee." . . . *I understood the Gita teaching of non-possession to mean that those who desired salvation should act like the trustee who though having control over great possessions, regards not an iota of them as his own. (Mahatma Gandhi, cited in Lakha, 1988)*

5. *Shashti* is a special vow taken by mothers for the protection of their children. Mothers have to keep fast and cannot accept other offerings until they have completed their *puja*. This was an excuse at least in one case since one of the three married women does not have children (but this minor point was not picked up by the Rabi Das). I believe that *mashtermoshai* was calming the Rabi Das down rather than confronting the teachers' behavior.

6. For a detailed discussion of the comparison between Freireian-inspired nonformal schools and the experience of children in the Rabi Das enclave, see Ganguly-Scrase, R. and Scrase, T.J. (1990)

7. I do not imply that the texts of the older students who did not seek my assistance were completely "pure" and "natural" (and thus do not suffer from the problems identified by Steedman). It should be obvious that the older students have assimilated many of the teachers' expectations over a long period of time and write within a well-defined school context. I encouraged the children to be free to express their views and write whatever they wished. I especially avoided punitive measures with respect to correcting their grammar, which was the standard practice of the school. Each child always wrote several drafts before putting them into their exercise books. The extracts in this chapter are the first drafts and the format has been retained as much as possible in the translation. It was not possible to retain grammatical and syntactical errors in translation.

8. Bengali *brahmanical* morning ritual to purify the house.

9.   Shoemaker or tanner by caste.

References

Bourdieu, Pierre (1984). *Distinction: A Social Critique of the Judgement of Taste*. Cambridge, Mass: Harvard University Press.

Freire, Paulo (1972). *Pedagogy of the Oppressed*. Harmondsworth: Penguin.

Ganguly-Scrase, Ruchira (1993). Labour Class and Community: An Ethnography of the Rabi Das of Krishnagar, India. Ph.D. thesis, University of Melbourne.

Ganguly-Scrase, Ruchira, and Timothy J. Scrase (1990). "Marginality in Third World Education: Towards an Ethnography of Indian Schooling." In R. Peddie (ed.), *Nationhood, Internationalism and Education*, Auckland: ANZIES.

Lakha, Salim (1988). *Capitalism and Class in Colonial India: The Case of Ahmedabad*. New Delhi: Sterling.

Mukherjee, S. (1975). "*Bhadralok* in Bengali Language and Literature: An Essay on the Language of Class and Status." *Bengal Past and Present*, vol. 95, no. 2.

Newman, Robert S. (1989). *Grassroots Education in India: A Challenge for Policy-Makers*. New Delhi: Sterling.

Scrase, Timothy J. (1993). *Image, Ideology and Inequality: Cultural Domination, Hegemony and Schooling in India*, New Delhi. Newbury Park, Calif.: Sage.

Sinha, S., and R. Bhattacharya (1969). "Bhadralok and Chotolok in a Rural Area of West Bengal." *Sociological Bulletin*, vol. 18.

Steedman, C. (1982). *The Tidy House: Little Girls Writing*. London: Virago.

Thapan, Meenakshi (1991). *Life at School: An Ethnographic Study*. New Delhi: Oxford University Press.

A Caribbean Experiment in Education for Social Justice
The Case of Grenada

Anne Hickling-Hudson

Introduction

The tragic internal and external events that brought to a traumatic
end the Grenadian revolution of 1979–1983 catapulted a hitherto
almost invisible society of 110,000 Caribbean people onto the world
stage. In October 1983, the U.S. invasion delivered the final death
blow to tiny Grenada's bold and radical challenge to America's imposition of regional hegemony in Latin America and the Caribbean. It is timely to reflect on the regional and international significance of this challenge. This chapter examines the revolution's
ideals of social justice, as seen in the reconceptualization and reor-
ganization of the education system. A component of any such reflection has to be the terrible tragedy that saw much of the revolutionary leadership forgetting or ignoring the ideals of the revolution
and turning against each other in fratricidal conflict, which ended
with the deaths of some of the Caribbean's outstanding young leaders and the life imprisonment of others in the ambit of the American invasion.

The outpouring of books and articles on the Grenadian revolution has focused mainly on a political and economic analysis of
the process and its defeat. This chapter, in discussing the social
justice ethos of education in the revolution, will provide a comprehensive overview of the educational goals, policies, and practices of the Grenada Revolution from 1979 to 1983. It draws on
documentary sources as well as on the author's personal involvement in teacher education and educational planning in Grenada
from September 1981 to August 1983. After describing briefly the
context of the Revolution, I examine the implications that revolutionary ideology and economic direction had on the educational

goals of the Peoples' Revolutionary Government (PRG). I then discuss the problems left by the colonial education system, describe the attempts made by the PRG between 1979 and 1983 to tackle these problems, and analyze the significance of the revolutionary policy of integrating educational development, political mobilization, and economic growth. Finally, I make some tentative, initial observations about the implications for developing countries of this process of educational change.

The Grenada Revolution and Its Effect on Educational Goals

Grenada consists of three small islands with a total area of 133 square miles, or 344 square km, and a population in 1979 of about 110,000. Like many other islands of the Eastern Caribbean, Grenada had been seized by the French from its native "Amerindian" inhabitants in the mid-seventeenth century, and in turn captured by the British in the late eighteenth century. After three hundred years of colonialism, it became in 1951 a semi-independent or self-governing colony within the British Empire. Self-government meant that it was responsible for its domestic affairs, but that the British continued to direct its foreign affairs including its economic alliances. Grenada became fully independent in 1974, twelve years later than Jamaica, which was the first Caribbean island to win its independence from the British. The educational pattern that Britain left in Grenada was the same as it had established in all of its Caribbean possessions. The majority of the population, largely peasants and estate laborers, received primary schooling or less in inadequate elementary schools, while a small minority received an academically imitative British "grammar" schooling. This prepared an elite for white-collar work in institutions such as the Civil Service and the schools, which helped to maintain the colonial and neocolonial system. The stratified and inadequate system of education (extremely vivid to any observer, yet unexplored by educational researchers) was a factor that had limited Grenada's economic and social development. This problematic legacy was one that the Peoples' Revolutionary Government of Grenada was determined to change.

Grenada's New Jewel Movement (NJM), led by Maurice Bishop,

was the first indigenous political grouping in the history of the English-speaking Caribbean to overthrow an existing government by armed force. The overthrown Prime Minister, Sir Eric Gairy, had been in power for three periods totaling nineteen years between 1951 and 1979. Although at first Gairy was a popular leader who won wage gains for the agricultural laborers, the 1967–1979 period of his regime was marked by economic stagnation, corrupt electoral practices, personal corruption, and repressive measures against any who tried to oppose him (Epica, 1982, pp. 42–50). His popularity diminished as he became more dictatorial. His government was frequently condemned, for example in the 1960s by an independent judicial commission of enquiry put in place by the British government and endorsed by many of the contemporary Caribbean governments, and in the 1970s not only by the young, radical, and Black Power–influenced members of the NJM, but also by several business interests (Jacobs and Jacobs, 1980, pp. 63–65, 96, 105–106).

By 1979, several factors combined to create a revolutionary situation. The majority of Grenadians were suffering economic distress, and many groups, including elements of the conservative middle class, were angry and embarrassed at the illegalities, the violence, and the "brand of vulgar superstition" that characterized Gairy's rule (Lewis, 1987, p. 18). The New Jewel Movement helped to organize and direct this opposition, on the one hand by carrying out many years of unorthodox, but effective political work among agricultural workers, school students, and the unemployed, and on the other hand by winning several seats as an opposition party in 1976. This has been described in detail by many analysts (Jacobs and Jacobs, 1980, ch. 5; Epica, 1982, pp. 44–50; Payne et al., 1984, pp. 1–16; Ambursley and Dunkerley, 1984, pp. 20–30; Mandle, 1985, pp. 14–18). The important point to note here is that the NJM correctly banked on the willingness of many Grenadians, including some key members of Gairy's army and police force, to assist them in bringing down Gairy's government.

A twofold reaction to the revolution, selective support or open hostility, was a reflection of Grenada's sharply stratified socioeconomic profile, which is characteristic of former European colonies. In the pyramid structure of Grenadian society, the mass of peasant, wage-laboring, and unemployed poor, almost all descendants of African slaves who had been transported to the region by the French and subsequently the British colonizers, lived at a subsistence level, socially, politically, and economically at the base of society. As in other Caribbean countries, their lives were characterized by "extreme poverty, high malnutrition, illiteracy, backwardness, superstition . . . and massive migration" (Bishop, 1979, p. 41). At the apex of society were the small elite groups who ran the institutions that kept the pyramid structure intact. This elite included the salaried, educated middle class, and an even smaller minority consisting of those who owned substantial land and business enterprises most of which were tied to powerful, privately owned British and North American firms.

It soon became clear that the PRG was initiating a revolutionary process that aimed to confront and change these inherited patterns, rather than the traditional Latin American coup that overthrows one government to replace it with another supporting the same system in spite of stylistic difference. The PRG's approach and programs showed a determination to challenge and overcome what they analyzed as the economic and psychological dependence that kept Grenada poverty stricken and politically and culturally backward. Their radical analysis and solutions were in line with those of Caribbean scholars, such as George Beckford (1972), Beckford and Witter (1980), and Norman Girvan (1972), and socialist-oriented Caribbean politicians, such as Michael Manley of Jamaica and Cheddi Jagan of Guyana. It was not surprising that their challenge to traditional structures evoked both the support of those who had experienced tradition as being oppressive and the antagonism of those who stood to lose substantial privilege, or who had been taught to revere tradition and fear radical change. The conflict engendered by these opposing political views was evident in education, as elsewhere, and will be discussed later in this chapter.

The impact of the Grenada Revolution on the political culture of the society had significant implications for education. As the NJM analyzed it, postcolonial societies suffered from a psychological dependence that made it difficult for them to challenge and emerge from their dependent economic status. This analysis was in accordance with the observation of Michael Manley that "post-colonial societies inherit the gross inequalities of the colonial system along with a view of the world that tends to the acceptance of this arrangement and an education system which works to perpetuate it" (Manley, 1974, p. 132). It was the dependent and imitative pattern of thought and the divided social and political relationships, said Bishop, which kept the Caribbean "wide open to domination . . . so drugged by the hypnosis of American television, American advertising, and capitalist consumerism that some really have no objection to becoming the backyard of the U.S." (Bishop, 1982, p. 196). At the same time, the NJM, through Bishop, was always careful to highlight the positive side of Caribbean and Grenadian culture. Its strength was the creative response forged over centuries by African workers to the challenge of survival in the oppressive social environment of slavery and the plantation system imposed upon them by the Europeans. Its weakness was its lack of confidence and its truncation within an elite-dominated society. As Bishop put it:

For centuries . . . this culture of the masses of Caribbean people has developed in limbo, unrecognised, unrecorded or at best viewed with contempt. This culture is yet to gain the approval of the very people who are creating it and practising it—the masses of Caribbean people. . . . Our cultures have never had the opportunity of developing to the point where they become the bulwark of our sovereignty. Education for Caribbean people has never meant the application of human knowledge to ensure the viability of our people's way of life. Education has meant the selection of an elite to be assimilated into the lifestyle and thought patterns of those whose interests lay in dominating us. Education has meant a mutually impoverishing divorce between the culture of the educated and that of the masses. . . . (1982, p. 186)

Stemming from this analysis, the NJM had three overlapping strategies to combat and overcome psychological dependence, to release and regenerate the people's culture. One strategy was to attempt to unite Grenadians in the tasks of national development, a process that would heal the political divisions of the people and "unlock (their) voices from centuries of obligation" (Bishop, 1982, p. 201). The new political organizations established to carry out this aim included the National Womens' Organisation, the National Youth Organisation, the Productive Farmers' Union, and the Zonal and Parish Councils. They attracted thousands of members and supporters of differing political views and loyalties by involving them in social and economic projects that were of obvious benefit to a wide cross-section of people in local communities. These mass organizations played an important role in contributing directly to the education of the people through courses and seminars, and in indirectly raising their levels of political and economic knowledge by such means as involving them in studying, discussing, and advising on the National Budget. The PRG saw these political structures as the basis for developing a new form of democratic and participatory government that would replace the neocolonial model of Westminster government, castigated by the revolutionaries as being a barrier to socioeconomic development and to "grassroots" or popular democracy (Hodge and Searle, 1982, pp. 86–89).

The PRG saw the quantitative and qualitative development of the formal education system as another vital strategy in laying the basis for overcoming psychological dependence, economic underdevelopment, and class division. As Bishop put it, "If we are to bring an end to the serious problems that we face, education must enable us to confront these problems . . . to end unemployment . . . to increase production . . : to defeat disease and poor health conditions . . . to overcome backwardness and poverty" (Bishop, 1980, p. 162).

Out of the new political structures and the expanded and improved educational system would flow the third strategy, that of refashioning education, the economy, constitutional forms, and culture in Grenada's own image. In this process, the long-submerged peoples' culture would be released to express itself. At the same time, it would be inspired by "the new contact between the educated elite and the masses" and by pride in the knowledge that "today in Grenada we are walking in new ways that are our ways" (Bishop, 1982, p. 204). Thus, the "cultural regeneration" of Grenadians would come out of "a twin process of increased self-expression and increased education" (Bishop, 1982, p. 200).

The growth of Grenada's economy as a result of the policies of the revolution also contributed to changing educational policy and practice. First, it made possible an increase in education spending, and second, it led to a demand for workers with higher levels of education. Increased expenditure made possible an expansion of places and a granting of subsidies for food, books, and clothing to many students who needed them. Even more important, the thousands of new jobs that grew out of economic expansion required much higher levels of general education and technical and vocational skills in the workforce. By 1982 it was clear that without such education, progress would be severely constrained in the many new projects in construction, in the hotel industry, in craft design, in food technology, in scientific agriculture, in forestry and fishing, in economic and environmental planning, and in financial and administrative management (Creft, 1983).

The PRG also aimed at providing for the development of higher levels of cultural skills: for example, in the recording and use of folk lore and traditional music for drama, dance, and literary development, and in book publishing. A new type of education and training was needed to "produce the producers" in all of these areas. Grenadian leaders and technocrats frequently stressed the connection between education and economic development, and urged the people both to take advantage of and to contribute to new opportunities for educational advancement. Quoting from the nineteenth-century Cuban philosopher, Jose Marti, Finance and Planning Minister Bernard Coard expressed the overall educational ethos of the revolution in this way: "'The new world,' [Jose Marti] said, 'requires the new school.' And that is our objective in Grenada. That is why we believe so strongly in education for *all* our people in our big and popular school, which is how our comrade leader, Maurice Bishop, sees the whole country, as one, big, popular school" (Coard, 1983, p. 23).

Some Problems of Postcolonial Development and Education

The PRG's goals of expanding education and refashioning it into an instrument that would help Grenada to achieve its aspirations for a better life were similar to those of other postcolonial Commonwealth Caribbean governments. These governments have done what they perceived to be possible in building schools and providing scholarships to expand primary and secondary places, training more teachers, developing new curricula and examination formats, and providing increased opportunities for technical and university education at the tertiary level (Miller, 1984, p. 36). Such changes, however, although expanding educational provision compared to the colonial system, did not effectively alter the stratification of colonial education that selected out an elite for the minority of well-endowed schools and consigned the majority of young people to a much larger number of poorly endowed schools, thus perpetuating the socioeconomic pyramid and economic underdevelopment (Persaud, 1975, p. 40). Similarly, although adult literacy campaigns were carried out in some countries, they had little impact on the access of the newly literate to improved economic opportunities.

It has become increasingly clear to most Caribbean countries that the hopes of universal education based on equal opportunity are unlikely to be achieved in the near future (Miller, 1984, p. 31). The hopes of the majority of people to transform their life chances through educational achievement have been widely thwarted. The provision of more schooling has fallen short of achieving the social aims of equality, justice, and the improvement of economic conditions for the majority. Some educational analysts argue that this situation has been caused by the problem of "educational inflation."

Educational inflation and curriculum unsuitability are both dangers of the modernization paradigm. This sees development almost entirely in the economic terms of striving for and eventually achieving the level of industrialization that will allow "take-off" into a Western model of a developed society. Many Caribbean governments have adopted wholesale the message of this model, popularized by U.S. economist W.W. Rostow (1960) in his self-proclaimed "non-communist manifesto" that prescribes certain stages of economic growth as being essential for "take-off" into development. In this model, education along Western lines is seen as one of the primary instruments that will modernize and develop the population to the point where national economic "take-off" becomes possible. Bacchus (1980, 1981) points out the main flaw in this thinking, which is that education cannot achieve development without a whole complex of other political and economic factors being present. An argument of this paper is that the Grenadian revolution saw the importance of the interlocking factors of development. Its striving to integrate educational development into this complex of factors made it more likely that aims of social justice and equity would move beyond the widely shared Caribbean political rhetoric and into the realm of possibility.

One important factor underlying the poor quality of schooling, as evidenced by poor performance and high dropout rates, was that a large proportion of teachers had no teacher training. In 1980, some 500, or 67%, of Primary, All Age, and Junior Secondary school teachers had no post-school education (Education Sector Survey, 1982, p. 101), and very slim chances of entering the Grenada Teachers' College to obtain it, since this institution could only take up to fifty students a year in its two-year Teacher Training Certificate program. Of the 218 teachers in Secondary (grammar) schools, 126 had no post-school education, 32 had Primary Teachers' Certificates, and 60 were university graduates, only 29 of these having postgraduate training in education (Education Sector Survey, 1982, p. 68). Thus, some 72% of secondary teachers were not suitably educated or qualified for the profession.

Since opportunities for tertiary education were few, Grenada had no way of producing the numbers of skilled and professional personnel needed for the development of the economy and of the educational system. Although some 352 Grenadians had been educated at universities abroad between 1946 and 1970 (Jacobs and Jacobs, 1980, p. 94), most of them were privately financed by their families. On graduation, many of them stayed abroad. By the mid-1970s, only two or three students per year could hope for government scholarships to pursue university education abroad (Coard, 1983, p. 8). The combination of few educational and economic opportunities led to massive migration. Some 300,000 Grenadians lived outside Grenada, particularly in the United States, Britain, and Trinidad, compared to the 110,000 who lived in Grenada (Coard, 1983, p. 11). The large migration of people each year further wasted, from the nation's perspective, the resources that had been spent on their education.

The PRG repeatedly committed itself to providing "mass education" in Grenada—the educational development "of all our people, not just a few" (Creft, 1981, p. 52). The aims were to counter the past educational neglect of the majority and to produce a system in

which an educated and politically aware working class would join
with trained and progressive professionals and administrators to reshape production and sociopolitical practices. Arguably, it is this
ideal of cultural unity, and the emphasis on the creative and leading
role of the working class within it, as well as the effort mentioned
above to integrate education into social, economic, and political goals,
that differentiated the PRG's vision of educational and national development from the goals and policies in other English-speaking
Caribbean territories.

Curriculum Change: The Dream of Resocialization

School curriculum reform was the educational area that remained
least developed in the Grenada Revolution, because the majority of
the resources were concentrated elsewhere at Stage 1 of the Education Plan. Qualitative change was started on only a small scale, and
indeed, proved much more difficult to implement than the expansion of school capacity. Yet, there were at least two areas that gave a
clear indication of the new emphasis on the everyday culture of the
Grenadian majority of small farmers, fisher folk, and manual workers. One was the production of the Marryshow Readers, a new series
of Infant Reading Primers that sought to foreground and validate
this worker-peasant culture. Another was the effort, not very successful, but clear in its ideological goals, to initiate a work-study
approach to education. An examination of these projects will allow
a glimpse into the possibility of developing a new kind of content in
the school curriculum. Following this, a consideration of other partially formulated initiatives at various levels of the curriculum will
illustrate some of the difficulties of comprehensive curriculum change.

The Marryshow Readers, developed by a group of teacher educators and student teachers in the new national teacher education
program, sought to portray drawings and stories of the lives of ordinary fishing and farming families in Grenada. Until then Grenadian
children had used standard English reading books developed in other
Caribbean islands, which portrayed middle-class Caribbean children
leading lives far removed from those of worker and peasant families.
Second, the Marryshow Readers presented a carefully developed
scheme of teaching English as a second language to Creole speakers.
Sentences were presented that allowed the children first to use their

Grenadian Creole speech patterns and then to move into standard English. Third, some of the stories placed little girls as the main focus, or as winning arguments with little boys, while others showed fathers helping with child care and domestic duties and others participating in production. The readers were printed in Cuba as part of Cuba's educational aid to Grenada, and distributed in sufficient numbers for each child to have one, perhaps for the first time in the history of many of the primary and All-Age schools, traditionally extremely resource-poor.

The political leaders constantly stressed the importance of integrating the school with the community and of developing a "work-study" approach in the curriculum, whereby the practical work of students should inspire their studies and vice versa (Bishop, 1980 in Searle, 1984, pp. 52, 60; Creft, 1981). A Community School Day Program (CSDP) was launched in which parents and other community volunteers helped to teach the children craft, farming, and other skills each Friday (Coard, 1983, p. 14), while the bulk of the teachers were being trained in the in-service teacher education program. An agricultural "work-study" program was started in three pilot schools where there was suitable land for farming, but this remained rudimentary and not well understood. The CSDP, too, was so beset by organizational and other problems that it was only successful in a few communities. In 1983, the Ministry of Education sought advice on how to improve the planning and organization of work-study in the schools, by inviting Cuban experts in work-study education to examine the CSDP and the agricultural pilot projects and hold discussions with the local teachers and organizers involved.

An attempt was made to initiate new projects and approaches, such as modern "child-centred" methods at the Preprimary level. The Ministry of Education continued the tradition of organizing several short methodology and curriculum development workshops for teachers. In secondary schools, there was an attempt to give students the beginnings of participation in school affairs through new student councils elected by secret ballot (Coard, 1983, p. 18). As part of the plan to rationalize secondary curricula, it was decided that the British GCE Cambridge "Ordinary Level" examinations would be phased out starting from the 1983–84 academic year. They were to be replaced with the regional secondary school-leaving examinations including "con-

tinuous assessment" coordinated by the Caribbean Examination Council (CXC), a process of evaluation that had already been adopted by
other Anglophone Caribbean territories. Secondary teachers were encouraged to form Subject Associations to launch the development of
curricula that would more suitably prepare students for the Caribbean Examinations. British GCE "Advanced Level" examinations
would be maintained in the foreseeable future, as they were the instrument of selecting students for entry to the University of the West
Indies with its three campuses in Jamaica, Trinidad, and Barbados.

However, most of the traditional weaknesses of the curriculum
continued unabated. There was still very little technical education:
Planning for the expansion of this was just beginning. The humanities curriculum still had virtually a colonialist orientation in many
schools. Literature and history, for example, were designed according to the Eurocentric perspective of the syllabi for the British external school-leaving GCE examinations, with their focus on British
writers, heroes, and exploits, and an often negative portrayal of Caribbean people. Mathematics and science teaching, and student performance in public examinations in these subjects, remained extremely weak, so weak that the government could not find enough
students to take up the increased number of university and technical
education scholarships offered abroad (Bishop, 1981, p. 235).

If the revolution had continued and had been able to implement its education plan along the lines envisaged, three vitally important areas of curriculum change would have helped to alter the
unsuitable curriculum inherited from the past. The first change would
have been to establish work-related technical, vocational, and agricultural education, by means of the interim plan to train students in
the Senior Forms of All Age schools as skilled apprentices in a variety of trades, as well as through plans to develop the CSDP and
other structures to enable all primary and secondary schools to offer
this kind of practical education. The combination of production
and study would have eventually become a compulsory component
of the curriculum (Education Sector Survey, 1982, pp. 245–249).
Second, the PRG stressed the importance of improving science and
mathematics education, starting with the formation in September
1982 of a Young Scientists' Association and the recruitment of more
science lecturers in teacher education. The government also negoti-

ated a personnel loan, from 1983, of several primary and secondary science and mathematics curriculum experts from Cuba and the Soviet Union. For example, two Cuban experts in primary curriculum planning (science and mathematics) visited Grenada in the summer of 1983. They worked together with teacher educators at the teachers' college, through a translator, to produce detailed analyses of the weaknesses in primary science and mathematics, and made recommendations as to how these could be tackled. Soviet curriculum experts in secondary school science and mathematics were to have arrived in the latter part of 1983 to help plan for and teach in the proposed Secondary In-Service Teacher Education Program in 1984, but these plans came to nothing after the collapse of the revolution and the U.S. invasion in October 1983. The third important area of curriculum change was that, with the introduction of the CXC curricula, the humanities would have become more Caribbean oriented. Additionally, the PRG was discussing with education officials plans to allow students to take school courses in political studies. It was hoped that this, together with the attempts at portraying working-class culture and revolutionary ideals through school texts such as the Marryshow Readers, would help to spread a more nationalist, regional, and "progressive" consciousness among school students.

By the 1990s, the education of all students in a unified secondary school system with a comprehensive and equal curriculum would be the basis for preparing them for the expanded tertiary education subsector. The equalization of the curriculum, and the expansion of its technical and vocational capacity, would be important factors in doing away with the problem noted by Bacchus (1981, pp. 219–220) and others of technical and vocational education remaining much less developed and less popular with most students than the traditional academic education leading to "white collar" jobs. These changes were intended to help build an education system that would encourage young people to qualify themselves for a particular job or career needed in the socioeconomic development of Grenada.

Within the context of these ambitious plans, the improvements by 1983 in the quantitative and qualitative provision of schooling represented only a modest start. Two thousand high school places had been added out of the nine thousand that were needed, the principle of subsidizing needy school children had been launched and there had been an increase in subsidized preschool places. Some key ideas such as guidance counseling, work-study, cultural relevance in the curriculum, student representation, and community involvement in schooling were put in place, but had to await further progress until the next stage of educational development. The PRG minimized budgetary allocation and skill deployment on these projects because it reasoned that at this initial stage of change, only limited progress could be made on them until the first priority was achieved—that of improving the general education and professional skills and attitudes of the majority of teachers through teacher training. The shortage of skilled teachers was part of the general problem of an acute shortage of trained professionals that led the PRG to lay enormous stress on the expansion of tertiary education, including teacher training (see Education Sector Survey, 1982, pp. 177, 181).

Literacy and Adult Education in the Re-Creation of Popular Culture

Among the high priorities of the PRG was to develop new systems of adult education for workers who had not necessarily had any secondary schooling, and for adults who were illiterate or subliterate. On-the-job training, usually in the form of six-month vocational courses, was provided for tourism workers at the Hotel School, craft workers at Grencraft, and farmers and fisher folk at the new Farm Schools and Fisheries School. In these adult vocational courses, productive work and the management of cooperative business enterprises were an integral part of the education offered (Education Sector Survey, 1982, pp. 145–155).

The PRG saw the education of illiterate and functionally illiterate adults as not only a moral and ethical responsibility, but also as being vital to the more efficient functioning of the economy. Their view was in accord with the observation of Bacchus (1981, p. 221) that, "People with an education seem to display a greater willingness and ability to participate more actively in the political decision-making process and in community development efforts. Education also increases the predisposition of the population to try out new ideas and practices such as improved health practices, family planning and the introduction of new crops and cultivation techniques." In

1980 the revolution introduced the provision of adult education for 3,500 illiterate adults through a new community-based structure, the Centre for Popular Education (CPE). A literacy campaign was carried out by the CPE's small core of paid organizers co-ordinating an initial number of 1,575 volunteer, unpaid teachers who each took responsibility for teaching one or more adults to read and write by regular visits to their homes (Brizan, 1981, pp. 138–145).

Because of organizational and resource problems in the CPE, more than half of the teachers dropped out in the first year and fewer than half of the entrants, just over a thousand adults, completed the basic literacy level of the program. Efforts were made to reorganize and improve the program, and by 1982 there were 1,500 adults studying at various levels of the CPE, which planned to bring them from basic literacy to the stage of the Primary School Leaving examination within three years. The target was that the CPE would have expanded, within the five years of Stage 2 of the Education Plan, to provide these and more adults with a secondary level education that had a strong vocational component (Creft, 1982). The CPE would therefore equip Grenada's traditionally most neglected adult workers with a primary and eventually a secondary education, from which point the best would be ready to enter the Institute for Further Education where they could matriculate for university or pursue a local Tertiary Diploma.

In addition to adult education in the formally structured and funded institutions established by the tevolution, nonformal education was further provided to rural and urban communities all over the country through the new mass organizations (of women, farmers, youth, and neighborhoods) described earlier. These held regular sessions of political and general-interest debate and discussion that contributed to raising the general level of informed awareness of local and international issues affecting Grenada.

The Integration of Educational Development, Economic Growth, and Mobilization

Because of the growth in the GDP that took place during the revolutionary period, Grenada was able to spend $23 million on education by 1983 instead of the $8 million spent in 1978. This, together with assistance from abroad, enabled the PRG to afford the educational expansion that it considered feasible and desirable in the first stage of its education plan.

Within the framework of educational growth, costs were held down and many programs, especially in adult education, were made possible by the effective mobilization of people and resources. Many school buildings were used day and night for education and community purposes. Hundreds of people gave voluntarily of their time and effort to contribute to education, for example, the volunteer literacy teachers responding to the CPE's campaign slogan "Each one teach one;" the parents who gave their labor, cash, and materials to the School Repair Drive; and the citizens who volunteered in the Community School Day Program to help teach children on the Fridays when their teachers were attending NISTEP (National In-Service Teacher Education Program) classes. Many trained educators not only willingly took on an increased workload, but also gave extra time and effort to do additional, unpaid tasks in education—for example, those who contributed their research to educational planning, their curriculum skills to the production of new materials, and their organizational skills to coordinating zonal council meetings on the national budget and the education programs of other community groups. Professional administrators and project leaders in the Civil Service devoted a regular part of their time to preparing material for public sessions in which parish and zonal councils were informed about economic and social development policies as a basis for the discussions that followed. There is little doubt that an important factor encouraging the mobilization of voluntary work was the team spirit engendered by frequent consultative and planning meetings between educators at all levels—principals, teachers, department heads, Ministry of Education officers, and others in the education field.

All of this should not lead us to forget that there was a current of opposition to many of the programs, and that ultimately the educational leaders may have failed to achieve the consensus that may have neutralized dissatisfaction. This will be discussed in the next section.

From the perspective of the "socialist orientation" path, the type of economic development that was undertaken by revolutionary Grenada would have made it likely to avoid the problem of producing educated people faster than the economy could absorb them. Key features of that path that may have encouraged a continuation of the initial high rate of job creation included the fact that a significant part of the economy (the public or state sector) could now be planned, that new sources of international assistance were being utilized beyond the traditional ties with Britain and the United States, and that the building of the new international airport could have greatly expanded tourism. Related to the development of the public sector was the PRG's effort to increase local scientific and technical capacity so that still more jobs could eventually result from the opening up of new fields, for example in the establishment of a mini hydroelectric power supply, of an improved water supply and telecommunications network, and of local geothermal energy. At the same time, the encouragement of the private sector by way of investment incentives also created new jobs, for example, with the increase in the capacity of privately owned garment factories and the growth of privately owned producer cooperatives. On the other hand, there are those who have pointed out that the many inherited areas of weakness in the economy could not easily have been overcome, and that the slowing down of growth that started from 1983 boded ill for the hopes of continuing economic expansion.

If there had been a continuation of the kind of economic development characterized the first three years of the revolution, it was highly likely that all those being trained at tertiary institutions would be immediately absorbed in the economy. Many would have the opportunity of helping to enlarge its productive capacity—using their professional skills in privately owned enterprises if they wanted, or in the enormously expanded public sector. The expansion of the economy also demanded more manual and middle-level workers with literacy and technical competencies: Many of these would be school graduates. From the point of view of the adult student undergoing vocational training or attending courses in the CPE or in their Community Organizations, education would not just be for its own sake. It was the kind of education that would help them obtain a job, set up a cooperative, or function more efficiently as enterprises became more technically developed. Against this background, Grenada would have been able to avoid the problem afflicting some other developing nations in which adult time and effort invested in acquiring literacy is largely wasted in terms of improving economic opportunity.

Several factors indicated the possibility of gradual success for the government's goal of laying the basis for acceptance of a new kind of socially conscious and development-oriented education. A most important factor was the enthusiasm with which much of the population supported the development goals and projects of the revolution. As Lewis (1987, pp. 33–34) points out, the extent and nature of volunteer participation in these programs "demonstrated that a whole population was serving the common cause with zeal and dedication, unaided by . . . material luxuries." People increasingly saw the connection between developing these programs and developing both the formal and the nonformal education system. The training of the country's teachers and the new opportunities for their participation in community work was to provide a basis for involving them in reorganizing the education system and developing more appropriate curricula in the humanities, sciences, and technical education. The education in socialist countries of several hundred young people who would return to take up deliberately planned positions of professional expertise and leadership in the society would have underpinned administrative understanding of a path of socialist orientation.

Conflicts and Problems

During my two year contract as a visiting lecturer in the National In-Service Teacher Education Program (NISTEP), I observed several of the conflicts and debates that arose out of the differing conceptions that educators had about the changes in education and the new role they were being asked to play. A brief discussion of a few of these conflicts suggests the enormous difficulties involved in the contested nature of educational change.

The first conflict arose out of NISTEP's commitment to training in its first phase the entire group of 67% unqualified primary and all-age school teachers, comprising five hundred teachers instead of the twenty-five a year trained in the former selective Grenada Teachers' College. The teachers entering NISTEP did not have to take an entrance examination or possess the matriculation certificate that had been formerly required for entry to teacher training. In fact, they were required to enroll in NISTEP regardless of their level of education, for the government decided to make teacher qualification compulsory instead of optional as it had been before. NISTEP started with hundreds of students, not enough lecturers, and not enough materials, but with the hope that these problems would be overcome as the revolutionary government sought and employed more lecturers and was able to put more resources into the program. From the beginning, NISTEP was contested terrain in which the struggles reflected the changing relations between the traditional stratified status quo and the new ideals of striving for equity even if this involved a large scale disruption of tradition.

On many levels, NISTEP challenged both local and regional tradition. NISTEP threw aside the old traditions of selectivity and optionality in teacher education, and this was contested. It also established some new pedagogical and curricular practices that evoked much anxiety and hostility. It seemed at times that the hostility to NISTEP innovations was so great that it was uncertain that it could survive. But it did survive the difficult stage of becoming established, and lasted long enough—three years—to carry out its major goal of training the primary and all-age teachers.

NISTEP was strongly criticized for eliminating the formerly rigorous entry requirements to teacher education, and for allowing the entry of more student teachers than there were resources to cope with. These criticisms were most articulately expressed by some of the lecturers from the former teachers college that had offered full-time training to a select few, and by faculty from the University of the West Indies who had been external examiners for the former college. It was said to be extremely unwise to allow students at such different levels of readiness admission into a single teacher education program, and Grenada was advised to limit entry only to those who had passed at least four subjects in the British school-leaving examinations. If this were done, the program would still have 153 students and be much larger than the former college was. The hundreds of teachers who had not passed the British exams should simply be kept out of teacher education until they had passed them. For the first year and a half of the program, the university put its views powerfully into practice by refusing to accredit NISTEP, which meant that the students would not be allowed to take the regional Eastern Caribbean teachers' college exams set and moderated by the university. Eventually, after much deliberation a compromise was reached: All of the student teachers would sit for exams that would qualify them for a local NISTEP certificate recognized only in Grenada, but the 153 matriculated students would be allowed to choose to take, in addition, the regional exams and be qualified with a regional, university accredited certificate.

The second case of resistance to NISTEP came, surprisingly, from some of the students in it. The fact that teacher training and qualification were made compulsory was very unpopular, even among many of the unqualified teachers who had pressed for the expansion of teacher education. A survey of their opinions found that some of these did not wish to be trained, as they saw themselves as being only temporarily in teaching until they could find another job. During the first term of NISTEP, nearly 150 dropped out of it to seek jobs other than teaching. However, even many of those who remained in NISTEP—some 70% of them in fact—argued that enforced training was an infringement of their freedom. Only about 30% of the NISTEP student-teachers expressed themselves as being solidly behind the program.

The revolutionary government reacted to both these questions by arguing that teachers, like doctors, nurses, and other professionals, had an obligation to their clients, and ultimately to the nation, to be trained for their profession. Children in the primary and elementary schools had been left long enough without adequate schooling; it was a commitment of the revolution that their education would be improved, and training all the teachers was a pivotal step in achieving this. Many serious teachers had been urgently pressing for training, and though NISTEP was bound to have problems, it was more important to make a start than to wait to solve them. These arguments reflected the government's choice that the interests of the poor, and of the nation as they interpreted it, should be treated as predominant and that change would be geared toward ensuring this.

How might we analyze the two cases of resistance to the inclusive structure of NISTEP? The theories of resistance developed in "First World" countries are of limited use in understanding them. The assertion of Giroux (1983, p. 267) that resistance theory "provides a new means for understanding the complex ways in which subordinate groups experience educational failure, pointing to new ways of thinking about and restructuring modes of critical pedagogy" makes it clear that he is not thinking about the resistance of professional groups to progressive educational reform. This approach of Giroux appears to be the main focus of the well-known "resistance theorists": Willis, looking at working-class school boys in England; Baudelet and Establet studying student resistance to hegemonic ideology in France; Weiler, discussing sexism and the resistance of school girls in the United States. These approaches do not explore resistance to the kind of educational change that challenges hegemonic education, whether in a revolutionary situation or not.

The first case, that of the resistance of some university and college lecturers to the mass nature of NISTEP, could be seen as an attempt to maintain the status quo in a modified form. They did not disagree with expanding teacher access to qualification, even by means of an in-service rather than a full-time program, but insisted that selectivity should be retained by requiring that teachers should pass a certain number of external school-leaving exams before entering NISTEP. Perhaps in-depth interview would be needed to explain the second case, the resistance of so many unqualified teachers to being "forced," as they saw it, into a teacher education program. Brizan (1981, p. 121), having conducted a questionnaire survey of teachers in the first year of NISTEP, pointed out that, "All teachers in Grenada admit the need for teachers to be trained but not all are willing to be trained." Why such resentment of compulsory training, when this is commonly taken to represent progress, and is a norm in most developed countries? Brizan says that some of the teachers gave as their reasons that the program was "too rushed and hurried," that their opinions and input during the planning phase were often limited, and that their concerns were unsatisfactorily dealt with. Even more significant, he felt, was the fact that 40% of the people who became (unqualified) teachers did so for economic reasons: Most of this number did not want to make it a career, and the vast majority of these saw NISTEP as "a type of confinement." I would suggest that further interviews may have uncovered among some of the teachers, traditionally a conservative body, a negative reaction to the Grenadian revolution in general and a desire to disassociate themselves from a program such as NISTEP created by the revolution. Some may have felt a resentment of the extra workload that NISTEP required of them. Their individualistic view that they should have "freedom" to choose or to reject professional training as teachers may have had something to do with a perceived low status accorded to primary school teaching, although even this supposition is problematic since everyone accepted the necessity of training requirements for careers such as nursing, which were of similar status. Finally, a point to consider is that if another interview had been conducted nearer the end of the program in 1983, when at least 150 unwilling participants had dropped out of NISTEP and out of teaching, a different view may have emerged.

The development and "working-class" content of the Marryshow Readers was another source of conflict. Some of the more traditional teachers criticized the readers as being too ideological. They expressed their chief concern as being over the use of Creole in the books, since Creole was regarded as undesirable speech. As soon as the revolution collapsed, the readers were withdrawn by the Ministry of Education. The questions of interest here are these. Why would some teachers of Creole-speaking children favor the previous types of readers over the Marryshow Readers when detailed scholarship and research at the University of the West Indies had shown that recognition and use of Creole first language patterns is the most effective way of teaching the second language of formal standard English? And why would there be such an extreme reaction as to withdraw collectively designed curriculum material of a high standard and of obvious cultural relevance? The literature on hegemonic culture in education helps us to develop some ways of thinking about this.

Developing the observations of European analysts Pierre Bourdieu (1973) and Basil Bernstein (1973), many educational researchers have shown how schools give legitimacy to certain groups through the language, knowledge, and patterns of interaction that are sanctioned as "proper" and valued. It is likely that the (mostly middle- or lower-middle-class) teachers in Grenada's working class schools regarded as "proper" and desirable the middle-class children portrayed in the previously used readers, although the smart clothes and two-parent nuclear family situation in which these children were shown were typical of perhaps less than 10% of any Caribbean society—certainly not of most of the children in the poorer primary schools. These teachers were obviously not influenced by Freire's advocacy that teachers should try to create the pedagogical situation in which students can articulate their understanding of the world. In most Caribbean countries, the children of workers have never seen themselves or their families as the subjects of texts. To see themselves in the Marryshow Readers would be likely not only to create an identification with the stories, a belief that they are worth writing about, but also an interest in the lively and problematic situations described in the readers. For teachers to reject material that encouraged this illustrates that they must be working from another perspective.

As Gramsci, however, reminds us, people have complex consciousness (Gramsci, 1971, quoted in Weiler, 1990). The conservative teachers and education officials who resisted the new readers may have had hegemonic ideas, but they may also have had a potential quality of critique that could lead them to a reevaluation of their actions and to positive, people-directed action. The NISTEP curriculum developers did hold workshops with teachers to introduce them to the new readers, but one might ask whether there was enough effort to tap this potential for critique, enough encouragement of a broad cross section of teachers to explore the issues brought up in the text in a way that developed their consciousness. It is also possible that the conservative teachers could have seen it as entirely justifiable to want their pupils to benefit by using the kinds of books and texts that have a high status in society, rather than revolutionary texts that gave legitimacy to Creole language patterns and foregrounded the poor.

There are some difficult questions here. Would it have been better, for the sake of consensus, to have presented more familiar images and stories and put less emphasis on Creole language structures in the Marryshow Infant Readers? Might this have ensured their wider popularity, and later saved them from the fate of abandonment? Could the texts of the CPE have been more neutral in tone, similar, perhaps, to those mild texts used in the long-running Jamaican adult literacy program (JAMAL) endorsed by both politi-

cal parties? Instead of creating a totally new teacher education structure, would it have been more prudent to have retained the old
Grenada Teachers' College, at least in form, while at the same time
expanding it, to have altered the curriculum less, to have taken in
only those teachers who desired the qualification, in the hope that
when the idea became more accepted the rest would also seek to
become qualified teachers? In other words, would a gradualist approach to educational change be more likely to ensure its widespread
acceptance than a sweeping, intense transformation? Some may argue that many of the educational changes put in place by the revolution represented a reckless radicalization that disobeyed the basic
imperative of laying foundations for their survival.

Paget Henry (1991, p. 66) puts the political dilemma, made
clearer by hindsight, in these words:

*At the symbolic level, the new political elites must secure the ongoing
reproduction of a Marxist–Leninist political culture that will support
the new socialist state, its economic reforms, and patterns of class exclu-
sion. However, given existing levels of transformation of political culture, literacy and the dominant role of religion in peripheral societies,
this is a major undertaking. These types of cultural changes are often
quite resistant to administrative manipulation or coercion. It took centuries of capitalist domination and inculcation to detach Afro-Grenadians
from their precapitalist cultural orientations.*

Yet, it must be observed that the NJM leaders, though themselves mostly Marxists, were always keenly aware that Grenada could
not become a socialist society for a considerable period during which
an ideologically mixed "noncapitalist path" had to be laid. It may
therefore have been somewhat premature, tactically, to have organized for radical educational changes at least in the formal education sector.

Apparently less conflict-ridden was education in the nonformal
sector (adult literacy and continuing education in the Centre for
Popular Education) and the informal sector (through community
workshops, such as those on the budget, and through mass organizations, such as the National Women's Organisation, the NWO).
As Jules (1991, p. 261) points out, "The development of a system of

adult education proved far easier than the transformation of the inherited configuration." Yet the high dropout rate from the CPE showed that there were deep-seated problems in the implementation of adult education. And in spite of the excellent community work of the NWO (for example, in helping to implement the school feeding program for needy children), an area which may be considered problematic, again with hindsight, is that of the social and educational status of women. The revolution encouraged women to take a much more prominent role in the society, with some women being in the NJM "vanguard" party and others having far more opportunity than before to play important leadership roles in administration and the organization of programs. New laws providing for equal pay and maternity leave sought to improve the status of women in the workplace. But women, particularly those within the political leadership, experienced great hardships because few or no concessions were made to the fact that they had to shoulder child care, domestic responsibilities, and workloads at home, as well as their careers and political tasks. Within family relations, the double standard of sexual behavior allowing men more freedom than women, continued unabated. Thus reforms on gender issues brought important material benefits for women but did not alter several problematic areas of daily life. In the education system, there was not yet much engagement with gender issues. There was no analysis of how, or whether, boys' and girls' schooling, performance, and career chances differed, although in the curriculum development process that produced the Marryshow Readers there were the beginnings of change that foregrounded a stronger and more visible role for women.

Finally, the notable case of conflict that must be considered, although it lies outside of the educational sphere, is the fatal conflict within the political leadership of the NJM that led the revolution to implode, laying itself open to the defeat that followed both in terms of the U.S. invasion and of the revulsion of many Grenadians from a process that could snuff out the lives of their popular leader Bishop and some of his supporters. Some commentators, such as Jorge Heine see this derailment of the revolution as being due to "a failure of political leadership of the highest order" (1990, p. 24), explaining the failure primarily in terms of the widely held conspiracy theory in which a "carefully orchestrated" plan by an envious Coard challenged an unsuspecting Bishop for the leadership of the party and the country (see Heine, pp. 217–255). Other analysts are skeptical of this personalistic interpretation (based, in Heine's article, largely on speculation and inference from a highly biased selection of sources). They point instead to the weaknesses of the NJM's party organization—for example, its somewhat arrogant image of itself as being a political "vanguard" that, as Bishop expressed it, was "way, way ahead" and "much more politically and ideologically developed than the masses," its secrecy and small size, its assumption of correctness—the latter leading it to become eventually disengaged from reality (Thorndike, 1990, pp. 46–48; Mills, 1991, esp. pp. 33–47). In my view, this interpretation seems the more likely one. The revolutionaries, seeing themselves as leaders of the forces of liberation trying to overthrow the injustices of domination and imperialism, fell into the trap of behaving like those forces of repression that have traditionally crushed others in the name of freedom, instead of seeking a consensual political process in their own party groups, and instead of tolerating and managing public dissent. Were there implications for education? Perhaps it could be argued that the leaders (many of whom were NJM members) of the education process made great efforts to achieve participant involvement and empowerment in bringing about change, but that there were within the process ominous signs of an inadequate ability to manage conflict, dissent, and resistance.

Conclusion

After the invasion, a series of elected Grenadian governments, backed by U.S. financial and political aid, tried to reverse or erase memories of the revolution. Examples of this erasure in education came in the abandonment of the revolution's experimental structures and programs that had any connection to the socialist-influenced ideas of developing and articulating the voice of the worker-peasant majority. Those that were abandoned in nonformal education included the CPE and the mass organizations, and in the formal educational sector, the Marryshow Readers and the curriculum development process that produced those and other texts, the university scholarships to socialist countries, and NISTEP (though some elements of NISTEP, such as an in-service component, have been retained in the new Teacher Education structure). There seems to be little left to show for the fervent effort and activity of the revolution to lay the basis for restructuring education according to its ideals of social justice for the majority. Brizan, in a 1991 analysis of Grenadian education, identifies as its main deficiencies many of the very problems that educational policy and planning in the revolution had sought to tackle, for example, a primary school teaching force of which 55%, including 57 principals, were untrained, a high drop-out rate from the teaching profession, lack of textbooks, low attendance, overcrowded classrooms, deteriorating school buildings, deteriorating performance standards in external school-leaving examinations, a low level of interest of students in the curriculum, a high level of repetition of grades due to failure, and (not surprisingly) a drop-out rate of 24% of the school-leaving population (Brizan, 1991, pp. 59–69).

It might be argued that this problematic record of postrevolutionary education seems to vindicate the educational policies and strategies of the Grenada Revolution. Even if few of them took root, their very existence as a comprehensive experiment has important implications for developing countries. Clearly, these implications can only be fully explored by a comparative study of postcolonial education in other structurally similar societies, a study that develops along the lines of both policy analysis and cultural analysis. This chapter has attempted to show that a major focus of educational change in Grenada was the attempt to correct the nation's educational underdevelopment in a manner that was consistent with the PRG's political objectives and with the growth of the economy. This, perhaps, is one of the most important considerations for other formerly colonial countries with the same kind of poverty and social deprivation that characterized Grenada in 1979. The revolutionary government set about pursuing its goal by restructuring the formal and nonformal educational systems in a way that would promote the development of the people and serve the needs of an expanded economy. Many radical and unusual strategies were used in improving the quality of secondary and tertiary education, in establishing structures for combating illiteracy and substandard schooling, and in planning for an education future that would give the traditionally poor and neglected the opportunity for learning that had throughout

Grenada's history been denied them. The government, in its determination to combine political with educational development, also gave thousands of people their first experience of active participation in the affairs of their country and nation, in itself an educative process. The target of establishing a qualitatively new type of education had been delineated, and some basic initial steps had been taken toward it.

References

Ambursley, F., and J. Dunkerley (1984). *Grenada: Whose Freedom?* London: Latin American Bureau.

Bacchus, M.K. (1980). *Education for Development or Underdevelopment?* Canada: Wilfred Laurier University Press.

———— (1981). "Education for Development in Underdeveloped Countries," *Comparative Education*, vol. 17, no. 2.

Beckford, George (1972). *Persistent Poverty*. Oxford: Oxford University Press.

Beckford, George, and Witter, Michael (1980). *Small Garden, Bitter Weed*. Jamaica: Maroon Publishing House.

Bernstein, Basil (1973). "Social Class, Language and Socialisation." In A.S. Abramson et al.(eds.) *Current Trends in Linguistics*, vol. 12.

Bishop, Maurice (late leader of the Peoples' Revolutionary Government, Grenada) (1979). "Imperialism Is Not Invincible." 6 September: Address to the Sixth Summit Conference of the Non-Aligned Movement, Havana, Cuba. In D. Jules and D. Rojas (eds.). *Maurice Bishop: Selected Speeches, 1979–1981*. Havana: Casas de Las Americas.

———— (1980). "Learning Together, Building Together." 27 July: National Broadcast to Declare the Literacy Campaign Open, Radio Free Grenada. In D. Jules and D. Rojas (eds.) (1982). *Maurice Bishop: Selected Speeches, 1979–1986*. Havana: Casas de las Americas.

———— (1981). "Education is production too!" 15 October: Feature address delivered at the official opening of the second year of NISTEP. In D. Jules and D. Rojas (eds). (1982). *Maurice Bishop: Selected Speeches, 1979–1981*. Havana: Casa de las Americas.

———— (1982). "For the Cultural Sovereignty of the Caribbean People." 20 November: Address at the Caribbean Conference of Intellectual Workers, St. Georges, Grenada. In C. Searle (ed.) (1984) *In Nobody's Backyard: Maurice Bishop's Speeches, 1979–1983*. London: Zed Books.

Bourdieu, Pierre (1973). "Cultural Reproduction and Social Reproduction." In R. Brown (ed.) *Knowledge, Education and Cultural Change*. London: Tavistock.

Brizan, George (1981). *The Education Reform Process in Grenada, 1979–1981*. Grenada: Institute for Further Education, November 1981 (Report).

———— (1991). "Education and Society in Grenada." In Errol Miller (ed.) *Education and Society in the Commonwealth Caribbean*. Jamaica: Institute of Social and Economic Research, University of the West Indies.

Coard, Bernard (former Minister of Finance and Planning in the Peoples' Revolutionary Government, Grenada) (1982). Unpublished opening address to the Education and Production Conference, Carriacou, Grenada, (November).

———— (1983; 1985). *Revolutionary Grenada: A Big and Popular School* (1983 speeches). London: NJM (UK Branch).

Creft, Jacqueline. (late Minister of Education in the Peoples' Revolutionary Government, Grenada) (1981; 1982). "The Building of Mass Education in Free Grenada." In *Grenada Is Not Alone*. Speeches by the People's Revolutionary

Government at the First International Conference in Solidarity with Grenada, November. Grenada: Fedon Publishers.

———— (1983). *The Importance of the Centre for Popular Education. Phase 2.* January 1983: National broadcast on Radio Free Grenada (unpublished).

Education Sector Survey (1982). St. George's, Grenada: Ministry of Education, Youth and Social Affairs, Government of Grenada. This report was researched and written by Caribbean personnel, and should be differentiated from the *Education Sector Survey,* written by UNESCO personnel in 1982.

Epica Task Force (1982). *Grenada: The Peaceful Revolution.* Epica: Washington, D.C.

Giroux, Henry (1983). "Theories of Reproduction and Resistance in the New Sociology of Education: A Critical Analysis." *Harvard Educational Review,* vol. 55, no. 3.

Girvan, Norman (1972). *Foreign Capital and Economic Underdevelopment in Jamaica,* Jamaica: University of the West Indies.

Gramsci, Antonio (1971). *Selection from Prison Notebooks.* In Kathleen Weiler (1990).*Women Teaching for Change.* Boston: Bergin and Garvey.

Heine, Jorge (ed.) (1990). *A Revolution Aborted: The Lessons of Grenada.* Pittsburgh: University of Pittsburgh Press.

Heine, Jorge (1990). "The Hero and the Apparatchik: Charismatic Leadership, Political Management and Crisis in Revolutionary Grenada." In Jorge Heine (ed.) *A Revolution Aborted: The Lessons of Grenada.* Pittsburgh: University of Pittsburgh Press.

———— (1990). "Socialism and Cultural Transformation in Grenada." In Jorge Heine (ed.) *A Revolution Aborted: The Lessons of Grenada.* Pittsburgh: University of Pittsburgh Press.

Henry, Paget (1991). "Socialism and Cultural Transformation in Grenada." In Jorge Heine (ed.) *A Revolution Aborted: The Lessons of Grenada.* Pittsburgh: University of Pittsburgh Press.

Hickling-Hudson, A. (1985). "In-Service Models of Teacher Education in Developing Countries." In *The Preparation of Teachers and Emerging Curriculum Issues,* Collected Papers of the Fifteenth Annual Conference of the South Pacific Association of Teacher Educators, Tasmania, Australia.

Hodge, M. and C. Searle (eds.) (1982). *"Is Freedom We Making." The New Democracy in Grenada.* Grenada: Government Information Service.

Jacobs, W., and R. Jacobs (1980). *Grenada, The Route to Revolution.* Havana: Casas de Las Americas.

Jules, Didacus (1991). "Building Democracy: Content and Ideology in Grenadian Educational Texts." In Michael Apple and Linda K. Christian-Smith (eds.)*The Politics of the Text Book.* New York: Routledge.

Jules, Didacus and Don Rojas (eds.) (1982). *Maurice Bishop: Selected Speeches, 1979–1981.* Havana: Casas de Las Americas.

Lewis, Gordon K. (1987). *Grenada: The Jewel Despoiled.* Baltimore: Johns Hopkins University Press.

Mandle, J.R. (1985). *Big Revolution, Small Country: The Rise and Fall of the Grenada Revolution.* New York: North South Publishing Company.

Manley, Michael (former Prime Minister of Jamaica) (1974). Keynote Address at Sixth Commonwealth Education Conference, Jamaica.

Miller, Errol (1984). *Educational Research: The English-Speaking Caribbean.* Ottawa, Canada, International Development Research Centre.

Mills, Charles (1991). "Marxism and Caribbean Development: A Contribution to Rethinking." In Judith Wedderburn (ed.) *Rethinking Development.* Jamaica: University of the West Indies.

Ministry of Education, Youth and Social Affairs, Government of Grenada. (1983). *Survey of Numbers of Grenadian Students at Tertiary Institutions Abroad* (unpublished manuscript), St. Georges, Grenada.

Ministry of Finance and Planning, Government of Grenada (1983). *An Overview of Economic Sectors in Grenada.* Document Prepared for Classes in the National In-

Service Teacher Education Programme, St. Georges, Grenada.

Olliverre, Irwin (1982). "NISTEP, a Revolutionary Approach to Teacher Training in Grenada." Paper presented at the Education and Production Conference, Carriacou, Grenada.

Olliverre, Irwin (1984). Interview on developments in teacher education (Personal interview with Ann Hickling-Hudson, St. Georges, Grenada, November).

Payne, A., P. Sutton, and T. Thorndike (1984). *Grenada: Revolution and Invasion*, London: Croom Helm.

Persaud, G. (1975)."The Socializing Functions of Teacher Education: System Maintenance or Change?" *Caribbean Journal of Education*, vol. 2, no. 1.

Rostow, W.W. (1960). *The Stages of Economic Growth: A Non-Communist Manifesto.* Cambridge, U.K.: Cambridge University Press.

Searle, Chris (ed.) (1984). *In Nobody's Backyard: Maurice Bishop's Speeches, 1979–1983.* London: Zed Books.

Searle, Chris, and Don Rojas (eds.) (1982). *"To Construct from Morning": Making the Peoples' Budget in Grenada*, Grenada: Fedon Publishers.

Sunshine, Catherine (1985). *The Caribbean: Survival, Struggle and Sovereignty.* Washington, D.C.: Epica.

Thorndike, Tony (1990). "People's Power in Theory and Practice." In Jorge Heine (ed.) *A Revolution Aborted: The Lessons of Grenada.* Pittsburgh: University of Pittsburgh Press.

Weiler, Kathleen (1990). *Women Teaching for Change.* Boston, Mass.: Bergin and Garvey.

Social Justice and Education in China

Ronald F. Price

Introduction

It hardly needs stating that what China is and how it will develop is of major importance for all of us. China is not only a culture that has contributed in different ways over a long period to world culture, but is today one of the most populous and potentially powerful countries in the world. Moreover, it has overseas populations of significant size in a number of other countries, all of whom to one degree or another look to their ancestral homeland and may be influenced by it. While, as I shall show, the ideas of social justice are foreign to China this does not mean that Chinese people do not suffer the same injustices and inequalities that have prompted the rhetoric of social justice elsewhere. They clearly have and, moreover, increasing numbers of Chinese are learning to use the same rhetoric to describe and challenge them. In this chapter, I shall set out some of the questions that need to be asked and something of the situations within which the moral–political conceptualizing of social justice takes place.

The model of education I shall be using is essentially that of a process of lifelong learning in which the teachers range from parents and close relatives and peers through schools of various kinds to the experiences of the work world. One must remember that China is still a largely rural society in which formal schooling plays a relatively minor to absent role for all but a small number of its population. Chinese have learned, and continue to learn, their worldview from a variety of sources outside the school. The dominant view from the past may be called Confucian, remembering that this is a complex strand of ideas stretching back some two and a half thousand years. Into this have been woven ideas taken from Europe, including, most importantly, those of Marxism–Leninism imported from the USSR. This learning has been selective, ideas being changed in the process, some simply added on and others blended into a new form. Learning has also been different, regionally, by class and by individual. Generalizations, particularly talk of "China" or "the Chinese," must be made with caution.

This is not the place to examine the complexities of the various abstractions that form our European-grounded concept of social justice. Two sources that, from different perspectives, bring out the variety of meanings involved and that both argue for the importance of ideas not included in the concept of justice are Heller (1987) and Kaufmann (1973). When it comes to understanding ideas across very different cultures and language groups the problems are compounded. Readers should beware of translations that equate Chinese terms with those of Europe, remembering that the more abstract the concept the more approximate the translation. That said, the important questions for education are the uses made of the rhetoric of social justice. We are familiar with the use of talk about "human rights" in the furtherance of U.S. policy (Kolko, 1988, pp. 262, 283–288). In the Chinese context, we need to ask who is talking; are concepts of social justice motivating people to action; are they a useful measure to be applied in judging Chinese society; or are they simply justification for particular group interests? No doubt we shall find elements of all of these in China today.

The Changing Tradition
Chinese today draw on a long and rich tradition. One complex strand, Confucianism, dominated Imperial China for some two thousand years. Other influences stem from the end of the Imperial stage and early Republican years as Chinese struggled to respond to the battering of the foreign imperial powers. Many today are reexamining this past as they search for solutions to current problems. Confucianism, which has been condemned as a cause of China's ills, is again being quarried for a cure. Limiting our consideration to concepts of social justice, we find no discussion of this term, or the wider one of "justice," in the standard English language works on Chinese philosophy.[1] What we do find is an obsession with hierarchy and order expressed in the familiar five social relationships, linked

in the *Doctrine of the Mean* with the ancient practice of filial respect: "the duties . . . between sovereign and minister, between father and son, between husband and wife, between elder brother and younger, and those belonging to the intercourse of friends" (cit. Price, 1970, p. 49). Some may wish to see here analogies to Kaufmann's first stage of *justice* (1973, p. 38) or the fifth of Perelman's definitions, "to each according to his rank" (cit. Heller, p. 24). But that is of little help in understanding the modern concept of *distributive justice*, the "common good or public interest" (Nicholas Rescher, cit. Heller, p. 25). More useful is the observation of a contemporary Chinese, Du Weiming:

T'ang Chün-i has pointed out that "to live in definite ethical relations with others in the actual world, practicing the morality of doing one's duty to others but not asking them to do their duties, reciprocally," is the Confucian way. We may add that the golden rule in Confucianism, which states, "Do not do to others what you would not want others to do to you," is basically "duty-consciousness." It does not lead to the demand of "rights consciousness," that the other reciprocate what my sense of duty has dictated me to perform. (Du, 1979, pp. 26–27)

These traditional ideas of hierarchy were supported rather than replaced with the formation of the People's Republic of China and the dictatorship of the Chinese Communist Party. While the power structure, personnel, and much else were changed, the traditional "village tyranny"[2] and belief in "benevolent despotism" continued. But before discussing the recent period a word should be said about the end of the imperial period and the May 4th Movement, periods when ideas of social justice were imported from Europe.

The reception of Euro-American ideas has to be seen against the internal and external disasters that befell China from about the middle of the 19th century. Internally, the greatest was the upheaval of the Taiping Rebellion, a struggle which lasted from 1850 to 1865 and resulted in the loss of life of between 20 and 40 million people and the devastation and depopulation of wide areas of southern China. Externally, China was humiliated in a series of some seven wars with foreign powers, beginning with the Anglo-Chinese (Opium) war of 1839–1842. These resulted in occupation of im-

portant coastal areas and other impositions. The response of the intelligentsia, the scholar-bureaucrats and their successors, was a search
for "self-strengthening" and "wealth and power."[3] After the turn of
the century, Euro-American ideas were introduced, both by the translation of foreign writings and by Chinese returning from study
abroad. Between 1895 and 1904, Yan Fu translated Thomas Huxley,
Adam Smith, J.S. Mill, and Herbert Spencer (Schwartz, 1964). Liang
Qichao introduced the ideas of Rousseau (Chang, 1971; Chow, 1960,
p. 294). Liang also played with Hegelian notions of "negation of the
negation," writing about a period when "no one has rights so they
are equal" and a future when "everyone has rights so you return to
equality" (cit. in Bernal, 1976, p. 92). Chow comments that "Liberalism was a catchword among the intellectuals in those early years"
and that "they talked of freedom in terms of human rights, and freedom of speech and the press" (Chow, 1960, p. 295). Inequalities
certainly featured in the discussions: inequalities of power; inequalities between urban and rural areas; inequalities between men and
women. It is to these inequalities that we will return, since it is these
that are among the major barriers to social justice as it is generally
understood. But before that we must look briefly at the ideology
that has dominated the period of the People's Republic.

Marxism–Leninism–Mao Zedong Thought

While some of the writings of Marx and information about a variety
of socialist movements was introduced into China before the Russian Revolution of 1917, it was developments in the latter that were
to have the greatest influence, not least in the formative period of
the People's Republic of China in the mid-1950s. This influence
helped consolidate the system of Communist Party domination of
the State and society and ensured that Marxism–Leninism has been
taught as a system of *scientific* socialism,[4] with a conception of history progressing through stages according to objective laws (Price,
1977; Price, 1987).

The official ideology has added Mao Zedong Thought to its
title and the writings of Mao have indeed formed an important part
of moral-political studies. But selection has varied over time since
the writings of Mao include a range of ideas, some of which have
not been compatible with current Party policy.[5] The thread of self-

strengthening and patriotism in Mao, has, of course, been always welcome. But some of his statements supporting genuine democracy with power to initiate and effect policy have been seen as a threat to Party leadership, especially in the post–Cultural Revolution period. It should be noted that Mao has always been concerned with power, both political and economic, and this may account for his avoidance of and even hostility toward the language of social justice that he regarded as "bourgeois liberal" (Mao, 1965, pp. 31–3; Schram, 1969, pp. 296–98).

In the writings of Mao Zedong, we encounter the realities of inequality many times, from the 1927 "Report on an Investigation of the Peasant Movement in Hunan" to his comment on China as "a socialist country" published in a separate pamphlet titled *Marx, Engels and Lenin on the Dictatorship of the Proletariat* (1965). In the former, he referred to "systems of authority" that dominated people, "political, clan, religious, and masculine" (Mao, 1965, p. 44), rather than inequalities, and throughout this and his other writings, though conceptions of "justice" and "equality" are present it is other concepts that are in the forefront, particularly in this case the question of class power. He uses the newly fashionable term "democracy" (Mao, 1965, p. 27) to describe the actions of the peasant associations against the landlords and former power holders. He also implies a concept of retributive justice when he comments that "the peasants keep clear accounts, and very seldom has the punishment exceeded the crime" (Mao, 1965, p. 28). In the latter case, Mao was commenting on the system of distribution under the "eight-grade wage system," saying that it was "scarcely different from (that of) the old society" (i.e., it was unequal). The two passages quoted are too short to infer anything beyond Mao's unease at this situation and his fears of a restoration of capitalism. But it would be wrong to see concepts of social justice as playing a major role in Mao's thinking. Rather, they are implied in his conceptions of class power and of China's people "standing up" and building a strong and wealthy country (Mao, 1965, pp. 15–18). He neither uses them to justify his own policies, nor other than in passing to condemn those of his opponents. It would probably be true generally that while conceptions of "equality" and "rights" were often spoken about in the various trends of the Chinese revolution of the past nearly a century, they seldom formed the motivation for action nor informed the content of that action.[6] However, in recent times "rights" have become embodied in various state documents and in teaching materials about the law.

The grounding of official ideology implied in the term *Marxism* raises important questions about the nature and significance of the ideas held by Marx himself.[7] In the present context, Peffer's *Marxism, Morality, and Social Justice* is most useful. He attempts to "develop at least the outlines of an adequate Marxist moral and social theory" which would allow one "to judge social arrangements and . . . provide criteria to decide between competing sets of historically possible social arrangements" (1990, p. 3). He explores Marx's writings and "reconstructs" from them a moral theory of social justice that he then develops further. Peffer regards the values of "freedom (as self-determination), human community and self-realization" as the more basic values that Marx espoused and that Marx implicitly held that these should be distributed (relatively) equally (1990, pp. 35–36). Comparison of Peffer's recommended list of principles with those in the Chinese Constitution illustrate the difficulties at this level of abstraction:

1.   Everyone's security rights and subsistence rights shall be respected.

2.   There is to be a maximum system of equal basic liberties, including freedom of speech and assembly; liberty of conscience and freedom of thought; freedom of the person along with the right to hold (personal) property; and freedom from arbitrary arrest and seizure as defined by the concept of the rule of law.

3.   There is to be (a) a right to an equal opportunity to attain social positions and offices and (b) an equal right to participate in all social decision-making processes within institutions of which one is a part.

4.   Social and economic inequalities are justified if, and only if, they benefit the least advantaged, consistent with the just savings principle, but *are not to exceed* levels that will seriously undermine equal worth of liberty or the good of self-respect. (Peffer, 1990, p. 418)

The theoretical treatment of social justice in China is perhaps best illustrated in the chapter on "Fundamental Rights and Duties of Citizens" of the state Constitution of the People's Republic of China, a document that closely follows its Soviet counterpart. This was first adopted by the First National People's Congress of the PRC in September 1954, and has been revised since then. But the "rights" and "freedoms" promised remain basically the same: equality before the law (1954; Art. 85); freedom of speech, the press, assembly, association, procession, and demonstration (1954; Art. 87); freedom of religious belief (1954; Art. 88); freedom of person (1954; Art. 89); inviolability of homes and privacy of correspondence (1954; Art. 90); the right to work (1954; Art. 91); and the right to leisure (1954; Art. 92). Women are said to "enjoy equal rights with men" (1954; Art. 96). In the 1978 version, "freedom to strike" and "the right to 'speak out freely, air their views fully, hold great debates and write big-character posters,'" the latter formulation a result of the Cultural Revolution of 1966–1976, appeared (1978; Art. 45).[8]

The important questions for Chinese to ask are what purpose is served by these formulations and to what degree are they carried out in practice. The items in Peffer's (2), listed above, seem adequately covered in the Chinese document (here we are not saying anything about practice). Peffer's (3a) is to some extent catered for in 54— Art. 86 where it speaks of the "right to vote and stand for election." But there is no equivalent for Peffer's (3b). Moreover, the democratic rights embodied in the Constitution are negated by the actual role of the Communist Party in the society, a role that was incorporated in the 1978 Constitution where Article 2 reads:

The Communist Party of China is the core of leadership of the whole Chinese people. The working class exercises leadership over the state through its vanguard, the Communist Party of China.

The guiding ideology of the People's Republic of China is Marxism– Leninism–Mao Tsetung Thought. (Documents . . ., p. 134).

That the present Chinese leadership clearly believes that the question of human rights is an important propaganda one is shown by the publication, by the Information Office of the State Council in Beijing in November 1991, of a document entitled: *Human Rights in China*. This was widely reproduced in the Chinese press and also distributed abroad in translation. Sixty-two pages long, the document has chapters with the titles: (1) The Right to Subsistence—the Foremost Human Right the Chinese People Long Fight For; (2) The Chinese People Have Gained Extensive Political Rights; (3) Citizens Enjoy Economic, Cultural and Social Rights; (4) Guarantee of Human Rights in Chin's Judicial Work; (5) Guarantee of the Right to Work; (6) Citizens Enjoy Freedom of Religious Belief; (7) Guarantee of the Rights of the Minority Nationalities; (8) Family Planning and Protection of Human Rights; (9) Guarantee of Human Rights for the Disabled; (10) Active Participation in International Human Rights Activities.

The Unequal Society

In looking at the past few decades in China, I am not implying that things are better or worse than either in China's past or compared with other countries. Such comparisons are difficult and require careful treatment beyond the scope of this chapter. I am only indicating what I see as continuities, and in some cases new phenomena, in need of further exploration. I shall particularly address questions of hierarchy, social class, gender, and regional differences. The question of poverty, whether as an overall evaluation or as a difference in the distribution of wealth between people and places, is a central question.

To those inclined to take Marx's democratic position seriously, the continued, even reinforced position of hierarchy in People's China is a depressing if not unexpected phenomenon. Deference to the old and male, especially where they also occupy party and state positions of power, continues to dominate society. This has been especially visible in the recent past in the case of the leading members of the Communist Party, some of whom exercise extensive power after having officially resigned from office. Kahn-Ackermann expresses nicely what others of us who have lived in China have observed when he writes:

In the eyes of many Chinese, the power that a person wields is still seen as legitimised directly by the position he holds. If he is sufficiently far up the hierarchy, then he is virtually impregnable. Our Chinese fellow-students were always irritated when they saw caricatures of leading politicians in the Western newspapers. . . . A member of the party leadership can be criticised or removed from office only by his equals or superiors; open criticism from below is confined to exceptional situations. (Kahn-Ackermann, 1982, pp. 107–108)

The "exceptional situations" remind one again of the *Mencius* and the "right to rebel" when the emperor's behavior is such that he can no longer be called emperor.[9] This is a far cry both from Marx's conception of democracy and from much of Mao's Thought.

Another irony of "communist" China has been the replacement of the former unequal and "unjust" class structure by new and officially legitimated divisions. Land reform and the subsequent commune system in the early and late 1950s respectively swept away the landlords in the villages, and contemporary changes in the towns eliminated many, but not all capitalists. But family origin was registered, and in one political "movement" after another the children of landlord and other labeled families were singled out for persecution of one kind or another. In traditional manner such families were referred to as the *wulei fenzi* ("five (bad) elements"). In the Cultural Revolution the intelligentsia were added to this list of suspected classes as the *choulaojiu* (Stinking Old Ninth), though they have subsequently been classed among the politically favored "working class." Another group that has suffered all kinds of discrimination has been that of contract workers, particularly those working on construction away from home. They have allegedly been denied various rights, including the right to join a trade union or the Communist Party.[10] On the other hand there have been various groups that have been given special favors including the families of revolutionary veterans and, more important, of party and state officials *(ganbu)*. An important aspect of these divisions is that many of the group labels were registered in the household registration books *(hukoubu)* and public security dossiers that have made life difficult for so many (White, 1989, pp. 10–15).

Another significant inequality has been that between different kinds of workers, with workers in the "modern" enterprises having better conditions than those in other sectors of the economy. During the first three years of the Cultural Revolution (1966–1969), the plight of contract workers came to public notice and recently Anita Chan et al. have given a depressing account of the migrant workers being used in Chen Village in Guangdong, the village they studied when it was under the commune system (Chan, Madsen, and Unger, 1992). Living in poor housing, the migrants earn low wages, pay a special residence tax, and are often threatened with violence from local youth gangs. They are prime suspects for all crimes and while doing all the hard work have none of the rights of residence. Furthermore, migrants are themselves hierarchized according to the work conditions, which range from female Hunan textile factory workers at the top to Sichuanese workers on the Hong Kong capitalist-owned vegetable farms at the bottom. The lessons that both locals and migrants learn in such conditions have nothing to do with democracy or equality, but rather with the resentments that fed the Great Proletarian Cultural Revolution (GPCR).

Whatever the Constitution and various policy statements might say about gender the gulf between males and females remains extremely wide. This is not to say that the situation is not better than in the past, but rather, in the words of one of the major writers on the subject, "the benefits for women frequently fell short of official goals and expectations" (Croll, 1983, p. 125). Suzanne Pepper, in her study of universities in the late 1970s and early 1980s, noted a number of assumptions among academic staff members "about the physical and intellectual inferiority of women," including the incredible statement by one schoolteacher, that girls' brains stop developing earlier than do those of boys! (Pepper, 1984, p. 113). An aspect of the continuing inequalities brought out by Delia Davin is the way in which women have been accepted in the public domain only within restricted spheres (Davin, 1976).

A further set of inequalities requiring attention are those associated with a person's place of birth. Much has been said about the gulf between urban and rural areas and between rich and poor rural areas. But differences of regional origins also confer inequalities, among them those described for the Subei people, natives of northern Jiangsu province, working in Shanghai today (Honig, 1990). In this case "Subei people suffer a subordinate status in the labor market" and are discriminated against in such social connections as marriage.

Unequal Schooling

In spite of the impressive increase in the number of schools and of students attending and graduating from schools since the founding of the People's Republic, there are still considerable inequalities in provision between urban and rural areas of the country, as well as others less often remarked. The law on compulsory schooling, passed for the first time by the 5th National Peoples' Congress in April, 1986, proposed a term of nine years from the age of six, but left it to "each province, autonomous region, or municipality" to decide on the exact implementation "in accordance with the conditions of local economic and cultural development" (SWB, 1986, FE.8239, 22 April). The statement of the Communist Party Central Committee on the "Reform of the Education System" put out the previous year divided the country into three regional categories. In the first, the economically advanced, compulsory schooling should be completed by 1990; in the second by 1995; while in the third, "economically backward areas, which account for about a quarter of the total population of the country" no date was suggested (FBIS Daily Report, China, 20 May 1985). Overall official figures for progress made in schooling are to be found in the annual reports of the State Statistical Bureau.[11] According to the 1990 Report, 97.9% of school-age children attended school, an increase of 0.5% over 1989. It also claimed that 75.6% of primary school graduates "study further in the secondary school," an increase of 3.1% over 1989 (*China aktuell*, March 1991, p. 183). It is a little hard to reconcile these figures with other information on the condition of rural schools and on the incentives, under the recent economic privatization policies, for parents to make use of their children's labor. The difficulties of establishing a true picture are sensitively handled by Suzanne Pepper (1990, chap. 5).

Figures for the schooling of girls and an overall figure for "national minority students" are published in the now annual China Education Yearbooks. But since no figures are given for the full cohort and such official figures in all countries are open to dispute, it would be unwise to take them too seriously. Henze, drawing attention to Farrell's distinction of equality of access (the measure that is commonly referred to), of survival, output, and outcome, comments that available statistics, dealing only with sex, class, and ethnic origin, "are often no more than rough estimates" (in Hayhoe, 1984, p. 144). The situation has hardly improved. One is left with impressions, such as those of Rosen (in Hayhoe, 1984, p. 80), or the Chinese specialist on youth problems who attributed rural youth suicide rates (70% of unmarried young female suicides live in rural areas) in part to poorer opportunities for education (*China aktuell*, February 1989, p. 79).

A major inequality of the school system that is seldom seen in those terms is the way in which it functions, as it does in all countries, to produce a small elite to fill the major positions of influence and power. In the process, many of us would argue, the great majority are trained to see themselves as failures and their subordinate and powerless position in society as a consequence of differences in natural ability. In China, as Suzanne Pepper so nicely re-argued (1990), there have been swings of official emphasis between schooling for everyone and schooling particularly for the elite reaching much further back into China's history than the period when a "two-line struggle" was supposed to operate.[12] Pepper refers to the two policy emphases as "reform" and "regularisation." One of the divisive features of the "regularisation" periods has been the establishment and official support for priority schools (*zhongdian xuexiao*)[13] at all three levels of the school system (Price, 1979, pp. 289–299), schools in which priority has been given over other schools for funding, provision of trained teachers, and the selection of students for "academic excellence" by examination. The competitive flavor of these "regular" schools is brought out by both Shirk (1982) and Unger (1982).

Social Justice in the Curriculum

The Chinese curriculum, from the early years of modern, European-style schooling, has been of the comprehensive kind, attempting to provide all students with an introduction to the major fields of human knowledge. In broad outline and in the proportion of time devoted to the different subjects it has not changed since the early 1920s, in spite of many reforms and diverse influences. Moral-political teaching has always been included as a separate course, with its content changing from Confucian through Nationalist (KMT) to Marxist–Leninist–Mao Zedong Thought. While in the People's Republic period some uniformity of standards was provided by the modeling of all textbooks on a national standard, in recent decades there have been different books and courses for priority schools and between schools specializing in the humanities or the natural sciences. All of these matters bear on one's view of social justice, on the provision of access to the human heritage of knowledge.

Examination of the textbooks for the various moral-political courses reveals very little that might be considered under social justice. In the primary school, all teaching is supposed to exemplify the following principles: Ardently love the people; ardently love the motherland; ardently love the Chinese Communist Party; ardently love labor; ardently love science; ardently love socialism; diligently study; ardently love the collective; protect public property; observe discipline; practice civilized courtesy; be honest, courageous, and lively; work hard, live simply. This list appeared in the "Teaching Outline for Character Training in the Full-Time Day 5-Year Primary School" issued by the Ministry of Education in Beijing in May 1982 (*Zhongguo Jiaoyo Nianjian*, 1981, p. 445). In the secondary school materials, one might have expected some mention of human rights in that section of the book *A Simple History of Social Development* devoted to "Capitalist Class Revolution" (vol. 2, chap. 10). But instead we find a highly abstract account of the events of 14 July 1789, the actors identified in class terms of peasant, artisan, and supporters of feudalism, followed by a longer account of the industrial revolution, still in very abstract terms. The one book in which social justice is discussed, and then only the question of rights, is the one entitled *Common Knowledge of Law*, the textbook for a course that was first introduced in 1981. Lesson 5 is on "The basic content of our country's Constitution (2)" and includes sections on: (1) The basic rights of the citizen; (2) The basic duties of the citizen; and (3) Correctly understand the relation between rights and duties. The last is worth citing in full:

In our country the citizen enjoys rights and at the same time must perform duties. At the same time that all citizens enjoy constitutionally and legally guaranteed rights they must perform their duties very well. Manifested in labour and education, they are inseparable, namely, there are rights and there are duties. Our country's people are the masters of the state, rights and duties are a unity. Only if there is very good performance of duties can rights be fully enjoyed, is the role of master manifested, is patriotism and love of socialism manifested, and can the great majority of the citizens consciously perform.

Our country's citizens' rights and freedoms are extensive and authentic, not to be compared with those in the capitalist countries. They include all aspects of rights and freedoms, extending to political life, economic life, cultural life and social life. The Constitution gives to people the rights and freedoms they have struggled and won over a long period. This is an important expression of the superiority of the socialist system.

Citizens, in the exercise of freedoms and rights must not damage the interests of the state, society or the collective or the lawful freedoms and rights of other citizens. There have not existed before in the world such absolute, unlimited freedoms and rights. The state guarantees the citizen's legal freedoms and rights, and will not permit any organization or individual to violate them, but it will also not permit any person to use these freedoms and rights to conduct anti-revolutionary activity or other destructive activity. (Common Knowledge of Law, *1985, pp. 34–35*)

The real meaning is in the last sentence and June 1989 was to be a demonstration of its force.

The Democratic Movement

Here I am using the term, *Democratic Movement,* to cover all those different, connected and unconnected voices who, during the post-Mao period, spoke out in favor of changes in the system in China. It is an unsatisfactory label, particularly because I can detect no voice in favor of empowerment of ordinary working people, of the kind of democracy that would satisfy the conception of Marx and Engels when they spoke of self-determination. On the contrary, Fang Lizhi, the physicist whose political comments have become internationally known, appears to equate democracy with individual human rights and the assertion of professional independence (Williams, 1990, pp. 478; 484). The comment by Li Cheng and Lynn White, that "while he is widely considered a great advocate for democracy, Fang has a clearly elitist outlook" (Williams, 1990, p. 13) would seem to be applicable to all those voices that have managed to reach the West. But this said, it is the best term we have. Who, then, are these "democrats" and what do they stand for?

On the broadest definition the Democratic Movement might embrace all those who have spoken out, from the participants in the

1979–1981 movement associated with the "Democracy Wall" in Beijing to the supporters of the student protests in Tiananmen Square in 1989. All classes of the population are represented, workers, cadres, and private entrepreneurs. But it is the academics and students whose protests, physical and verbal, have been conveyed round the world on television and through academic channels.

The immediate object of protests has varied from the parochial (conditions in particular tertiary colleges) to those that directly concerned the highest levels of government. The language of social justice was used in the open letter by forty-two prominent members of the intelligentsia to Zhao Ziyang and other national leaders on 26 February 1989. Proclaiming their support for the policy of "modernization" they called for political democracy to support the already started economic and cultural reforms; the full implementation of the rights proclaimed in the Constitution, especially those of freedom of speech, publication, and the press; and the release of political prisoners of conscience. At the same time they urged attention to the standard of living of the intelligentsia, at present one of considerable material difficulty.[14]

Conclusion

In spite of European influence, the language of social justice has not become widely used in China. For most Chinese the term *bu gongping*, used during land reform and to protest other situations, is preferred, a term implying conformity with social hierarchy and custom (cf. Kaufmann's first stage of justice, 1973, p. 38). Today's demands for better living standards and control of the corruption and crime that are growing with the development of capitalist forms of economy are commonly expressed in more concrete terms. It remains to be seen whether the language of social justice, which has been used outside China to obtain and maintain privileges for the minority, will be used differently in China, to help the further Liberation of *all* the Chinese people.

Notes

1. One of the five classical virtues, *yi*, is sometimes translated as "justice," e.g., by Needham (1956, p. 24), but other writers use "sense of duty" (Watson, 1963, p. 45), "righteousness," or "uprightness."

2. With the organization of *danwei* (units) in which people not only worked, but also

for the most part lived, this "tyranny" was extended into the city and its most "modern" sectors, including the universities and other tertiary schools. For a description of this system see Kahn-Ackermann (1980, pp. 73–100).

3. This search is described and documented in a number of works, among them Teng and Fairbank, *China's Response to the West* and de Bary et al., *Sources of Chinese Tradition*, vol. 2. The later period is described in Chow, *The May Fourth Movement*. Y.C. Wang, *Chinese Intellectuals and the West, 1872–1949*, is also helpful.

4. This is the title of the final course of moral-political education in the junior secondary school, *Kexue Shehuizhuyi Changshi (Common Knowledge of Scientific Socialism)* published by the Education Publishing House, Beijing, first in 1979 and 1980 in two volumes.

5. For example, many of the ideas translated in Schram (1974), expressing Mao's emphasis on grassroots democracy.

6. Chang, writing about Liang Qichao, sees his concern to be with collective rather than individual rights, and this merging with a conception of "a vigorous citizenry" constituting "a strong and independent state" (Chang, 1971, p. 194).

7. This has been a constant theme of my writings on Chinese education, e.g., Price (1977). Other useful starting points are Draper (1977–1990) and Sayer (1979; 1987).

8. The numbering of Articles in the two versions is different. In 1978 the chapter on "Rights and Duties" runs from Article 44–59 (See *Constitution . . .* and *Documents . . .* respectively).

9. During the Cultural Revolution the "right to rebel" was widely used as a slogan and the Confucian classic, the *Mencius*, was referred to as well as Mao (Lau, 1970, p. 68 [8]; Schram, 1969, pp. 427–428).

10. One of the few public meetings I was able to attend during the Cultural Revolution in 1966 in Beijing was a protest by contract workers about their conditions, attended by Jiang Qing and other leaders.

11. Texts are to be found in English in *Beijing Review,* summarized in the Quarterly Chronicle and Documentation section of *China Quarterly* and a German language version is given in *China aktuell.*

12. A two-line analysis, with Mao Zedong posed against a series of enemies, during the Cultural Revolution. A key document on this is published in Seybolt (1973). My own analysis concentrated on the concept of "combining education with productive labour" and "part-work schooling" (Price, 1970, pp. 211–220; 1977, pp. 203–219).

13. These schools are also translated as "key schools" or "keypoint schools," a translation that fails to situate them in the English schooling terminology.

14. The Chinese text is given in Zhang Jingyu (1989). Besides a very full collection of Chinese documents, this also contains a number of English language texts. For the English text of the letter see FE/0404. The letter is put in context in Henze (1989).

References

Bernal, Martin (1976). *Chinese Socialism to 1907*. Ithaca: Cornell University Press.

Chan, Anita, Richard Madsen, and Jonathon Unger (1992). *Chen Village under Mao and Deng*. Berkeley: University of California Press.

Chang, Hao (1971). *Liang Ch'i-ch'ao and Intellectual Transition in China, 1890–1907.* Cambridge, Mass: Harvard University Press.

China aktvell (monthly). Hamburg: Institut für Asienkunde.

Chow Tse-tsung (1960). *The May Fourth Movement: Intellectual Revolution in Modern China.* Stanford, Calif.: Stanford University Press.

Common Knowledge of Law, (Falü Changshi) (1985). Beijing: Renmin Jiaoyu Chubanshe.

Constitution of the People's Republic of China (1961). Peking: Foreign Languages Press.

Croll, Elizabeth (1983). *Chinese Women Since Mao*. London: Zed Books.

Davin, Delia (1976). *Women-Work: Women and the Party in Revolutionary China*. Oxford: Clarendon Press.

de Bary, W.T., Wing-tsit Chan, and Chester Tan (eds.) (1960). *Sources of Chinese Tradition*, 2 vols. New York: Columbia University Press.

Documents of the First Session of the Fifth National People's Congress of the People's Republic of China. (1978) Peking: Foreign Languages Press.

Draper, Hal (1977–90). *Karl Marx's Theory of Revolution*, (4 vols.), New York: Monthly Review Press.

Du Weiming (Tu Wei-ming) (1979). *Humanity and Self-Cultivation: Essays in Confucian Thought*. Berkeley, Calif.: Asian Humanities Press.

FBIS (Foreign Broadcast Information Service: Daily Report of the People's Republic of China). Washington, D.C.: United States Government.

Hayhoe, Ruth (1984). *Contemporary Chinese Education*. London: Croom Helm.

Heller, Agnes (1987). *Beyond Justice*. Oxford: Basil Blackwell.

Henze, Jurgen (1989). *Studentendemonstrationen in der Volksrepublik China: Verlauf und Gesellschaftlicher Hintergrund*. Arbeitsstelle fur vergleichende Bildungsforschung. Ruhr-Universitat: Bochum.

Honig, Emily (1990). "Invisible Inequalities: The Status of the Subei People in Contemporary Shanghai." *The China Quarterly*, no. 122, June.

Kahn-Ackermann, Michael (1980). *China within the Outer Gate*. London: Marco Polo Press.

Kaufmann, Walter (1973). *Without Guilt and Justice: From Decidophobia to Autonomy*. New York: Dell.

Kolko, Gabriel (1988). *Confronting the Third World: United States Foreign Policy, 1945–1980*. New York: Pantheon Books.

Lau, D.C. (1970). *Mencius*. Harmondsworth: Penguin Books.

Li Cheng, and Lynn White (1990). "Elite Transformation and Modern Change in Mainland China and Taiwan: Empirical Data and the Theory of Technocracy." *The China Quarterly*, no. 121, March.

Mao Zedong (Mao Tse-tung) (1965). *Selected Works of Mao Tse-tung*, vol. 2. Peking: Foreign Languages Press.

Needham, Joseph, (1956). *Science and Civilisation in China: vol. 2. History of Scientific Thought*. Cambridge, Mass.: Harvard University Press.

Peffer, R.G. (1990). *Marxism, Morality and Social Justice*, Princeton, N.J.: Princeton University Press.

Pepper, Suzanne (1984). *Chinese Universities: Post-Mao Enrolment Policies and Their Impact on the Structure of Secondary Education. A Research Report*. Ann Arbor: University of Michigan Press.

Pepper, Suzanne (1990). *China's Education Reform in the 1980s: Policies, Issues and Historical Perspectives*. Berkeley: California Institute of East Asian Studies; China Research Monograph, University of California Press.

Price, R.F. (1970). *Education in Communist China*. London: Routledge and Kegan Paul.

—— (1979). *Education in Modern China*. London: Routledge and Kegan Paul.

—— (1977). *Marx and Education in Russia and China*. London: Croom Helm.

—— (1987). "Convergence or Copying: China and the Soviet Union." In Ruth Hayhoe and Marianne Bastid (eds.) *China's Education and the Industrialized World: Studies in Cultural Transfer*. New York: M.E. Sharpe.

Sayer, Derek (1979). *Marx's Method: Ideology, Science and Critique in "Capital."* Hassocks, Sussex: Harvester Press.

—— (1987). *The Violence of Abstraction: the Analytic Foundations of Historical Materialism*, Oxford: Basil Blackwell.

Schram, Stuart R. (ed.) (1969). *The Political Thought of Mao Tse-tung*. Harmondsworth: Penguin Books.

—— (ed.) (1974). *Mao Tse-tung Unrehearsed: Talks and Letters: 1956–71*.

Harmondsworth: Penguin Books.

Schwartz, Benjamin (1964). *In Search of Wealth and Power: Yen Fu and the West.* New York: Harper and Row.

Seybolt, Peter J. (1973). *Revolutionary Education in China: Documents and Commentary.* White Plains, N.Y.: International Arts and Sciences Press.

Shirk, Susan L. (1982). *Competitive Comrades: Career Incentives & Student Strategies in China,* Berkeley: University of California Press.

A Simple History of Social Development (Shehui Fazhan Jianxhi), 2 vols., (1985). Beijing: Renmin Jiaoyu Chubanshe.

SWB (Summary of World Broadcasts, daily reports). The Far East British Broadcasting Corporation monitoring service, Reading, England.

Teng, Ssu-yu, and John K. Fairbank (1954). *China's Response to the West: A Documentary Survey 1839–1923.* New York: Atheneum.

Unger, Jonathan (1982). *Education under Mao: Class and Competition in Canton Schools, 1960–1980.* New York: Columbia University Press.

Wang, Y.C. (1966). *Chinese Intellectuals and the West, 1872–1949.* Chapel Hill: University of North Carolina Press.

Watson, Burton (1963). *Hsün Tzu: Basic Writings, (Xunzi).* New York: Columbia University Press.

White, Lynn P., III (1989). *Policies of Chaos: The Organizational Causes of Violence in China's Cultural Revolution.* Princeton, N.J.: Princeton University Press.

William, James H. (1990) "Fang Lizhi's Expanding Universe." *The China Quarterly,* no. 123, September.

Zhang Jingyu (ed.) (1989). *Ziyou zhi Xiu Minzhu zhi Hua.* Taibei: Guoli Zhengzhi Daxue.

Zhongguo Jiaoyu Nianjian 1949–1981 (1981). Shanghai: Zhongguo Baike Quanshu Chubanshe.

Arab Women and Social Justice
Redistributive-Based Educational and Employment Opportunities (1970–1990)

Khadiga M. Safwat

Introduction

The main thrust of this chapter is to examine situations where economic and social justice in the area of women's education and job opportunities can be positively correlated with redistribution and with political democracy. Historically, social justice and political democracy ought to be based on economic democracy—the redistribution of wealth. The majority of Arab women's gains fall within the period between post-independence and the mid-1970s whereby relatively liberal social and popular programs were possible. Statistics relating to women's completion of schooling and subsequent entrance into the labor market show that in some instances, like in Syria, North Yemen, Lebanon, Jordan, and Egypt, women's participation in the labor market increased as did their wages and working conditions

Women's entry into the labor force doubled, in the public and mixed sectors, between the mid-1970s and the beginning of the 1980s. The labor force in rural areas came to be dominated by women. This development was dictated by the demand of men for recruitment in the first Gulf War (GW I) between Iraq and Iran. Additionally, pressure on the male skilled labor force followed the increased demand in the gulf labor market that had significantly been restructured to cater to the many construction projects triggered by massive oil revenues. In Kuwait, for example, female employment went as high as 88% of the skilled labor force. Thus, dramatic changes in the Arab male and female labor force structure occurred. Moreover, increased economic redistribution informed certain changes in the work place. For instance, in family law, and the relationship between the sexes more generally, the prerogative of male authority was to varying degrees modified, manifesting in a relative mutual interaction between the public and the personal, and the economic and the societal, leading to economic and political equality for many women. However, *negative* correlation between the two variables—social justice and economic democracy—figure most during subsequent periods between the mid-1980s and particularly after the Gulf War II (GW II). These events must therefore be read with two significant variables in mind—time and (geographic) space.

Thus, the argument I propose in this chapter seeks to decipher the most significant points of deviation in the accepted hypothesis that economic democracy leads to political democracy and social justice, illustrated by increases in women's education and labor force participation by attempting to:

(1) decode the changes in women's status-role position in the light of the complex Arab socioeconomic developments from the mid-1970s to the Gulf War II (GW II);

(2) define or redefine the operational concepts of social justice and political democracy keeping in mind that the concept of social justice in Arab society, having operationally undergone recurring changes, which may not necessarily correlate with the notion of simple economic redistribution;

(3) degroup Arab women by providing examples of gains made to Arab women's status and role positions, especially in terms of achievements of certain equality indicators like educational achievement and a higher share in the low-paid and the professional white collar labor market.

Development, Women, and the State

In a scale of gradation, women's status-role position ought to generally show positively consistent correlation with the democratic process. This correlation, however, cannot readily, universally be applied to all Arab societies at all times. To over simplistically draw on often dismissive generalizations of grouping together an Arab *world*, is both misleading and harmful (see, for instance, Said, 1979). Despite the mid-1970s boom, with the emergence of petrodollar Arab multinationals, or because of that, the presumed

homogeneity of the Arab world has become increasingly question-
able. Examples of significant developments in women's status-role
position, from oil rich on the one hand to capital-starving Arab
societies on the other is, as stated above, contingent in terms of
time and space. For example, expressed on a scale of gradation,
inconsistencies and contrasts between Sudan and Saudi Arabia stand
at extremes. Iraq, an oil rich economy and a historically, culturally
developed society, represents yet another deviation from a hypo-
thetical positive correlation between economic and political democracy.

The growing importance of petrodollar capital accumulated
during the 1970s, as a result of the monopoly over the oil market
by Arab Gulf states and the subsequent rise of oil prices, marks an
important development in the region and worldwide. The Gulf
Labor Market generated what in some cases amounted to between
30% and 35% of total foreign currency earnings of some countries. With the near collapse of oil prices in 1986, a general financial crisis ensued leading to capital drain through the syphoning of
profits on foreign aid and payment of interest on borrowing, which
in turn lead to unprecedented constraints on public spending. In
some instances, servicing aid interest repayments reached somewhere between 40% and 115% of Gross National Product (GNP).
Moreover, the subsequent dramatic diminishment of such aid following GW I, and particularly after Gulf War II, coupled with
disengagement of the gulf labor market and loss of foreign currency earnings in remittances from gulf labor employment, further hastened economic ruin. In this context, the widespread gender intolerance in almost all Arab societies can partly be explained
by the following:

(1) The syndrome of the recent rise of political Islamic programs, concentrating on the relationship between the sexes, is to a
large extent concurrent with and informs the subsequent negation
of women's gains everywhere in the Arab world.

(2) Petrodollar wealth became a catalyst in socioeconomic engineering throughout the Arab world. Once peripheral and insig-
nificant, a number of states increasingly began to exert pressures on
the broader Arab states to adopt socially conservative, cultural prac-

tices. The Hijab became a hallmark of those tendencies while anti-west, anti-left, and anti-women Islamic political programs centered around the relationship between the sexes.

State expansion and economic affluence informed both increasing state intervention and social engineering. Despite relative economic liberalism, expressed in some Arab countries by the entrance of many more women into the labor market during the decade between 1970–1980, family laws continue to be based on the traditional sexual divisions of labor leading to a double burden for working women with little or no change in their status position except in urban areas, among middle- to upper-middle-class women. Thus despite provisions of sophisticated public goods and social services, particularly during the decade from 1975–1985 in Arab Gulf societies such as Saudi Arabia, Kuwait, and the United Arab Emirates, these did not inform a fundamental change to women's status-role positions.

In middle- to low-income Arab societies, women's status role positions were marked by significant developments traced by some writers to the so-called shift of the women's dependence on the man to a dependence on the state. Yet women's status-role position in general remained functional to, and a function of, a certain model of political (cultural) development. This developmental model is particular to rich donor Gulf Arab states, especially Saudi Arabia.

Relatively high standards of provision by the state in a so-called socialist society such as Algeria, up to the mid-1970s, led to the implementation of programs to encourage increased educational participation for women and subsequent increased participation by women in the labor market especially in urban and professional sectors. These programs, however, progressively diminished by the early 1980s under pressure form both the National Liberation Front (FNL) (due to debt demands) and the conservative, Islamic Reconciliation Front (FIS), which gained its support largely from the Gulf states, Saudi Arabia and Iran. Both fronts, however, offer no more than variations of degrees in more or less the same articulated language of anti-democratic, anti-women-based programs, in the absence of, or in response to, solutions to the growing economic problems in the country.

Education, Job Opportunities, and Social Justice

Despite the difficulties in obtaining clear, up-to-date statistics on educational participation and literacy rates, for both Arab men and women, what is available paints a fairly dim picture with respect to women, especially rural Arab women. An Arab League of Nations Report (1980) highlighted the fact that literacy is still around 50% throughout the Arab world, although a slight fall was projected during the 1980s and 1990s. Figures obviously vary according to country and may indeed have changed somewhat in recent years. For example, the report showed that in the United Arab Emirates (UAE), women's participation in primary education was 43%, 33% at secondary level, and about 39% for higher education. Both Qatar and Kuwait had slightly higher rates. Illiteracy in Syria is much higher for women than men, with many of the illiterate women outside the gainfully employed labor force.

Some of the worst statistics came from Saudi Arabia where only about 30% of girls were enrolled in secondary school during the 1970s. Interestingly, far more men than women in Saudi Arabia are today entering higher education, predominantly in "traditional" female courses like teaching, nursing, and so forth. The Fourth Five Years Plan states that: ". . . it is important to expand women's education qualitatively and quantitatively. . . ." The report, however, goes on to say: "One of the challenges facing the Five Year Plan in education is to find a way to make use of the numbers of qualified individuals in this section of the population within the teachings and edicts of the Islamic Sharia regardful of the increasing needs of Saudization (of jobs) on all levels" (cited in Abu Khalid, 1988).

Education and social justice in the Arab world are not mutually productive and neither are they necessarily, positively correlated. Indeed, there is often a negative correlation between education and social justice in certain regimes. Selected examples of Arab women's education and social or political democracy shown below may dispel the over simplistic and misleading assumption that economic and social justice are mutually exclusive. The stark example of Saudi Arabian women illustrates a positive correlation between extra social compulsion and pecuniary affluence. Saudi Arabia, moreover, plays a progressively important role in the engineering of the family and subsequent effects on women's status and role positions through its increasing financial prowess in the Arab world.

Saudi Arabia: A Gulf Oil–Rich Big Brother

It is perhaps useful to note that Saudi Arabia can be an important regional variable in terms of constraints on, and the shaping of, developmental processes by constraining hitherto historically achieved gains by women in the region's socioeconomic and cultural centers. Undoubtedly, Saudi Arabia exerts both financial and ideological influence. Certain family and personal laws are infinitely engineered by Saudi Arabia, through implicit and/or explicit pressure. The outcomes are rather complex and cannot be simplistically concluded.

The relatively economically poor Arab societies, like Jordan, Egypt, Sudan, Algeria, Iraq, Tunisia, and Palestine, are historically much more politically and culturally developed, whereas the economically rich are traditionally politically conservative and remain culturally and socially poor. Nevertheless, oil rich, extra statal/regional institutions exert direct influence on outlaying Arab extensions through cross-boarder economic activity. Granting and denying favors puts sociopolitical developments in the region in the conservative, oil-rich straitjacket.

In light of this, a women's social movement—the Saudi Arabian women's empire—has emerged. This "empire" may be compared and contrasted to the radical Western feminist ideological scheme that calls for a separatist society as the ultimate gain women can achieve in the battle between the sexes. Since the mid-1980s, progressive fiscal problems led Saudi Arabia to reconsider gigantic developmental schemes in foreign labor employment. At the same time, the female skilled-labor force has outgrown any feasible demand on a labor force that is not designed for employment. The percentages of women graduates outstrips the openings in a labor market confined to male labor. Subsequent social problems, which will not be dwelled upon here, inspired the creation of a women's empire by women for the servicing of women's interests. For these, and other reasons, the Saudi women's empire is incomparable to the ideals and goals of radical Western feminist movements.

The radical Western feminist concept of segregation of women into women-only society bases itself on a gender struggle as opposed to a class struggle. When arbitrarily projected on non-Western women, this concept generalizes about stages of social development and dismisses history with outrageous insensitivity to history everywhere. The Saudi women's empire exists at the heart of women's social segregation in Saudi Arabia and is predominantly a middle-class phenomenon.

The women's empire has until recently been a cultural and social empire. It is currently being engineered to fulfill a functional role for an increasingly problematic educational program; that is, the unemployment of an increasingly well educated and articulate group. An employment sector specifically created for women, serviced by women, becomes a subtle and expedient solution for both a dangerously frustrated women's labor force and expensive labor imports. This "event," the emergence of the women's empire, does not change things. It continues to sustain the system without so much as changing it. Moreover, it may have revitalized the system through cosmetic or window dressing. From 1987 onward the Saudi economy began to suffer serious fiscal contradictions as a result of compulsive integration to the world system of capitalism, the globalization of capital, and the circuit of financial accumulation based on the transnationalized banking system, the money and shares market. The massive foreign labor force in the Gulf costs Gulf States dearly. The women's empire cushions those problems without altering the division of labor or the need for radical social changes.

Job Opportunities, Resilient Division of Labor, and the Relationship between the Sexes

Political Islamic programs drew their undeniable appeal from: (a) the absence of an effective, alternative program to the debt and foreign investment policies of free-market economies where mass unemployment, displacement of rural population, and widespread poverty, coupled with the threat of civil wars were widespread; and (b) the jobs created under the so-called free-market economies in Free Trade Zones (FTZs) or free production zones or, indeed, free processing zones (FPZs) were largely tailored for deskilled, deunionized, cheap women's labor. Women seem to have had access to the majority of those jobs. In the 1980s, for instance, Moroccan and Tunisian women were estimated to comprise 30% and 40% of the industrial labor force, respectively. By comparison, women's labor comprised 4.8% in Jordan, 7% in Algeria, 6.8% in Syria, 18% in Algeria, and 22% in Kuwait. As female marriage age became higher, and the demand for female labor in the above industrial pockets increased, pressure was placed on women in certain age groups. Female labor in FTZs and FPZs is concentrated on women in the age groups 15–29. Tunisia shows a 30% female labor force in the age group 15–34 in contrast with Kuwait and Qatar (37% in the age group of 25–49). Thus, females employed in the FTZs and FPZs are lower paid, generally untrained, or slightly trained, and poorly educated. This labor force is thereby characterized by so-called naturalized, feminine occupational traits.

Female occupational opportunities come across in the women in development or the women and development (WAD) program literature as the epitome of women's emancipation through economic independence. However, I would argue that the economic variable alone has not accounted for women's emancipation in societies where the culture is patriarchal and legitimized through the sexual division of labor; where the priority, if not monopoly, of positions of power are held by men; and where men gain social honor through their bread-earning capacity and headship of household. In chronic, urban unemployment situations, the newly created women's labor market would naturally antagonize men by exacerbating competition in a shrinking labor market where women seem to get the jobs men should have had. Neither economic independence, nor the seeming rise to power of women in the labor market, have served women's interests, since the preconditions for equality were seriously deflected within general economic ruin and decline through the 1980s. Coupled with this, the appeal of political Islamic is based principally on the battle between the sexes in education, job opportunities, and status roles.

Conclusion

In this chapter, I have pointed to some of the complexities of the intersection between women, education, and justice within the Arab region. It is against these above-mentioned details that an analysis of Arab women's educational and employment opportunities, along with their overall status position, needs to be discussed. Under social systems inclined to frequent periodical digression into a distorted, colonially informed image of themselves, together with neocolonialism or global recession, there seems to be a recurrence of some general system collapse and system stress. Contemporary, protracted social, cultural, and economic regression seems to be characterized by universal cuts in redistributive social policies and increased pressure to reduce other socially enjoyed popular programs. Expressions of popularly felt concern during this era of global recession often have resulted in self-inflicted bloodletting and forms of self-condemnation throughout the Arab region. Women, especially, seem to be meted the most significant share of injustice, under periodic or seemingly unrelenting sociocultural digressions.

Political Islam (which is not the same thing as fundamental Islam, meaning reverting to the fundamentals of Islam) is commonly euphemized in the Western media. Political Islam borrows from and re-creates imagined Islamic schemes for an imagined Islamic society. These schemes are entirely politically motivated. They merely appeal to current issues such as anti-Westernization, opposition to an existing authority and its policies, intolerance of widespread unemployment and austerity measures, the rise in crime rates, and the violent displacement of people and cultures. They are implicitly anti-democratic and explicitly anti-women programs. They do not base themselves on anything near the fundamentals of justice and equality that any religion, including Islam, is based on.

It is during such times that the class struggle is replaced by national, ethnic, and cultural struggles, invoking the past with its tradition and decrying the loss of privileges. The battle centers around women as guardians; custodians of culture and honor of the nation under an imagined or real threat. Curiously, it is around women as the least emancipated, the most perpetually alienated, and the longest subjugated, that the Islamic struggles revolve. The gender struggle feeds into and reinforces the mainstream, male struggles, and so creates the preconditions for an increased onslaught on women during such periods of social digression.

The Trajectory of Injustices

The current self-image is particularly marked by reactionary political, religious, and xenophobic discourse among the impoverished population and so contrasts with the social image of the 1960s.

Women's gains were made possible during the independence and post-independence periods in the historic centers of cultural and political gravity, and their satellite extensions, in the region. Popular participation and gains were possible for wider sections of the population, women, and minorities.

The 1970s witnessed the genesis of the progressive decline in a brief, but historic period of achievement for both men and women in the Arab countries. Economic affluence enabled the provision of sophisticated social goods and services, which benefited both men and women benefited particularly during the decade from 1975 to 1985 in some countries of the Arab Gulf, Saudi Arabia, Kuwait, and the United Arab Emirates. Iraq stands out as both oil and culturally rich, yet women's status and role positions have more to do with a particular model of political development than with economic, historical, and evolutionary cultural developments. Moreover, relatively high standards of provision by the state implemented in the so-called socialist programs, initiated in Algeria for example, progressively diminished by the early 1980s and have thereafter heightened the tensions between women and men. At least in the case of Algeria, the Algerian form of political Islam should been seen in the light of the French occupation as much, or indeed more, than in light of the natural development of Islam up until the rise of the petrodollar, exported brand of political Islam from the Gulf, Saudi Arabia, and Iran.

Women's gains must also be seen in light of the current economic climate in a number of Arab states. For many Arab states, there is an emerging growth of (foreign) export-oriented industries. There remains, however, a dependence on a traditional and somewhat backward rural economy. Notable in the region is the high rate of population growth, and high or chronic unemployment. The estimated unemployment rate for Algeria is 22%; in Sudan more than 35%; in Egypt about 23%; Jordan around 28%, Morocco 18–25%; and in Tunisia 28–30%. Increasing social inequality is evident in middle- to low-income societies like Egypt, Tunisia, Jordan, Syria, Morocco, Lebanon, and to a far lesser degree, Yemen and Sudan.

The jobs that are currently being made available in the region are deskilled, deunionized jobs, which require no formal training or prior education. These jobs are often tailored for women in cheap labor sweat shops, such as those to be found in Morocco, Tunisia, Egypt, and Palestine. With the high rate of North African urban unemployment, the women's labor market merely feeds into the hands of anti-women, political Islamic programs in the sense that women are seen to be competing with men, considered traditionally to be the providers for the family.

In contrast, in Gulf oil societies, particularly in Saudi Arabia, women's skilled labor becomes functional at times of economic recession. Women are needed to service the market created (and favored) for women by women, as my description of the women's empire illustrated. This also sorts out the issue of having to engage foreign and, or expensive expatriate personnel, as well as providing the necessary job avenue for the increasingly educated Saudi women. As the examples cited above illustrate, particularly in the case of Saudi Arabia, education and social justice in the Arab world, especially for women, are not necessarily positively correlated.

References

Abu Khalid, Fawzia (1988). "Afro-Asian Solidarity Women's Group: Cairo Conference on the Oil Boom Decade and Arab Women" (Unpublished monograph).

Al Khayat Sana'a Al (1990). *Honour and Shame: Women in Modern Iraq*. London: Saqi Books

Arab League of Nations (1980). Report from the conference "Women and Development in the Arab World."

Commonwealth Secretariat (1989). *Engendering Adjustment for the 1990s*. London: The Commonwealth Secretariat.

Elson, Diane, and Ruth Person (1981). "The Subordination of Women and the Internationalization of Factory Production." In Kate Young et al. (eds.) *Of Marriage and the Market: Women's Subordination in International Perspective*. London: CSE Books.

Gerami, Shahin (1990). "The Role, Place and Power of Middle Class Women and the Islamic Republic." Paper prepared for the Round Table on Identity, Politics and Women, UNU/WIDER, Helsinki.

Safwat, Khadiga M. (1991). "Review of Patriarchy and Class." *Development Studies Journal*, vol. 4, no.27.

Said, Edward (1979). *Orientalism*. New York: Vintage.

Strichter, Sharon B., and Jane Parpart (1988). *Patriarchy and Class: African Women in the Home and the Work Place*. London: Westview Press.

Education and Social Justice in South America

Carlos Marin

A History Scarcely Begun

For five decades, historically a very short period, South Americans like people from other continents have spoken of, written about, and discussed *development* in the broadest possible range of forums. The first thing we were confronted with was that, in the name of truth, there was a great deal more that we had to learn about ourselves than we could ask of others. Our initial concern was to define the nature, significance, and profound causes of our *underdevelopment*.

A comparison with other peoples and continents was unavoidable. We discovered there were others, situated to our north, with standards of living better than ours, and who were more advanced, more wealthy, more industrialized, and more organized than us. Thus, with a cursory glance at quantitative indicators—the GNP, income per capita, and economic growth—we have come to accept categories that inexplicably continue having relevance as First, Second, and Third Worlds.

Diagnosis was never easy; nor was there identification of the real causes, or consensus in the design and proposal of solutions. Having scrutinized history, economic development, and processes, as well as systems of government, our discussion came to focus on concepts like dependence, marginalization, economic development, on countries' levels of wealth and poverty, industrialization, and on models of development. Our point of reference always centered on the relationship between the North and the South.

Sociologists, politicians, economists, and even anthropologists

Translated by Andrew Batchelor.

took prime responsibility for the diagnosis and subsequently any feasible solution. Bold questions with difficult answers emerged. For example:

- Is it true that the Third World is poor because the North is rich?
- Need the Third World follow the same path and try to imitate the North?
- Is it true that underdevelopment is a state of mind?
- Is aid the solution, entailing money or depriving poor of a little less than the rich?

Of most concern is the lack of any response acceptable to both parties, to the North and to the South. To be honest, there have been more mistakes than successes. The most recent political and historical mistake has been manifest in financial assistance.

Initially, our solution was thought to be found in money. Multilateral credit organizations took the lead: They not only generously offered money, but succeeded in relating debt to policy decisions. Capitalizing on lending strength, they could recommend what was best for the poor. In other words, they dictated what the Third World had to do to overcome underdevelopment. Now we are paying the price. Today, the external debt of Latin America, which exceeds U.S. $420 billion, is considered unpayable and puts a brake on development.

Nevertheless investigation, dialogue, and the experiences of these recent decades have helped us to understand and defend some propositions or conclusions:

- Development does not necessarily or exclusively mean economic growth.
- The search for development does not imply imitating rich countries, as though one simply copies a model.
- To affirm that the Third World's inhabitants have and will continue to possess any particular characteristics is, to say the least, glib and an expedient and evasive notion.

Affirmations of this kind, which imply a coherent perception and a different discourse with regard to development, have compelled us to search for a new international order based on equity, cooperation, and solidarity; and not on *confrontation*. They have helped us in understanding our duty to create an authentic *democracy* within our countries, complete with human rights for all our citizens and countries, and to urgently design and affect a global strategy to fight our endemic woes, among which are not only illiteracy, tropical illness, and poverty, but also social irresponsibility, administrative corruption, political instability, and unequal opportunities in law and life.

In other words, it has taken us several decades to understand that development is not possible without a purpose, a will, an option, a national and continental political decision facing human rights and justice. If the new name for peace is development, then the only means is through realizing the demands of social justice. Development, like peace, is the fruit of justice. This grand conclusion, which the Third World has come to reach, suggests, justifies, and explains another which is the logical consequence of the first: Education for development demands, means, and is identified with another task: *education in and for social justice.*

Both the North and the South must be educated in and for the practice of justice if they are to reach completion of the first debate. But on completion, the second will have to begin. If we are convinced that *education* and specifically *education for justice* is the key, a qualitatively different focus on the theme and the problem of development prevails.

The countries of our America live in an internal situation that has a long way to go to be *just*. If one thinks about the progressive concentration of national wealth and living conditions of farmers, aborigines, Negroes, children, women, one would easily reach a conclusion that at the base of our dilemma lies social injustice.

Historically, it is certain that capitalism has been unable to solve the problems of poverty that exist in the Third World. We have already stated on previous pages: Economic growth does not necessarily bring with it distribution of wealth, nor equality of opportunity for all. To the contrary, in our America, wealth continues to concentrate in the hands of few, and poverty worsens in a way that is not only worrisome, but critical and menacing.

Herein lies our rationale. We seek to develop and clarify knowledge that inseparably ties *development* with *democracy, human rights, social justice,* and *peace,* and that recognizes the absolute necessity to prepare South American men and women, through a systemic and permanent educative process, for the practice and vigilance of values, rights, and virtues, which comprise the basis and inspiration of a utopia: a new society.

Each and every one of us is raised to naturally uphold a fundamental view of justice: that all receive their dues as human beings, to give and receive and be treated equally regardless of age, position, or circumstances. Although this is what we may call a sense of justice, it must evolve in humanity, be affirmed and placed in practice in each and every human claim and rationalization. Furthermore, social life must be inspired and organized according to the assumptions and requirements of social justice: if not, we can never speak of a healthy, fair, and kind social life for all. This indicates that it is time our America questioned the means, degree of quality, underlying principles, necessary decisions, and objectives that social justice means with respect to its national education projects, plans, and laws. Or, at the very least, we need to ensure that there exist in South American countries well-designed national education policies in social justice.

If, in the final diagnosis, at the root of underdevelopment lies a problem of justice, then in order for there to be equality, order, and peace (both now and in the future), educational reforms are urgently needed. Pressing is the need for an educational proposal and a pedagogic project that includes social justice as an integral part of a curriculum and provides learning opportunities for the attainment of *sustainable development.* Any such sustained development would have to be at a level acceptable across the continent for the 1990s and into the twenty-first century.

All this happens at a time when in countries like Colombia, with 42% of its inhabitants age eighteen years or under, the number of unschooled children and the number of illiterates increases. Will not the task to educate in and for social justice be informed by historical responsibility?

Principles for a Response
Responding to these questions is no easy matter. On the one hand,

there appear no studies that might throw light on the level of consciousness about the relationship between education and justice in the context of Latin America, nor on the experiences within the student's classroom or beyond it. On the other hand, it would serve little to simply affirm that we are (or are not) educating in social justice and are treating it as a slow and difficult process due to its very nature. Furthermore, what is truly interesting is not to know whether countries like Bolivia or Ecuador's school programs include the subject Social Justice, but to determine the criteria by which it is possible to judge whether or not it serves a purpose within national educational plans, and what such a subject may aim to achieve.

There remains, if it were only possible, instead of making distinctions between basic education and university, formal and informal schooling, public and private, to think of the continent as an "educational city" or at least to have sufficient reason to refer to ourselves in each nation as an "educational community." Achieving this as we may, there still remains a long way to go.

If our America were able to speak of education as an *integral* goal, rapid response could proceed. That is to say, education in and for social justice could be adopted as a single task that implicates not only school, but the whole fabric of society, the church, and the family: political parties, trade unions, government departments, as well as the media. In other words, the subject itself is not sufficient; the school classroom is not all there is; there exist other relevant places beyond the classroom. Tomorrow's justice is paved and built upon the justice of the school, the family, and the very same community as that of educational environment. Importantly, formal education is only one of the elements or factors that make us what we really are or what we aspire to be. It is life in its most global sense, daily life, that *educates* us: family, church, community, values, traditions, tribe, nation, company, political parties, sport, art, what we read, hear, or see through the media.

There is evidence that all these factors or realities have as significant an impact on the child and youth, and consequently their behavior in civil society, as formal schooling received in the classroom. Needed is a resolution that all life—personal or communal, private or public—embodies or stands for an experience of justice within the refuge of society. Such refuge equates with that found from the outset of constant education as an evolving process for all individuals during the stages of their life, their daily tasks, and their educational experiences.

Intimately linked to that discussed so far is another relevant aspect: that of quality, or more precisely, the truth or purity of the very educational act. By this we mean the content, the act's intention, and the teachers themselves. The truth must be told, not only what is said or written on justice, but in the actual practice of teaching itself. Every educator in justice must act as a defender, as a promoter who is truthful and is impassioned by the realization of social justice, and is capable of expressing his or her personal experience in daily relations with others.

Finally, we would say that the relationship between education and justice is not exhausted with the identification of unjust situations, nor in their denunciation or denial. Fruit borne of that relationship can be none other than the sign to love justice; to opt for justice and tirelessly work for a society inspired and governed by social justice.

What's Clear So Far

The panorama is not totally obscured; clarity is making its way. Despite all of our deficiencies, our slowness, and perhaps our shyness to act, we can enumerate and explain by heart certain things, facts, and propositions.

Speaking, for example, of our countries' *development*, it is clear that it is not simply a matter of eradicating absolute poverty, as we once thought, but of achieving and guaranteeing a form of development that would sustain in a continuous way, that would satisfy the population's legitimate aspirations, that would respect the principle of equilibrium or equal distribution of benefits, and that would be able to reduce ecological costs.

It should be noted that, although living conditions have improved for a growing proportion of the population in Latin America, the number of poor, illiterate, and undernourished have continued to increase. In our continent of 130 million poor in 1970, we exceeded 144 in 1980, and in 1990 a total of 204 was estimated. By the year 2000 a total of 232 million is predicted.

What is the connection between all these issues and education? As we have previously mentioned, economic growth does not necessarily and automatically bring with it an improvement in the quality of human life. We now know that those countries that have given priority to policies and programs oriented toward investment of a social nature and that focus their efforts on education and the capacity of human potential have achieved massive progress with regard to *human development* as well as in economic growth. In a word: it's clear that raised investment in *education* program provisions follows economic development, not the reverse. Along the way we have managed to discover the causal relationship that exists between *development* and *education,* between *education* and *justice.* In our continent, we are unable to continue speaking of development as though it could simply be treated as a fashion or intellectual indulgence; in order to avoid it, the only open avenue is to educate people.

Simultaneously, we must now recognize that absolute material poverty does not constitute, so we say, the essence of underdevelopment. Many among us complain of being barefooted, yet do not understand the value of having healthy feet with which to tread; and to be able to walk, in the context of development, could mean one or a hundred opportunities to make sense of human life. Healthy arms and hands could mean one or a thousand opportunities to produce wealth, well-being, and needed community services.

Considerations of this nature lead us to reiterate: If integral development is not just about things, but human beings, then education is the key to it all. Turn Latin America into an immense and unique educational project. This may be taken as mere rhetoric, but nobody could deny that this is the great challenge not only for this decade, but, above all else, if we wish to reach the approaching century on equal footing with the countries of the North.

Distribution of the existing wealth is certainly an imperative, and to do it equitably without excluding anyone is a requirement of social justice. But the creation of wealth, in a context like ours, must be adopted as an indispensable condition for integral and sustainable development. And, in this, education again has a role. It is only possible to create a culture of productive working people, of individuality and association, in which wealth is seen as an opportunity for both personal and community growth, if we hasten to unpack our curricula—formal and informal basic, intermediatory, and tertiary—in a way that would allow us as Latin Americans to learn what is needed in terms of justice and human development. In this sense, it is clear that all educational intent must be an essential or integral part of the national or continental development plan. Although currently this is not so, it must one day be the case because if we do not school ourselves in justice, we suddenly jeopardize our selfsame right to development.

Today, we know with scientific certainty that education for social justice is irreplaceable if we wish to stimulate growth in critical thought and self-expression, all of which has been silenced under several centuries of cultural oppression. In this way, one may quickly leave behind silence, find a voice, freely say what one must, and thereby take a place as a real actor, in all senses, and capable of intent to change the reality within which one lives. And in discovering one's own voice, in having things to say and do, ideas become reality through the intentional creation of situations in which persons and groups realize conscious acts through an open and reflective dialogue and the use of techniques and problem-posing educational aids, all ultimately aiming for the development of a critical consciousness that would enable the conversion of guilt and associated injustice into constructive action in the service of justice.

We understand perfectly well that to educate for social justice in our America means to lay the foundations of and inspire the construction of an authentic "culture of human life," a culture of human rights and duties and of the fundamental liberties, a healthy understanding of the human being and of life in society, to train youth and adults—men and women who are free, responsible, and united and who pledge themselves to building a civil, healthy, just, and kind life for all.

From this perspective, education for social justice can not be a process structured from simple conceptualization or from good advice, nor from simple propaganda for something to be desired, but which at no time reviews the nature of *what should be*. In order to do so, education in and for social justice demands planning and the development of an active, practical pedagogy: compromised and compromising.

At issue, then, is not an optional nor supplementary task; neither can *education* in justice be conceived of as a neutral process. No educational action can be neutral; several Latin Americans would wish it were, though it cannot be. If we aspire to educate in justice, we have to decide among ourselves on an open and broad pedagogic action that would stimulate critical and reflective thought about the requirements for social justice, and decide to really enlarge upon that space transformed by thought.

This cannot happen, however, while scholarly education continues being authoritarian and elitist; it cannot happen unless current costs of education in our continent cease to be an instrument of social discrimination; it will not happen unless we severely criticize prevailing educational models in our America; it will not happen unless the school, the family, and the enterprise change to be true laboratories where the relationship between education and justice is discovered and practiced; it will not happen if our educational model is not informed by that meaning, that dimension, that fundamental focus. It will not come to be if we do not safely and rapidly progress with the conviction that *democracy* is not simply a form or system of government, but rather a philosophy of civil society, a lifestyle, everyday living that promotes the essential forms of freedom, participation, responsibility, and solidarity. This we declare because it cannot be, save the benefits derived from social justice. We say it because with each step along the way in Latin America the content, quality, and transforming force of education are weakened and impoverished by the governments' political instability and by the civil or military authorities' frequent totalitarian expressions.

A Hazy Dawning

It cannot be denied that within our America there is an irreversible awakening in terms of the discovery of the intimate relationship between *education* and *justice.* A circumstance in which we must alone face the North, which needs nothing of us other than to consume their products, requires us to *learn to live* and the formula is education for development and consequently for the practical application of justice. But above all, it is growth's uncontrollable impulse that is leading us to educate ourselves in justice; the very demands of human development—right, duty, and calling—encourage us to learn much more about justice and to try to live it without dishonesty because, over time, we will not be forgiven.

Nobody would deny that there have been, are, and will be, at an ever-increasing pace, a great many educational innovations and worthwhile experiments to take into account, in the search for the relationship between education and justice and for a valid proposal for educational action according to the needs of social justice. These changes are not merely concerned with methodology, educational planning, or curricular improvement; rather, they incorporate a healthy conception of humankind and social life that responds more completely to an ideal of social justice.

We are thus surpassing the scholarly conception of education. The various communities and organized groups actively participate in the educational task, and they do it in such a way that in Latin America today it is impossible to think of educational plans without taking into account the grassroots or popular sector. This popular participation is exercised in all of our countries—Nicaragua, Brazil, Peru, Colombia, Costa Rica, Chile—an influence mobilized and inspired by educational concepts and programs.

The history of popular education is short, but intense. Like everything, if we analyze the prevailing ideas, the lived experiences, the focuses, and the objectives that are at the very core of the people's education, we find strong social justice content. Popular education promotes popular participation and social change, naturally conditioned, that is participatory. It is an educational job not to diminish specifically scholarly dimensions; not to instruct, but to raise one's consciousness and through it construct a popular identity. It may be said that persons live a moment of popular education each time organized groups, or groups in the process of organizing, in a shared critical reflection, undertake a common experience or intentionally construct their own historical project through an educational process, not in an authoritarian, but liberating sense.

To study and learn, in the sphere of popular education, is primarily to actively and consciously participate in social processes of discovery, in participatory practice and solidarity in civic life, and in the exercise of politics and economics. In this way popular education converts reality and the very process of transforming that reality in an educational fact, in what is internalized; so the demands of social justice are put into practice. It is the process of changing living as a community that really educates.

Conclusion

Nobody will dare deny that there remains a great deal to be done in terms of research into discovering the role of education and its relationship to social justice in order to serve humankind. It cannot be said that there exists in the different states a political will to improve education that leads us all to interpret research findings from educational plans and programs and propositions of a pedagogic nature.

Equally, although we have made ground in identifying and understanding the profound meaning as well as the social and political implications of the Ecuador Mission, we have still not managed to draw the outline of exactly what educates in terms of the demands of social justice. The same would have to be said in relation to the subject matter and to the educational action's design. In the former as well as the latter, we must advance decidedly. Content must be enriched, and the educational process must become intentionally clear.

Weak and unstable governments, more speculative than productive economies, overly rigid and hierarchical educational models: These retard and burden a program of educational action and a pedagogic project throughout the continent that would empower us to unhesitatingly affirm that in our America: *education* prepares and builds a better future through *social justice*.

References

Agulla, Juan Carlos (1983). *Education, Society, and Social Change.* Buenos Aires: Kapelusz.

Angel Perez, Rafael et al. (1991). *Education Processes in a Democratic Society,* San Jose, n.p.

Faure, Edgar (1973). *Learning to Be: Education of the Future.* (Spanish version by C. Paredes de Castro). Paris: UNESCO.

Jara, Oscar, et al. (1990). *Contributions to the History of Popular Education in Peru.* Lima: Tarea.

Nunez H., Carlos (1989). "Education for Change." In *Transform in order to Educate,* (8th ed.). Mexico: IMDS.

Peresson, Mario, et al. (1983). *The People's Education and Illiteracy in Latin America.* Bogota: Education Dimension.

World Bank (1991). *World Development Report.* Washington D.C.

Wren, Brian (1975). *Education for Justice.* London: SCM Press.

List of Contributors

Ibrahim Alladin, Ph.D., is currently the Director of Cambrian International at Cambrian College of Applied Arts and Technology in Sudbury, Ontario, Canada. He was formerly a professor in International Education and Development at the University of Alberta. His areas of interest include education for minorities and global education. He is the author of several books, including *Racism in Canadian Schools* (Harcourt Brace, 1996), *Multiculturalism in the 1990s: Policies, Practices and Implications* (EISA Publishers, 1993), and *Teaching in a Global Society* (Ginn Press, 1992).

M.K. Bacchus, Ph.D., is the Director of the Institute for Educational Development, The Aga Khan University, Karachi, Pakistan. Born in Guyana, Dr. Bacchus received his tertiary education in England, principally at the LSE and the Institute of Education, University of London. He has published extensively on issues of development and education and has served for many years as a consultant on problems of development with a number of government and nongovernment bodies in a variety of countries. He has been a Leverhulme Scholar at the LSE and more recently he held the THB Symons Senior Fellowship in Commonwealth Studies. He was for a number of years Professor of Education and Director, Centre for International Education and Development, University of Alberta.

Lynn Davies, Ph.D., is Director of the International Unit, School of Education, University of Birmingham. She has acted as consultant on equity issues in various parts of Africa, developing a particular link with the University of Botswana to promote women in development. Her current teaching centers around school management in developing countries, with particular focus on equity and democracy and her present research project is on management and school effectiveness in contexts of economic stringency. Her books include: *Pupil Power: Deviance and Gender in School* (Falmer Press, 1984) and, with C. Gunawardena, *Women and Men in Educational Management* (IIEP, 1992).

Christine Fox, Ph.D., is a Lecturer in Education at the University of Wollongong, Australia. She has had a long-standing research interest in education and social justice issues and has worked in South America and the Pacific. Dr. Fox is currently engaged in research on multicultural classrooms in Australia and is looking at ways in which staff development programs may enhance anti-racist practices in education. Dr. Fox was the National Coordinator of the Australian Peace Education and Research Association between 1989 and 1993, and is the President of the Australian and New Zealand Comparative and International Education Society.

Ruchira Ganguly-Scrase, Ph.D., is currently Lecturer in Anthropology, Charles Sturt University in Albury, Australia. Born in India, she grew up in Melbourne and holds degrees in sociology and anthropology. Her doctoral dissertation, from the University of Melbourne, was an ethnographic study of a community of leather workers in West Bengal, India. She has taught in a range of courses in both sociology and anthropology in a number of Australian universities. Her research interests include ethnographic writing, childhood and schooling, gender relations in the Third World, and the sociology of race and ethnicity. Dr. Ganguly-Scrase's most recent published articles include: "Global Manufacturing and Indian Leather Workers" in *A New World Order? Global Transformations in the Late Twentieth Century,* edited by D. Smith and J. Böröcz (Praeger, 1995) and "Engendering Marginality: Women, Work and Femininity in West Bengal, India" in *Anthropology: Voices from the Margins,* edited by J. Perry and J. Hughes (Deakin University Press, 1995).

Anne Hickling-Hudson, Ph.D., is Lecturer in Social and Policy Studies, Faculty of Education, Queensland University of Technology, Australia. Dr. Hickling-Hudson has extensive experience in education, development and gender with a special interest in the problems of development within the Caribbean and has published widely in these areas. Recently she was awarded a fellowship to the Centre for Puerto Rican Studies, Hunter College, the City University of New York (September 1995–June 1996).

Carlos Marin is the Assistant Director of CODECAL (Corporacion Integral Para El Desarrollo Cultural y Social) based in Bogota, Colombia. He has had extensive university teaching experience in Colombia in Social Work and has held a range of advisory positions for various nongovernment bodies. He has published numerous articles on peace, human rights, education, and the family and in his current position he is researching human rights and peace in the context of social education.

John Martino, Ph.D., is currently a research analyst with the Public Sector Research Centre at the University of New South Wales. He has extensive teaching experience in both the secondary and tertiary education sector. He was previously employed as Policy Analyst, Australian Council of State Schools Organisations, Canberra, Australia and as researcher with the Centre for Citizenship and Human Rights, Deakin University. He has also taught history method to graduate education students at La Trobe University in Melbourne.

Ronald F. Price, Ph.D., is currently an Honorary Research Fellow in the School of Education, La Trobe University in Melbourne, Australia. Originally from England, where he undertook his doctoral studies at the Institute of Education, University of London, he moved to Australia in the early 1970s to become one of the first members of the Centre for Comparative and International Studies in Education. He was for many years senior lecturer in the school and taught courses including "Comparative Education" and "Education in Russia and China." Apart from Australia, he has taught in many countries including England, China, Bulgaria, and Ghana. He has published numerous articles and a number of books including: *Education in Modern China* (Routledge, 1978) and *Marx and Education in Late Capitalism* (Croom Helm, 1986).

Khadiga M. Safwat, Ph.D., is Executive Director of MERAWEC (Middle East and African Research Centre, Wales) University College, Swansea. She has had extensive teaching and research experience in many countries including Sudan, Italy, Mozambique, Algeria, and Egypt. She has professional status and membership of some thirty national and international organizations. Her current research and writing focuses on patriarchy and class, development, labor migration, and multicultural education.

Timothy J. Scrase, Ph.D., is currently Lecturer in Sociology, Department of Sociology, University of Tasmania, Hobart, Australia. He teaches a range of courses including "Globalization and Culture" and "Social Justice, Marginality and Difference." His research interests are also in these areas. His doctoral dissertation, undertaken at the Centre for Comparative and International Studies in Education, La Trobe University, was a social and cultural analysis of school textbooks in India. It has been subsequently published as *Image, Ideology and Inequality: Cultural Domination, Hegemony and Schooling in India* (Sage, 1993). He has published numerous articles, the most recent being "Globalization, India and the Struggle for Justice" in *A New World Order? Global Tranformations in the Late Twentieth Century,* edited by D. Smith and J. Böröcz. (Praegar, 1995).

Index

Reference Books
in International Education

Edward R. Beauchamp, Series Editor

Education in England and Wales
An Annotated Bibliography
by Franklin Parker and Betty June Parker

Chinese Education
Problems, Policies, and Prospects
edited, with an introduction by Irving Epstein

Understanding Educational Reform in Global Context
Economy, Ideology, and the State
edited by Mark B. Ginsburg

Education and Social Change in Korea
by Don Adams and Esther E. Gottlieb

Three Decades of Peace Education Around the World
An Anthology
edited by Robin J. Burns and Robert Aspeslagh

Education and Disability in Cross-Cultural Perspective
edited by Susan J. Peters

Russian Education
Tradition and Transition
by Brian Holmes, Gerald H. Read, and Natalya Voskresenskaya

Learning to Teach in Two Cultures
Japan and the United States
by Nobuo K. Shimahara and Akira Sakai

Educating Immigrant Children
Schools and Language Minorities in Twelve Nations
by Charles L. Glenn with Ester J. de Jong

Teacher Education in Industrialized Nations
Issues in Changing Social Contexts
edited by Nobuo K. Shimahara and Ivan Z. Holowinsky

Education and Development in East Asia
edited by Paul Morris and Anthony Sweeting

The Unification of German Education
by Val D. Rust and Diane Rust

Women, Education, and Development in Asia
Cross-National Perspectives
edited by Grace C.L. Mak

Qualitative Educational Research in Developing Countries
Current Perspectives
edited by Michael Crossley and Graham Vulliamy

Social Cartography
Mapping Ways of Seeing Social and Educational Change
edited by Rolland G. Paulston

Social Justice and Third World Education
edited by Timothy J. Scrase